Springer Proceedings in Business and Economics

Springer Proceedings in Business and Economics brings the most current research presented at conferences and workshops to a global readership. The series features volumes (in electronic and print formats) of selected contributions from conferences in all areas of economics, business, management, and finance. In addition to an overall evaluation by the publisher of the topical interest, scientific quality, and timeliness of each volume, each contribution is refereed to standards comparable to those of leading journals, resulting in authoritative contributions to the respective fields. Springer's production and distribution infrastructure ensures rapid publication and wide circulation of the latest developments in the most compelling and promising areas of research today.

The editorial development of volumes may be managed using Springer's innovative Online Conference Service (OCS), a proven online manuscript management and review system. This system is designed to ensure an efficient timeline for your publication, making Springer Proceedings in Business and Economics the premier series to publish your workshop or conference volume.

More information about this series at https://link.springer.com/bookseries/11960

Alina Mihaela Dima · Mihaela Kelemen
Editors

Digitalization and Big Data for Resilience and Economic Intelligence

4th International Conference on Economics and Social Sciences, ICESS 2021, Bucharest, Romania

Springer

Editors
Alina Mihaela Dima
Faculty of Business Administration
in foreign languages
Bucharest University of Economic Studies
Bucharest, Bucuresti, Romania

Mihaela Kelemen
Nottingham University Business School
University of Nottingham
Nottingham, UK

ISSN 2198-7246 ISSN 2198-7254 (electronic)
Springer Proceedings in Business and Economics
ISBN 978-3-030-93285-5 ISBN 978-3-030-93286-2 (eBook)
https://doi.org/10.1007/978-3-030-93286-2

This Springer imprint is published by the registered company Springer Nature Switzerland AG
The registered company address is: Gewerbestrasse 11, 6330 Cham, Switzerland

Preface

The COVID-19 pandemic has brought into sharp relief the importance of "resilience" as a concept that can bridge disaster recovery and business continuity. 'Building back better' has been transformed into 'building back sustainably' to ensure the development of more effective solutions within the interconnected economic, environmental, and social systems and to avoid cascading failure during similar future shocks.

The process of digital transformation has accelerated during these unprecedented times, with artificial intelligence and big data starting to have a more critical and widespread impact within the entrepreneurial and public sector decision process mechanisms.

The global crisis has also encouraged companies to become more agile and innovative by adopting digital business models, while the development of new methods for strengthening regional development, redesigning social contracts, revitalizing global cooperation and harnessing Industry 4.0, has become essential for streamlining economic recovery.

The fourth edition of the International Conference on Economics and Social Sciences (ICESS 2021) stimulated the exchange and co-production of valuable ideas on the theme of Digitalization and Big Data for Resilience and Economic Intelligence. This issue of the proceedings includes a series of selected papers dealing with relevant topics, as follows:

- Grand challenges, such as global issues, demand that businesses alter their business models to reflect current events. The paper *The Impact of Data Science, Big Data, Forecasting and Predictive Analytics on the Efficiency of Business System* discusses the latest quantitative methods and technologies afforded by Big Data analytics for organizational efficiency and productivity increase. The value of this field is demonstrated by examples of forecasting and estimating future values of indicators including Management Key Performance Indicators, based on defined forecasting algorithms, in tandem with predictive analytics for business strategies.
- Digitalization has been a steady driver of the global standard of life, providing mechanisms for simplifying daily routines, reducing errors, and speeding up the growth of nations. In this regard, the article *High-Tech Industries Performance in*

the European Union analyses the performance of knowledge-intensive companies in the service sector in the European Union.

- The emergence and frequency of situations of uncertainty and risk are becoming more common in the global macroeconomic framework. The *article Analysis of Fluctuations of Aggregate Indicators and Persistence of Business Cycles in the Caspian Countries* explores the extent to which the existence of business cycles causes a series of disturbances at the level of each examined state, as well as how their persistence leads to a number of consequences that may impair their macroeconomic performance. The study's novelty lies in the examination of Caspian region's countries, which have specific competitive advantages, due to international transactions with petroleum products.
- A wide range of political, economic, social, environmental, and public health concerns are putting tremendous strain on the global economy. The COVID-19 outbreak has quickly evolved from a medical emergency to a threat to global supply chains and economic recession in nearly every country on the planet. The paper *Solutions for Post-Pandemic Economic Recovery: The Case of China* compares the performance of China's major macroeconomic parameters in 2020 to previous periods, discusses the efficacy of China's government's economic, fiscal, and investment solutions during the pandemic, and evaluates how these measures have affected China's recovery in terms of GDP, fixed asset investment, exports and imports, money supply, and the price index. The paper *Resilience and Recovery: The Impact of Covid-19 Pandemic on the Global Cruise Tourism* provides insights into the cruise industry's resilience by bringing together theoretical developments within the cruising sector as well as the newly emerging practices underlining the counteractive measures recently adopted in order to improve risk mitigation strategies and enhance decision-making processes in unpredictable circumstances. On a more specific note, the study *Fiscal Consolidation in Romania in the Wake of the COVID-19 Pandemic: How Much and How Fast?* projects Romania's public debt evolution from 2021 to 2030, based on the declared fiscal consolidation plans for 2021–2024 and then proposes a continuation of the budgetary deficit reduction. A sensitivity analysis is carried out to account for probable fluctuations in the causes of public debt, taking into consideration both optimistic and pessimistic scenarios.
- Risk has always been a part of the global agri-food value chain. Food safety issues arose at many levels as the open global market became more intense. Both inside and outside of Europe, food quality was frequently questioned in relation to regulation and management. The article *Risk Management of Agri-Food Value Chains—Exploring Research Trends from the Web of Science* explores emerging research trends concerning risk management approaches in the literature related to agri-food value chains.
- Migrations require a long-term or permanent change of residence, and they frequently result in significant changes in the lives of those involved. The study *Implications of the Migration Phenomenon in Romania* aims to identify the working relationships between the migration phenomenon and its implications on the Romanian economy, in the context of the global health crisis.

- Within a sustainable development context, companies are willingly participating in various CSR initiatives to enhance their contribution to the transition to a green economy. Related to this issue, the research *Non-Financial Performance of Energy Companies Listed on the Bucharest Stock Exchange and Relevance for Stakeholders* explores the sustainability activities of Romanian companies from the energy sector.
- Technological advancement has enabled citizens' interactions with local authorities and the government. The positive influence of digital technology could be seen in the quality of government-provided public services by increasing the efficiency and transparency of public-sector organizations. Therefore, the article *E-Government and the General Population's Digital Skills in the European Union and OECD Member States* used both visual analysis and analytical methods to determine the type of relationship between the Digital Government Index and the number of individuals with digital skills in countries that are members of both the OECD and of the European Union. The study entitled *The Context of Digital Entrepreneurship: New Technologies between Evolution and Revolution* aims to provide relevant answers to the challenges of the digital technology used by entrepreneurs to improve business strategy decisions.
- The paper *Factors Affecting Consumers' Attitude and Intentions towards Online Events during the COVID-19 Pandemic* aims to identify the factors affecting consumer attitudes and intentions towards online events during the COVID-19 pandemic. Under the same circumstances, the agri-food sector in Romania and Europe suffered due to slow consumers market and the restrictions imposed to reduce the spread of the virus. The main goal of the study *The Impact of Covid-19 on Food Prices in Romania* is to assess the influence of the pandemic on the Romanian food market, the consequences of the economic changes, as well as the link between the consumer price index and GDP.
- Higher education institutions had to rapidly adapt their teaching and learning processes, the research activity, and the programs for the society development, by embracing virtual on line platforms. The purpose of the study *Civic University Challenges in Romanian Higher Education; Students' Perceptions of Civic Engagement* is to present how Romanian universities have adapted to the civic university model by exploring whether student civic involvement is connected to academic performance and extracurricular activities. This study focuses on the concept and features of the civic university, on the institutional practices and leadership efforts underpinning civic engagement efforts and on a survey of students' perceptions on civic engagement.
- Comparing competitor prices, assessing expenditures incurred, and estimating the value given to the investor/client are the three most common methods for valuing one's labor. The aim of the paper *Individual Work Valuation in a Digital World—the Case of Personal Token's Pricing* is to identify the types of individual work that are valued by means of personal tokens and offered in the virtual world.

  - Family business is defined as the "backbone" of the world economy. In terms of globalization, the family's decades-long brand recognition is one of the most

intriguing marketing strategies on which the family has constantly worked on. In this regard, the paper entitled *The Importance of the Family Brand* addresses the relationship between R&D investments and revenues in successful family company brands.
- Tax evasion or avoidance is a global problem that affects societies all over the world. The paper *Is Trust a Valid Indicator of Tax Compliance Behaviour? A Study on Taxpayers' Public Perception Using Sentiment Analysis Tools* aims to identify those variables relating to taxpayers' behavior that could be tackled by the Tax Authority in order to control this phenomenon. The main results of the study reveal that the negative, pessimistic attitude of Romanian residents toward the fiscal system is fueled by a perceived lack of transparency, poor quality of public services, and a greater tax burden, which erodes faith in the government.

A resilient response to the impact of the COVID-19 pandemic necessitates stable governance, political leadership, community participation, business continuity, and a focus on long-term recovery. Businesses, policymakers, and academics must work together to ensure that the communication between all stakeholders becomes more transparent and inclusive with the view to mitigate the negative consequences of the COVID-19 pandemic and move toward long-term recovery in a more sustainable way. We hope you find the collection of evidence based research papers presented in this book thought provoking, illuminating and useful in providing a first step toward pursuing a 'common good' and 'building back better and more sustainably'.

Bucharest, Romania Alina Mihaela Dima
Nottingham, UK Mihaela Kelemen

Contents

High-Tech Industries Performance in the European Union

Horobeţ Alexandra, Gîlcă Melisa, and Belaşcu Lucian

Abstract Digitalization has been a constantly increasing driver of the standard of living worldwide, providing mechanisms through which quotidian activities are simplified, errors reduced, and development of nations accelerated. Therefore, people, businesses and governments became dependent on the good functionality of technological advances integrated in the system. In this framework, the performance of companies in the high-tech sector is vital to maintain and promote progress at country or region level. In the last decades, we have seen a complete transformation of the way the high-tech sector is perceived, especially considering how digitalization penetrates more developed countries versus less developed ones. In this respect, the current paper analyses the performance of knowledge-intensive companies in the services sector headquartered in the European Union, with relatively homogenous macroeconomic situation. Firstly, we investigated the performance of these knowledge-intensive services between 2011 and 2017 using productivity and profitability indicators, aiming at gaining insight into the behaviour of these services under normal economic conditions, and at revealing the relations between performance and location. We analyse the information extracted from the Eurostat database with a panel data approach, using an ordinary least squares (OLS) model, taking into consideration industry and country-specific variables. The results imply that industry factors are more prominent than geographical position as drivers of knowledge-intensive industries' performance, but further research is needed to have more conclusive estimations. Secondly, we analysed the current pandemic, and the way social

H. Alexandra (✉) · G. Melisa
Bucharest University of Economic Studies, Bucharest, Romania
e-mail: alexandra.horobet@rei.ase.ro

G. Melisa
e-mail: gilcamelisa17@stud.ase.ro

B. Lucian
"Lucian Blaga" University of Sibiu, Sibiu, Romania
e-mail: lucian.belascu@ulbsibiu.ro

A. M. Dima and M. Kelemen (eds.), *Digitalization and Big Data for Resilience and Economic Intelligence*, Springer Proceedings in Business and Economics, https://doi.org/10.1007/978-3-030-93286-2_1

distancing is pushing towards finding fast and efficient solution to maintain communication, work in appropriate conditions and have easy access to any information necessary. From here, we discuss the implications of our previous findings for the knowledge-intensive services business performance in the years to come.

Keywords High-technology · Knowledge-intensive services · Location · Performance · Productivity

1 Introduction

The change towards highly industrialized manufacturing processes and intensive trade between nations increased the growth rate of developed countries and created a bigger gap between states that did not have the political, social and economic environment to sustain the remodelling of operating procedures and those that adapted promptly. After the extensive developments in research and innovations in the technological field, throughout the twentieth century, there can be a distinguished shift from tangible to intangible goods, or information goods (Shapiro and Varian 1999).

Digitalization has changed the way consumers perceive goods, the incentives to buy and companies' approach to business practices. Due to increased improvement in information technology worldwide, traditional manufacturing operations are combined with smart technology. The automatization of factories, logistics and even human capital is designed to enhance consumer experience and streamline procedures. A constant relocation of the employment field can be a consequence of the robotization of processes (Schwab 2016). Because certain jobs have become obsolete, especially in the production lines, there is currently an increase in service-based businesses. The tertiary sector of economies has enlarged rapidly—according to estimates for the European Union (2014) 73% of the workforce works in the service sector, in Belgium (2013)—80%, in Netherlands (2015)—81% and in Germany (2016)—74% (CIA 2020). This phenomenon can be explained by the increase of economic output in the developed countries, large-scale investments in education and investments in research institutions, therefore higher labour productivity; higher wages, decrease in the number of hours worked per week, resulting in the creation of new interests and desire for experiences provided by the service industries. A major consequence of the expansion of the service sector is the regional agglomeration of economic growth, leading to amplified socio-economic inequality (Evans and Timberlake 1980).

The knowledge economy is the result of technological advances and information goods proliferation. These evolutions have led to the demand for highly skilled and educated workers who could meet the upgraded standards, being rewarded with higher wages (Powell and Snellman 2004). Research and development in universities is another factor that could determine the performance of a country in the service sector, especially because of the cluster effect of start-ups near universities and conglomerates of similar firms, such as Silicon Valley (Kerr et al. 2019).

This paper investigates the performance of high-tech knowledge-intensive services in the European Union and represents an inquiry regarding the correlation between the geographical location and the performance of this sector, i.e., we are interested in assessing whether the location of a business can determine its productivity and profitability and debates the results in relation to the current economic environment. It is of interest for investors (redirect financing towards more advantageous opportunities), entrepreneurs (market penetration), consultancy firms (risk evaluation for companies, Human Resources planning—employment based on location advantages), governmental entities (reallocation of funds) and corporations (selective offshoring or outsourcing).

The objective of our research is to understand the connection between high-tech knowledge-intensive services' (HTKIS) performance, productivity and innovation, and whether location is a determinant for these aspects. The research hypothesis is that location is a significant factor for the performance of HTKIS—based on outreach, education levels and standard of living. The alternative hypothesis is that the geographical position does not impact performance. After examining the database selected for the study, we expected to identify a link between location and performance, because of the significant differences in opportunities, labour productivity and economic development between the developed and the developing countries. However, the subject will be debated from more perspectives to fully comprehend the phenomenon and identify possible shortcomings and elements that should be taken into consideration in further examinations.

Our paper is organized as follows: the next section presents the problem statement and is accompanied by a section that discusses the aims of our research. Further, we describe our research methods, show the most important results and conclude by outlining the most important implications of our research and suggesting avenues for future research.

2 Literature Review

The literature is vast in what concerns the knowledge/information economy, the digitalization of labour and "servicification of manufacturing" (Lanz and Maurer 2015; Rainer and Andreas 2015), as well as high-tech industry and knowledge-intensive businesses. Research on high-tech knowledge-intensive services that analyses their performance is scarce, especially in what concerns empirical approaches. The subject of whether the location has been a determinant of performance in the high-tech and/or knowledge-intensive industries has not been debated at length, but Audretsch and Feldman (1996), Fischer et al. (2009), and Wang et al. (2016) considered the geographical factor as an influence on profitability. The results differ as the scope of the analyses and timeframes were different throughout the studies. Hence, the current literature is insufficient to conclude whether or not the geographical location of a high-tech knowledge-intensive service determines its performance, and is even contradictory in some respects. The literature is inconsistent across the years because of the high digitalization of the economy, thus the findings at the beginning of the century may differ quite substantially from more recent ones because data was quantified and qualified differently, the approaches authors used lacked the research methodology that can be accessed today, or their understandings of knowledge-intensive services were dissimilar.

An early study of Audretsch and Feldman (1996) referred to innovation's spatial distribution and geographical agglomeration of production, noting the spillovers from research and development. They used a correlation matrix and ordinary least squares (OLS) method and three-stage least squares (3SLS) estimation methods for the regression. The authors concluded that innovation concentrates in sectors where spillovers of knowledge were a key factor, despite the geographic clustering of production. Also, industry R&D (Research and Development), educated workforce and university research contribute to the increase in innovation. The paper lacks updated data, but the theoretical conclusion applies to the current status of society. It provides a thorough historical background to comprehend the situation of high-tech services before digitalization—which has increased in the last decade, at least when measured by the Internet use in the European Union—see Fig. 1.

Capello et al. (2012) investigated whether the presence of large, urbanized cities represents a factor for increased performance in innovation, regarding knowledge-intensive services (KIS) and knowledge spillovers. The study proposed an inquiry concerning agglomerated regions and their level of innovation, proving that those specializing in KIS were more innovatory than the ones specializing in manufacturing. The authors used the method elaborated by George Jenks and Fred Caspall of natural breaks (Jenks and Caspall 1971), which draws maps to present the dynamic behaviour of each country in the selected industries. They found that rural regions tend to focus on low-tech activities and that there is a concordant autocorrelation between innovation performance in Europe and spatial distribution, i.e., largely populated regions, especially metropolitan ones, attract process innovation due to a more imaginative and diversified environment. Their remarks help in creating a

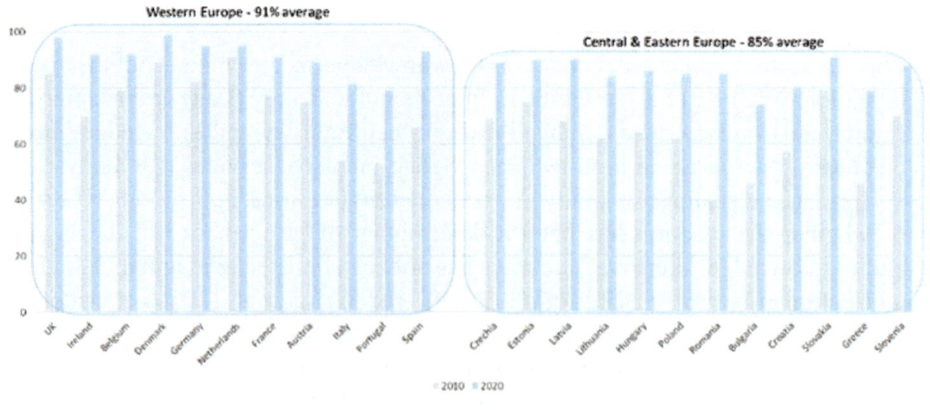

Fig. 1 Internet use measured in percentage [%] of individuals in the European Union—2010 versus 2020. *Source* Authors' calculations based on Eurostat data

context for the way knowledge-intensive services have punctual concentration rates, are more accentuated in very urbanized areas and their localization yields different innovation performance. However, it fails to consider other location factors that may have an impact on the results and does not provide extensive research on possible particularities.

The way high-tech sector innovation performance is determined by R&D expenses, the number of employees in R&D, the expenditure in education and the level of exports were analysed by Baesu et al. (2015). They used panels with fixed and random effects models and concluded that the number of patents rises directly with the number of employees and diminishes when the R&D expenditure amplifies. However, their database is not complete for all the European countries, therefore it is difficult to generalize the results. Also, they do not analyse in-depth the applicability of their results and how they are relevant in improving the high-tech sector. Their research concentrates on patents as an important innovation indicator. Similar approaches have been undertaken by Maurseth and Verspagen (2002), Thompson and Fox-Kean (2005), Fischer et al. (2009). Other authors remark that geographical location is an important negative factor on knowledge flows, which are maintained at a national level, within countries (Maurseth and Verspagen 2002). Despite this, Fischer et al. (2009) concluded that geographical proximity no longer plays such an important role, and technological distance is more relevant when considering knowledge spillovers. The difference in results may be explained by the change in economics and technology between the two studies' publishing dates, the difference in timeframes analysed and specific indicators used.

Taking into account the effect of inbound open innovation, Wang et al. (2015) researched firm performances in the high-tech sector. They focus on the acquisition of knowledge resources and the way innovation and performance are distorted depending on the obtainment of external technologies. The paper aims at finding correlations between technology scouting, horizontal/vertical collaboration and firm performance. They use a large-scale survey, five control variables and descriptive statistics to explain what factors could upgrade the innovation operations (cooperation with suppliers, competitors and customers) and the way firms can obtain technical knowledge and information to innovate by concentrating on external sources, such as customer communities. The study focuses on the managerial inferences of innovation and performance increases, therefore there is an abundance of theoretical frameworks and little empirical data for performance indicators. Thus, it provides managerial guidelines in order to draw on frameworks for reallocations of knowledge resources and acquisition of such goods in a manner that would induce the most performant scenarios for companies.

Schmidt (2015) measured the level of knowledge spillovers by accounting for the exact spillover mechanism. The methodology of the paper consists of a quantitative survey and qualitative interviews undertaken with biotechnology, architecture and engineering entrepreneurs from Germany. One shortcoming of this research is that the data selected are biased based on the firms' studies and the timeframe in which the interviews were taken. Therefore, the findings may not be completely applicable when it comes to other regions and could have been overruled by recent developments in technology and the way it affects knowledge transfer and innovation practices. Still, it creates a useful research method to assess the level of knowledge spillovers, providing more meaningful insights from the industry due to the qualitative data it entails. We can talk about positive spillovers because of the benefits they may offer, such as productivity growth, help in the decision process for specific subjects, relationships based on knowledge and enriched strategic decisions. Schmidt also found that spillovers may occur over a large regional distance, thus not being necessarily related to metropolitan areas or very urbanized regions. The study acknowledges the importance of R&D establishments and companies' regional proximity but questions the matter of spatial localization of knowledge spillovers as regional clusters in KIBS—an idea supported by many studies in the field of economic geography before. It finds that spillovers can occur in larger spatial distances when considering vertical business relations and in the case of social ties based on trust.

Given the high volatility in the service economy, changes are inevitable and occur with increased intensity. Wang et al. (2016) analyse the way KIBS have changed in the Pearl River Delta (PRD) of China, focusing on location patterns and vicinity. The paper takes into consideration Western practices and findings, and it helps the current paper with methodological structure and in generating patterns that can be further identified in other locations, consequently resulting in possible worldwide trends. The paper chose a highly economically developed, industrialized and globalized area for the study of a complex phenomenon, which may cause the data to be impractical for other regions. The authors classify the firms assessed as state-owned enterprises (SOEs) and foreign-owned enterprises (FOEs) and aim at understanding whether KIBS concentrate in the centre of cities, if their intensity depends on the closeness to large SOEs or FOEs, if entrants in this sector will converge close to already existing firms (the cumulative causation mechanism) and how manufacturing companies nearby are affecting the number of new KIBS companies. The authors employ the DO approach—a distance-based test of spatial concentration, analysing spatial concentration with kernel density estimation and a binomial regression model. They discovered that the businesses in the study based on KIS concentrate towards a centre, as a consequence of newly entered companies' propensity to locate near already established and profitable KIBS firms. An interesting conclusion was the bipolar dispersion of KIBS entrants, either the placement near SOEs—resulting in increased concentration, or near FOEs—the concentration is decentralized.

Horobet et al. (2018) examined the European high-tech sector, with the aim of finding whether competitiveness in this industry is impelled by location. They looked at performance indicators and considered a classification of companies based on their ownership (foreign or domestic). Their study is relevant at the European Union level, but the methodology used could be applied to other regions as well, considering the difference in indicators and classifications of sectors. The indicators chosen to measure the performance and competitiveness of the studied firms are labour productivity and gross operating rate, which were included alongside industry and country characteristics in a panel least squares. A strong point of this method of research is that, because of the presence of both manufacturing and services (secondary and tertiary sector of the economy), it can easily be observed if there are any correlations between the two, ergo studies could be continued to see if there is a relevant connection along with performance and is determined by the presence of the other. In another order of ideas, a weak point of the study is represented by the selected countries, although this issue was independent of researchers as it was based on data availability. Even though they are all EU member states, their economic development is very different, political and social factors do not correspond, not even in neighbouring countries. These aspects may lead to inconclusive results. The authors found important disparities between old and new EU countries, as appears to be increased labour productivity in older member states, which can easily be explained by the economic environment present in more developed countries and its attractiveness in terms of financing and technological advancement. It is also relevant to mention that performance increases are directly proportional to the level of development of the respective country. The current paper will focus extensively on this research, attempting to continue their investigation, specializing in the tertiary sector and spatial proximity, rather than ownership aspects.

The changes in the KIBS that do not necessarily follow classic economic theories were evaluated by Mol and Brandl (2018). The authors assess cognitive distance and the breach created by offshoring influencing KIBS. The paper focuses to a high extent on predictions, which may be inefficient in some cases or more difficult to implement if the subject is not properly explored. The authors concluded that KIBS are comprised of modular stages—conducted either onshore or offshore. Also, production processes present high heterogeneity and "are likely to involve significant learning, discovery, and experimentation" (Mol and Brandl 2018).

Foreign-owned and locally owned companies in the European Union (EU) were analysed in the study of Horobet and Popvici (2018) to see if there are any correlations between technological intensity and performance gaps in the analysed companies during a post-crisis period. The authors brought into discussion the hypothesis of the specific advantage of multinational enterprises overrunning the liability of foreignness, setting the argument for a mutually beneficial relationship between foreign and local ownership. The analysis covered medium high-technology industries, medium–low-technology industries and low technology industries. Their findings do not indicate a link between performance gaps and the technological level of the industries. Yet, it is noted that the performance of foreign-owned companies is inclined to be more homogenous compared to locally owned firms and improved performance in locally owned companies can be associated with higher profitability and productivity levels in foreign-owned companies, conceivably due to positive spillovers. The paper did not insist on the theoretical aspects of the spillover effect and could have taken into consideration or point towards future research regarding factors that lead to spillovers and to what degree they encourage innovation rather than theft of information goods. This research helps the current paper by providing a model for analysing the performance of high-tech sectors and insights into the spillover effects present in the European Union.

Gil et al. (2019) considered the Europe "2020 Strategy" to increase the growth rate of economic development and high-skilled workers in the high-tech sector. They investigated whether the two are correlated using a directed-technical-change model, accounting for horizontal and vertical R&D. Their analysis points towards certain policy implications for economic growth—educational (motivation to improve the qualification level, decrease brain-drain effect) and industrial (ease the entry costs, diminish the regulations and bureaucratic efforts). The paper presents a detailed evaluation of the high-skilled sector in terms of workers, analysing determinants for performance and providing an ample theoretical framework on which the authors base their conclusions.

Related studies were made regarding land use and the concentration of KIS in large urban areas by Lu et al. (2020) and Lee and Jung (2020). Overall, they provide information about the localization of KIS and how the planning of land use can influence industries' performance. Because of the impact land-use policies can have on a firm's development, concentrations of KIS may occur more likely in countries with better regulations in this sense. Their research analyses data from Asia [China and Seul, Korea], but the results could be interpreted and useful for other countries as well. On a theoretical framework, they use panel data analysis, Slack-based measure model, a local indicator of spatial autocorrelation (LISA) analysis and multivariate regression and discover that clustering of high-tech companies in national high-tech zones (NHTZ) has led to knowledge spillovers between foreign and domestic ones. Hence, the increase of impact of NHTZs can be done through policies aiming at creating multiple mature zones for high-tech and regional development of KIS can be boosted by land-use planning.

Horobet et al. (2020) contributed to the literature research regarding factors determining competitiveness and performance in EU high-tech industries by analysing twelve countries through a panel approach with ordinary least squares (OLS) and autoregressive integrated moving average (ARIMA) frameworks over the period 2008–2015. There are significant differences between older and new EU member states, mainly because of their development level. Consequently, older members have a bigger focus on knowledge-intensive activities, whereas the new ones are used as affiliates for multinational companies (MNCs) specializing in labour-intensive activities (manufacturing). These findings will help in better understanding the results in the current paper, especially since it only focuses on services, so there might be a clear distinction between performances in the countries analysed. Figure 2 shows the differences between older and newer EU members in terms of the importance of the ICT Services sector in countries' GDP, including the comparison with the EU average.

Despite the early technological advances in the Western Europe, Central and Eastern Europe have increased tremendously in the past years the share of ICT services—as seen in Fig. 2 (from 3.38% of GDP in 2008 to 3.89% in 2018, in line with Western Europe Average in 2018 of 3.91% of GDP). The current paper comes with a similar approach in methodology as other previous ones, but addresses a different question, looking more in-depth at the correlation between knowledge and geography or location, and the way they are influenced by different factors. It aims at understanding the development potential of a sector with respect to economic, social and location environment.

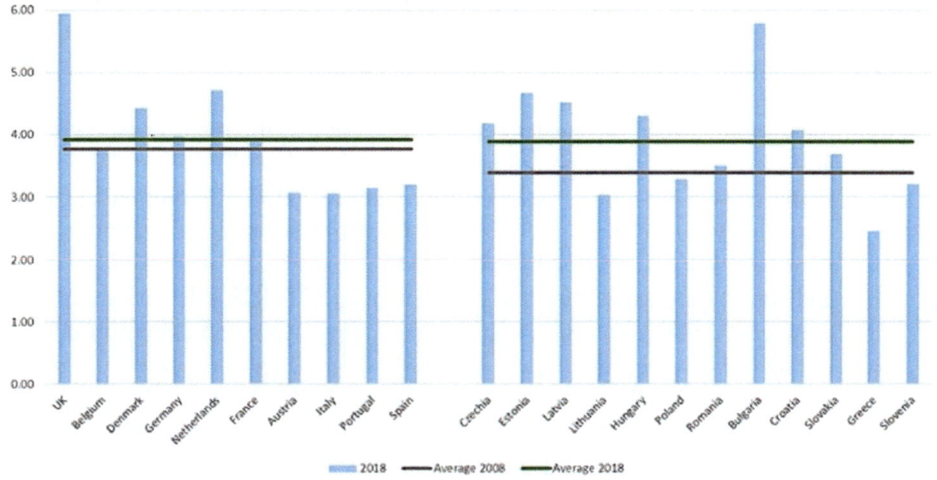

Fig. 2 Percentage [%] of the ICT services sector in GDP in the European Union in 2018 versus 2008. *Source* Authors' calculations based on Eurostat data

3 Methodology

The objective of our research is to understand the connection between high-tech knowledge-intensive services' (HTKIS) performance, productivity, and innovation and location as a potential determinant. The null hypothesis is that location—i.e., the country of headquarters of HTKIS companies—is a factor for performance. The alternative hypothesis is that the geographical position of firms in this sector does not impact performance. After examining the database selected for the study, we expected to identify a significant correlation between location and performance, because of the significant differences in opportunities, labour productivity and economic development between the developed and the developing countries in the European Union, which represents the area of research. However, the subject will be debated from more perspectives, to fully comprehend the phenomenon, explain possible shortcomings in this paper and elements that should be taken into consideration in further examinations.

The current investigation analyses data for the period 2011–2017 and refers to twenty-one countries, member states of the European Union (EU), for which there was the highest availability of information. The countries are classified as older member states (11)—Belgium, France, Germany, Italy, Netherlands, Denmark, Greece, Portugal, Spain, Austria and Sweden—and new member states (10): Czech Republic, Hungary, Latvia, Lithuania, Poland, Slovakia, Slovenia, Bulgaria, Romania and Croatia. For the sake of relevance in further research, despite data availability, the United Kingdom (UK) has been removed from the data set because of its withdrawal from the European Union on 31st of January 2020.

The paper focuses on the investigation of the high-technology (high-tech) sectors in the EU considering the Eurostat classification by sector approach, which groups manufacturing and services activities. This analysis will concentrate on services activities, more specifically on the high-tech knowledge-intensive services (HTKIS) as described in the High-tech aggregation by NACE Rev. 2—at 2 digit level, with the following industries: "Motion picture, video and television programme production, sound recording and music publishing activities" (J59), "Programming and broadcasting activities" (J60), "Telecommunications" (J61), "Computer programming, consultancy and related activities" (J62), "Information service activities" (J63) and "Scientific research and development" (M72).

The indicators used to measure the performance of HTKIS activities in the European Union were collected from Eurostat. They are: (i) Apparent labour productivity (ALP) defined as "value added at factor costs divided by the number of persons employed"; (ii) Wage-adjusted labour productivity (WALP), which is calculated as "value-added divided by personnel costs [...] adjusted by the share of paid employees"; and (iii) Gross operating surplus/person employed (GOSPE) representing the ratio between gross operating surplus—"the remuneration of the production factor capital" and persons employed—"total number of persons who work in and outside the observation unit who belong to it and are paid by it"—definitions extracted from Eurostat. The first two indicators address labour productivity at large as this aspect can denote the performance of an industry. The last indicator (GOSPE) introduces a combination of profitability and productivity. There is a bigger emphasis on labour productivity because the paper focuses on services and competitiveness, which could be better assessed through innovation rather than financial indicators.

The specific variables for countries or at a regional level considered in this essay are: (i) Gross domestic product at current market prices measured in thousands of euro per capita (GDP_C); (ii) Trade balance for services, calculated as the difference between exports and imports of services, expressed in million euro (TRADEBAL); (iii) The percentage of the population with tertiary education, from 15 to 74 years, expressed as a percentage (TERTED); (iv) The expenditure on R&D by businesses per inhabitant only in the HTKIS sectors adjusted by the number of enterprises (RDEXP_ENT). These variables have been chosen to assess a country's level of development, trade openness with regard to services, the level of education of the average individual—as it assumed that more advanced education will most likely provide a job in HTKIS; and the attention given to the studied sectors. These indicators should help integrate the variables into a regional context.

The performance of the high-tech knowledge-intensive services in the European Union can be illustrated with the help of industry and country-specific factors. This paper assesses the relevance of these variables in what concerns the chosen indicators for the performance of HTKIS using a balanced panel with the general form of:

$$Y_{it} = \alpha_{it} + \beta_{it} \cdot X'_{it} + \delta_{it} \cdot Z'_{it} + \gamma_{it} + u_{it} + \varepsilon_{it} \tag{1}$$

with Y_{it} the dependent variable—it will be successively a variable for performance: ALP, WALP and GOSPE; αit represents the constant for the given model, X'_{it} is the industry specifics vector; Zit' is the vector for location characteristics that helps understand the differences across countries; y_{it} describes the cross-section distinct fixed effects, u_{it} captures the period-specific fixed effects; ε_{it} is the error term for $i = 1, 2, \ldots$, M cross-section units monitored for the periods $t = 1, 2, \ldots$, T; in which case $M = 21$ and $t = 6$. T is not equal to seven, even though there are 7 years analysed because the data was constructed using the first difference of logarithmic data, thus having the effect of lowering t from 7 to 6.

The vector for industry characteristics includes the following variables: (i) Turnover per number of enterprises, expressed in million euro (TURN_ENT)—calculated as the turnover for each industry divided by the number of companies in the industry; (ii) The number of persons employed per enterprise (PERSEM_ENT)—the indicator for persons employed was adapted to the number of enterprises registered for each sector; (iii) The average personnel costs or personnel costs per employee —defined by Eurostat as "total remuneration, in cash or in kind, payable by an employer to an employee in return for work done by the latter", adjusted to the number of enterprises for every industry measured in thousands euro (PERSCOST_ENT); (iv) The business investment rate (INVR)—defined by Eurostat as "gross investment divided by gross value added of non-financial corporations". The first three indicators have been adjusted to the number of enterprises present in every sector because of the high correlations they had initially with the dependent variables and between each other. This accommodation has largely resolved the issue, with very few exceptions. Overall, it is expected that the coefficients will be positive for TURN_ENT and PERSEM_ENT—because a higher number of persons employed is usually present in larger corporations that generate higher rates of profitability, and negative for PERSCOST_ENT—we hypothesize that higher personnel costs, caused by the services nature, governmental requirements, or social conditions, diminish business profitability. Moreover, we expect either a negative coefficient for INVR—given that most of the new companies in the investigated industries attract fewer investments rates, which can lead to very low growth rates, or a positive one, building on the impact that investments have on long-term business growth, jointly with profitability.

4 Analysis and Results Interpretation

The difference between pooled and panel data is that for the latter we have the same cross-sections analysed over a specified period, whereas for the first category the observations are more dispersed. Panel data provides a better overview of the dynamics of the variables. A balanced panel is done when for every cross-section there is the same sum of time units (Zulfikar 2018). In our case, there is the same period studied for all the countries and sectors. The model uses the Ordinary Least Squares Method (OLS) to minimize the sum of residual points from the plotted curve. The coefficient of determination (R^2) expresses how well the regression in the analysis fits the data. The adjusted R^2 also considers the way independent variables contribute to the model and creates a better overview of the correlation. R^2 and the standard error of the regression are goodness-of-fit measures. The difference between the two indicators is that the standard error gives absolute values for measurements, while R^2 is expressed as percentages. F-statistic is the critical value obtained from an F-test used to compare statistical models to find out which one fits a given population better (Gujarati 2004). The results for all the estimations are presented below. There are the coefficients and their respective probability for every variable under the panel specifications NO—no effects, FCE—fixed-cross-sections effects and FPE—fixed-period effects (Fig. 3). The outcomes are discussed with regard to industry and country-specific variables, following an overall analysis for every sector.

Dependent	panel	α	TURN_ENT	PERSEM_ENT	PERSCOST_ENT	INVR	GDP_CAP	TRADEBAL	TERTED	RDEXP_ENT	R2	Adj. R2	St.E	F-stat	Prob F-stat
J59 Motion picture, video and television programme production, sound recording and music publishing activities															
ALP	NO	-0.040	0.674	-0.670	0.069	-0.093	1.239	0.000	0.001	0.080	0.199	0.144	0.206	3.627	0.001
		0.228	0.001	0.004	0.654	0.026	0.064	0.119	0.998	0.215					
ALP	FCE	-0.032	0.630	-0.586	0.047	-0.077	1.109	0.000	-0.107	0.129	0.267	0.056	0.216	1.263	0.201
		0.410	0.004	0.034	0.786	0.089	0.188	0.159	0.842	0.075					
ALP	FPE	-0.046	0.844	-0.597	-0.040	-0.103	1.723	0.000	-0.205	0.058	0.269	0.184	0.201	3.163	0.000
		0.176	0.000	0.010	0.803	0.016	0.029	0.107	0.655	0.373					
J60 Programming and broadcasting activities															
ALP	NO	-3.077	22.412	-32.381	25.226	0.179	88.424	0.000	-10.682	-3.356	0.307	0.260	11.466	6.480	0.000
		0.085	0.011	0.000	0.004	0.036	0.017	0.706	0.678	0.385					
ALP	FCE	-4.223	18.603	-30.353	27.776	0.188	137.529	0.000	-12.664	-3.631	0.356	0.170	12.138	1.916	0.010
		0.051	0.056	0.001	0.004	0.039	0.005	0.738	0.678	0.401					
ALP	FPE	-1.865	19.792	-34.290	28.266	0.206	44.879	0.000	-15.103	-1.802	0.395	0.324	10.954	5.615	0.000
		0.291	0.022	0.000	0.001	0.013	0.276	0.610	0.547	0.633					
J61 Telecommunications															
ALP	NO	-0.022	0.682	-0.798	0.151	-0.064	0.175	0.000	0.137	0.013	0.582	0.553	0.054	20.322	0.000
		0.012	0.000	0.000	0.001	0.008	0.346	0.215	0.258	0.446					
ALP	FCE	-0.024	0.608	-0.740	0.154	-0.070	0.249	0.000	0.110	0.019	0.617	0.507	0.056	5.584	0.000
		0.021	0.000	0.000	0.002	0.009	0.290	0.353	0.442	0.333					
ALP	FPE	-0.019	0.661	-0.793	0.160	-0.076	0.042	0.000	0.133	0.015	0.592	0.545	0.054	12.515	0.000
		0.042	0.000	0.000	0.001	0.004	0.840	0.241	0.287	0.405					
J62 Computer programming, consultancy and related activities															
ALP	NO	0.000	0.439	-0.541	0.087	0.006	0.527	0.000	0.042	0.008	0.370	0.327	0.050	8.590	0.000
		0.996	0.000	0.000	0.203	0.696	0.001	0.610	0.713	0.619					
ALP	FCE	0.000	0.455	-0.588	0.067	0.012	0.481	0.000	0.041	0.014	0.478	0.327	0.050	3.173	0.000
		0.989	0.000	0.000	0.361	0.476	0.020	0.562	0.746	0.418					
ALP	FPE	0.000	0.455	-0.542	0.102	0.006	0.604	0.000	0.012	0.008	0.394	0.324	0.051	5.603	0.000
		0.997	0.000	0.000	0.144	0.723	0.002	0.502	0.916	0.628					
J63 Information service activities															
ALP	NO	0.001	0.218	-0.471	0.174	-0.092	0.825	0.000	0.012	0.009	0.186	0.130	0.152	3.334	0.002
		0.957	0.054	0.016	0.108	0.001	0.084	0.763	0.972	0.854					
ALP	FCE	0.001	0.256	-0.532	0.170	-0.086	0.724	0.000	0.053	0.010	0.248	0.031	0.161	1.142	0.310
		0.964	0.046	0.017	0.158	0.006	0.242	0.749	0.896	0.852					
ALP	FPE	-0.002	0.206	-0.510	0.188	-0.099	1.026	0.000	-0.017	0.018	0.211	0.120	0.153	2.306	0.010
		0.929	0.075	0.011	0.092	0.001	0.069	0.806	0.962	0.732					
M72 Scientific research and development															
ALP	NO	0.127	0.555	-0.402	0.252	-0.095	-1.414	0.000	-1.225	0.052	0.388	0.346	0.222	9.280	0.000
		0.000	0.000	0.003	0.009	0.007	0.042	0.972	0.015	0.477					
ALP	FCE	0.170	0.542	-0.319	0.240	-0.080	-2.650	0.000	-1.435	0.078	0.482	0.333	0.225	3.224	0.000
		0.000	0.000	0.029	0.022	0.029	0.003	0.930	0.012	0.310					
ALP	FPE	0.123	0.541	-0.407	0.266	-0.097	-1.153	0.000	-1.295	0.054	0.394	0.324	0.226	5.607	0.000
		0.001	0.000	0.005	0.010	0.010	0.167	0.986	0.014	0.478					

Fig. 3 Panel least square results for ALP, WALP and GOSPE, respectively, as the dependent variable. *Source* Authors' calculations based on Eurostat data

Dependent	panel	α	TURN_ENT	PERSEM_ENT	PERSCOST_ENT	INVR	GDP_CAP	TRADEBAL	TERTED	RDEXP_ENT	R2	Adj. R2	St.E	F-stat	Prob F-stat
J59 Motion picture, video and television programme production, sound recording and music publishing activities															
WALP	NO	-0.047	0.769	-0.210	-0.518	-0.083	0.395	0.000	0.027	0.123	0.191	0.136	0.213	3.456	0.001
		0.169	0.000	0.373	0.001	0.054	0.566	0.244	0.955	0.067					
WALP	FCE	-0.053	0.724	-0.173	-0.575	-0.065	0.581	0.000	-0.032	0.164	0.280	0.073	0.221	1.349	0.143
		0.186	0.001	0.536	0.002	0.156	0.498	0.237	0.954	0.027					
WALP	FPE	-0.058	0.975	-0.102	-0.670	-0.094	1.086	0.000	-0.204	0.092	0.278	0.195	0.205	3.326	0.000
		0.092	0.000	0.661	0.000	0.031	0.175	0.191	0.664	0.168					
J60 Programming and broadcasting activities															
WALP	NO	-7.481	75.388	-70.518	-29.819	0.243	287.563	0.001	-34.025	2.277	0.161	0.103	36.990	2.802	0.007
		0.194	0.008	0.007	0.285	0.374	0.016	0.389	0.682	0.855					
WALP	FCE	-10.113	69.737	-65.003	-28.987	0.281	417.765	0.001	-49.095	3.971	0.212	-0.015	39.364	0.932	0.569
		0.148	0.027	0.023	0.348	0.339	0.009	0.449	0.619	0.777					
WALP	FPE	-3.579	62.186	-72.009	-17.725	0.319	162.329	0.001	-54.874	7.529	0.277	0.193	35.086	3.305	0.000
		0.526	0.025	0.005	0.507	0.225	0.219	0.348	0.495	0.534					
J61 Telecommunications															
WALP	NO	-0.008	1.175	-0.473	-0.697	-0.091	-0.314	0.000	0.214	0.028	0.635	0.610	0.068	25.490	0.000
		0.459	0.000	0.000	0.000	0.003	0.183	0.262	0.166	0.192					
WALP	FCE	-0.008	1.097	-0.411	-0.705	-0.094	-0.338	0.000	0.192	0.038	0.677	0.584	0.070	7.271	0.000
		0.532	0.000	0.002	0.000	0.005	0.249	0.454	0.279	0.118					
WALP	FPE	-0.005	1.233	-0.523	-0.702	-0.094	-0.367	0.000	0.181	0.028	0.641	0.599	0.069	15.391	0.000
		0.646	0.000	0.000	0.000	0.005	0.170	0.271	0.256	0.223					
J62 Computer programming, consultancy and related activities															
WALP	NO	-0.016	0.390	-0.213	-0.206	0.007	-0.216	0.000	0.059	0.009	0.215	0.161	0.052	3.995	0.000
		0.058	0.000	0.075	0.004	0.663	0.197	0.484	0.610	0.576					
WALP	FCE	-0.023	0.405	-0.207	-0.251	0.007	-0.070	0.000	0.081	0.012	0.329	0.135	0.053	1.699	0.030
		0.019	0.000	0.136	0.001	0.698	0.743	0.623	0.540	0.518					
WALP	FPE	-0.014	0.387	-0.218	-0.188	0.006	-0.235	0.000	0.036	0.008	0.231	0.142	0.052	2.585	0.004
		0.121	0.000	0.076	0.010	0.708	0.238	0.494	0.767	0.657					
J63 Information service activities															
WALP	NO	-0.017	0.129	-0.198	-0.073	-0.093	0.276	0.000	-0.063	0.009	0.117	0.056	0.151	1.931	0.062
		0.465	0.246	0.300	0.495	0.001	0.557	0.736	0.855	0.863					
WALP	FCE	-0.025	0.159	-0.212	-0.111	-0.094	0.441	0.000	-0.035	0.005	0.215	-0.011	0.156	0.951	0.543
		0.361	0.198	0.321	0.342	0.002	0.462	0.803	0.930	0.927					
WALP	FPE	-0.015	0.116	-0.228	-0.063	-0.099	0.222	0.000	-0.082	0.017	0.132	0.031	0.153	1.307	0.219
		0.555	0.312	0.248	0.566	0.001	0.690	0.785	0.818	0.736					
M72 Scientific research and development															
WALP	NO	0.097	0.510	0.039	-0.194	-0.085	-1.934	0.000	-1.138	0.025	0.302	0.254	0.220	6.331	0.000
		0.006	0.000	0.769	0.041	0.014	0.005	0.756	0.022	0.730					
WALP	FCE	0.125	0.464	0.128	-0.197	-0.068	-2.538	0.000	-1.338	0.058	0.389	0.212	0.226	2.201	0.002
		0.002	0.001	0.380	0.061	0.064	0.004	0.931	0.019	0.449					
WALP	FPE	0.098	0.505	0.025	-0.199	-0.082	-2.006	0.000	-1.110	0.020	0.306	0.226	0.224	3.806	0.000
		0.009	0.000	0.860	0.050	0.026	0.016	0.749	0.032	0.789					

Fig. 3 (continued)

4.1 Industry Characteristics

The attributes for industry picked for this analysis were turnover per number of enterprises (TURN_ENT), the number of persons employed per number of enterprises (PERSEM_ENT), the average personnel cost per number of enterprises (PERSCOST_ENT) and investment rate (INVR). From this range of variables, the turnover and persons employed showed the most statistically significant coefficients at least at 5% level for all the industries and the panel specifications. However, there is a positive connection between turnover and productivity in almost all the cases (except J63), but a negative link for almost all industries between productivity and the number of persons employed, the personnel cost (except J63) and investment

Dependent panel		α	TURN_ENT	PERSEM_ENT	PERSCOST_ENT	INVR	GDP_CAP	TRADEBAL	TERTED	RDEXP_ENT	R2	Adj. R2	St.E	F-stat	Prob F-stat
J59 Motion picture, video and television programme production, sound recording and music publishing activities															
GOSPE	NO	-0.081	1.123	-1.032	-0.248	-0.147	2.173	0.000	0.027	0.198	0.174	0.118	0.357	3.086	0.003
		0.157	0.001	0.010	0.354	0.043	0.062	0.152	0.973	0.079					
GOSPE	FCE	-0.081	1.073	-0.931	-0.308	-0.123	2.192	0.000	-0.055	0.263	0.233	0.012	0.378	1.055	0.408
		0.239	0.005	0.054	0.313	0.117	0.138	0.167	0.954	0.038					
GOSPE	FPE	-0.095	1.460	-0.867	-0.487	-0.165	3.152	0.000	-0.375	0.152	0.259	0.173	0.346	3.014	0.001
		0.104	0.000	0.029	0.082	0.025	0.020	0.115	0.635	0.176					
J60 Programming and broadcasting activities															
GOSPE	NO	-2.318	16.256	-23.985	7.566	0.157	89.249	0.000	-15.940	-2.220	0.199	0.144	11.085	3.639	0.001
		0.179	0.056	0.002	0.365	0.057	0.013	0.601	0.522	0.552					
GOSPE	FCE	-3.147	12.612	-21.025	9.192	0.168	137.965	0.000	-25.426	-2.256	0.269	0.058	11.632	1.275	0.192
		0.128	0.174	0.013	0.315	0.054	0.004	0.648	0.384	0.585					
GOSPE	FPE	-1.118	13.697	-25.608	10.365	0.186	44.894	0.000	-19.018	-0.284	0.310	0.230	10.515	3.876	0.000
		0.509	0.098	0.001	0.197	0.019	0.256	0.548	0.430	0.937					
J61 Telecommunications															
GOSPE	NO	-0.017	1.363	-1.070	-0.271	-0.165	-0.014	0.000	0.184	0.026	0.349	0.305	0.124	7.845	0.000
		0.405	0.000	0.000	0.009	0.003	0.973	0.311	0.512	0.515					
GOSPE	FCE	-0.016	1.245	-0.994	-0.268	-0.173	0.017	0.000	0.103	0.037	0.392	0.217	0.131	2.235	0.002
		0.482	0.000	0.000	0.021	0.005	0.975	0.490	0.757	0.412					
GOSPE	FPE	-0.006	1.444	-1.146	-0.281	-0.176	-0.391	0.000	0.151	0.018	0.377	0.304	0.124	5.204	0.000
		0.780	0.000	0.000	0.011	0.003	0.416	0.398	0.597	0.664					
J62 Computer programming, consultancy and related activities															
GOSPE	NO	-0.298	20.812	-18.271	-6.884	0.232	-7.644	0.000	2.360	0.017	0.209	0.155	2.684	3.870	0.000
		0.496	0.000	0.004	0.060	0.784	0.377	0.348	0.695	0.985					
GOSPE	FCE	-0.442	22.241	-16.626	-8.676	0.372	-7.666	0.000	3.904	0.140	0.349	0.161	2.674	1.858	0.014
		0.376	0.000	0.020	0.027	0.668	0.480	0.365	0.561	0.878					
GOSPE	FPE	-0.325	21.405	-18.409	-6.397	0.245	-4.401	0.000	1.515	0.049	0.227	0.137	2.713	2.523	0.004
		0.480	0.000	0.004	0.090	0.784	0.669	0.306	0.807	0.957					
J63 Information service activities															
GOSPE	NO	-0.045	0.874	-1.187	-0.471	-0.061	0.680	0.000	0.359	0.105	0.139	0.080	0.351	2.364	0.021
		0.413	0.001	0.008	0.060	0.336	0.534	0.555	0.654	0.364					
GOSPE	FCE	-0.060	0.939	-1.319	-0.574	-0.060	0.790	0.000	0.523	0.110	0.184	-0.051	0.375	0.782	0.767
		0.358	0.002	0.011	0.043	0.403	0.585	0.697	0.581	0.397					
GOSPE	FPE	-0.050	0.935	-1.430	-0.392	-0.091	0.962	0.000	0.337	0.175	0.199	0.106	0.346	2.134	0.017
		0.379	0.000	0.002	0.120	0.152	0.448	0.373	0.677	0.138					
M72 Scientific research and development															
GOSPE	NO	4.617	37.963	-29.294	-9.020	-3.408	-45.563	0.000	-76.810	1.812	0.242	0.190	14.162	4.659	0.000
		0.040	0.000	0.001	0.139	0.121	0.301	0.643	0.017	0.695					
GOSPE	FCE	6.013	32.390	-24.572	-9.969	-2.120	-76.971	0.000	-84.941	4.250	0.443	0.282	13.329	2.755	0.000
		0.011	0.000	0.005	0.106	0.325	0.132	0.788	0.012	0.348					
GOSPE	FPE	5.032	38.659	-28.111	-8.120	-2.298	-57.259	0.000	-75.067	1.580	0.267	0.182	14.232	3.134	0.001
		0.034	0.000	0.002	0.205	0.322	0.275	0.809	0.023	0.739					

Fig. 3 (continued)

rate (except J62), when measuring with the help of ALP and WALP. For profitability, measured by GOSPE, turnover seems to have a positive effect for all industries, except J60 where the estimations are not statistically significant. The number of persons employed has a negative effect on profitability in all cases and the average personnel cost negatively affects profit in J61 for all panel specifications and in J62 and J63 for cross-fixed effects estimations. Also, the investment rate seems to negatively impact J61 and J59 and positive for J60 in period-fixed effect estimations.

Overall, the panels show that the size of the company determined by turnover and persons employed are clear indicators for profitability, with the turnover increasing profit and the persons employed decreasing the gross operating surplus. The same effects are present for profitability as well, but it can be added that the personnel costs increase productivity, and the investment rate decreases it. In other words, with the increase in the number of employees, the wages expenses rise, and the companies lose from their share of profit. Yet, if the average personnel costs increase, the workers' productivity increases, generating a bigger turnover that can compensate for the previous losses. It is interesting how the investment rate seems to decrease productivity and this aspect could be further researched. A possible explanation for this phenomenon could be the Solow paradox that will be discussed later on in this essay.

The turnover per number of enterprises shows positive links for all panel specifications and indicators for J59, J61, J62, and M72, meaning that for these industries the gross revenue is an important aspect influencing profitability and productivity. For J60 "Programming and broadcasting activities", turnover only influences productivity and for GOSPE the results were not statistically significant. Meanwhile, the opposite is true for J63 "Information service activities", in which the income only affects profitability. The number of persons employed negatively affects productivity and profitability for all the sectors and the panel specification with the highest coefficients in the case of J60. From this matter, it can be deduced that a lower number of employees can generate higher profits and bigger labour productivity.

The results are not conclusive for the average personnel costs as they positively affect ALP (for J60, J61, and M72) and have a negative link with WALP in J59, J61, J62 and M72. Furthermore, PERSCOST harms profitability in J61 and, considering only cross-fixed effects estimation, in J62 and J63. This means that these last industries' personnel costs are strongly related to their regional characteristics. The investment rate has a negative link with productivity in J59 (except for FCE), J61, J63 and M72. However, it has a positive effect on J60 which can mean that the investments in this industry have a faster return on investment. Also, INVR and productivity are negatively correlated for J59 and J61 and positively correlated in J60. The above-found observations indicate the existence of more indicators that could help understand a firm's profitability and productivity in these sectors in terms of industry-specific attributes.

4.2 Country Characteristics

The country-related attributes chosen were gross domestic product per capita (GDP_CAP), trade balance (TRADEBAL), the percentage of the population with tertiary education (TERTED) and businesses' R&D expenditure adjusted by the number of enterprises in the HTKIS sector (RDEXP_ENT). The results were not statistically significant for TRADEBAL and RDEXP_ENT, which could mean that the geographical localization of a company in the selected industries is not relevant for its productivity and profitability. From another perspective, there could be more country-specific indicators analysed to better understand whether the location is not a determinant for a company's performance or it has only been a matter of inefficiently selected variables. The other two attributes have only a few statistically significant observations.

GDP per capita has a positive effect on J59 for period-fixed effects, meaning that for the selected period, the economic development has helped the profitability and productivity of the companies in this industry. There is also a positive link with ALP, WALP and GOSPE for J60 under the specifications of no effects and fixed-cross-sections estimations (in this case with a significant increase in coefficients and decrease in p-values). Therefore, the location for this sector is relevant when measuring performance. GDP_CAP had a positive effect on productivity in J62 and a negative one for M72. In the case of the population with tertiary education, the only significant observations are for M72, in which it had a negative effect on productivity and profitability, possibly because of the lack of employment in this sector. Regarding the country characteristics, the results are not satisfactory enough to make a precise conclusion. It is clear that the proposed variables do not determine profitability and productivity as measured by the dependent variables, indicating either towards an argument for the lack of influence of the geographical location in an industry's performance in the high-tech knowledge-intensive sector or towards research for attributes that could better describe a countries' specifics to analyse their effects on this sector.

4.3 Performance with Respect to the Specific Industries

For the J59 "Motion picture, video and television programme production, sound recording and music publishing activities" sector the panel estimations show that there were no statistically significant results for the cross-fixed panels for either of the dependent variables, adding to the idea that location does not influence performance. The measures for goodness-of-fit also denote that the fittest and precise data appears in the fixed-period estimations. J60 also has fixed cross panel effects that are not statistically significant for WALP and GOSPE and in the case of ALP, the measure for goodness-of-fit is the lowest for FCE, and highest for all dependent variables for FPE. It could also be noted that this sector has the highest standard of deviation, which indicates a lack of preciseness when compared to the others. J61 "Telecommunications" continues the trend of poor results for FCE considering the adjusted R2, standard of error and F-stat, thus contributing to the idea of a weak relation between countries and performance. This sector also has the best scores for all the measures compared to the other industries—for WALP, no effects estimations: adjusted R2 (0.61) and F-stat (25.49), and for FCE: R2 of (67.7%) and for ALP, no effects: standard error—0.054 (ALP, NO). These aspects show that this industry has the most precise and relevant data.

J62 "Computer programming, consultancy and related activities" does not follow the previous trend, as it has significant observations, yet it has the best scores for goodness-of-fit in the FCE for ALP and GOSPE. For this industry is seems to be a certain correlation between regions and the companies' performance. For "Information service activities" there are no significant estimations for FCE for all the dependent variables and FPE for WALP. Moreover, despite having the lowest values for R2—19.9%, adjusted R2—0.05 and F-stat—1.93, it has the highest values for productivity indicators in the no effects panel and for profitability in the fixed-period effects panel. M72 has statistically significant observations, with higher-than-average coefficients of determination, which denotes a better fit for the regression data. The values for all the measures for goodness-of-fit in this sector are very similar, but with clear distinctions in terms of profitability—highest values for no effects panel, and regarding profitability—highest in the fixed cross-section effects panel.

It can be deduced that for the majority of industries in the high-tech knowledge-intensive services, location is not a determinant according to the previous results. However, the performance in the analysed period seems to be correlated with the location in the case of J62 "Computer programming". This is also the case for profitability, measured in GOSPE for M72 "Scientific research and development".

4.4 Discussion on the Relevance of the Inferences in a Global Context

The current work aims at discovering if there is a link between the geographical localization of an industry and its performance. Generally, this should be the case, considering all the factors that could influence the wellbeing of a company. However, the inquiry comes from the desire to analyse the effects of digitalization and how it reshapes the business and economic environment, thus assuming that in the knowledge economy there are enormous data transfers regardless of nations, region or social status. The purpose was to reject the hypothesis according to which the geographical localization determines the performance in the high-tech service sector and this idea was sustained by two factors: the level of digitalization and technological advance seems to be highest in the industries analysed and the fact that only services were taken into consideration, some factors that would have made manufacturing high-tech to be more prone to be influenced by the regions it operates in be diminished (e.g., larger areas required the need for a developed infrastructure).

Certain favourable conditions can improve a firm's performance, which also creates a basis for entry-mode strategies in the context of possible expansions or relocations. The ownership advantage refers to the idea that a firm should have a valuable and unique product or service that provides a competitive advantage. This is assessed in comparison with the other companies on the market to diminish the liability of foreignness (the disadvantage foreign companies have when entering another nation's market). The location advantage refers to specificities of any state, either geographical position—for instance, the resources it can access or relation to neighbouring developed economies, or related to their attributes, such as the labour force productivity or governmental regulation that ease the entry taxes as compared to other places. The last advantage is internalization referring to the choice of producing internally or choosing the best possible strategy of outsourcing or offshoring to increase efficiency. All of these advantages structure the OLI paradigm discussed by Dunning (1979, 2001).

As the location advantage is more significant in the current study, it should be noted that an important tool with which it can be better assessed is Porter's Diamond Model, known as the theory of national competitive advantages of industries (Porter 1990). It provides a structure for explaining the way certain industries become more competitive in the international market, depending on their original location. The framework used is composed of (i) Firm strategy, structure and rivalry—managerial structure and strategies, (ii) Factor conditions—specific resources to that country (raw materials, financial and human capital), (iii) Demand conditions—the size of the market, level of competitiveness and opportunities for innovation (which could be visualized with the help of the cultural dimensions described by Hofstede (2001), (iv) Related and supporting industries—valuable for creating a partnership or alliances, e.g., Silicon Valley, (v) Government—the entity that can help improve the economic environment or be the cause of its inefficiency, (vi) Chance—referring to events that cannot be predicted, such as natural disasters.

The previously discussed factors may imply that for the industry to perform better, a more welcoming environment of a developed country is needed. However, for services, this may not necessarily be the case as the data shows that country-specific attributes are not relevant for the productivity and profitability of the high-tech knowledge-intensive services. Another aspect that has not been conclusive from the data is the inverse relation between the investment rate and productivity levels, which may bring up the Solow Paradox—according to which even though information technology is developing, the productivity growth is slowing down in the same period (Solow, 1957). However, Krishnan et al. (2018) debate the matter of the return of this paradox. They explain how digital technology is changing process optimizations and business models, and generates innovation that brings new products and services to consumers. It is very likely that we are experiencing a second wave of the productivity (Solow) paradox caused by difficulties in adaption for international firms, lag effects for innovations to reach their most efficient phase and the costs of transitioning to a new environment that has disruptive tendencies.

The HTKIS sector had a good performance in the analysed period, which could be a result of the Innovation Union plan, a part of the Europe 2020 Strategy for a more sustainable, inclusive and smart economy, which is meant to significantly speed up and improve the process of developing and accessing technological advances. A product of the previously mentioned plan is the European Institute for Innovation and Technology (EIT) that has the purpose of creating new Knowledge and Innovation Communities (KICs), promoting knowledge partnerships with education, research, the private sector and providing support for entrepreneurs. Alongside these strategies, productivity should grow more rapidly in the following years, also considering the possible increase in competitiveness and the economic development of the EU.

It is difficult to predict how any sector will perform in the near future because of the current pandemic, which will most likely dissolve into a worldwide economic crisis.

However, it might cause a general shift towards technological solutions, especially in telecommunication and information service activities. Ergo, the HTKIS may suffer less damage in the profitability section because of the rapid increase in consumers and market accessibility. This rise in digital consumers and innovations might not be a short-term one, as the adaptation to the technology was smooth, fast and it has proved to be practical, efficient and increased the average number of working hours. The desire to continue with the digital habits created throughout the restrictive period of 2020 has already been recorded by Child et al. (2020). Other side-effects of the COVID-19 crisis could be the increase in competitiveness due to the hostile environment and the need to maintain the business operational, as wages decrease, unemployment rate increases and market prices increase from regulations and taxes. Entrepreneurs might have to exit the market given the inability to meet the established objectives, and start-ups are more vulnerable and have to stop operating temporarily or permanently.

Another technological risk that could affect HTKIS businesses is the threat of cybersecurity that increases with the number of users and individuals, especially in the context of home working and studying. Personal data issues have already affected all business sectors when the General Data Protection Regulation (GDPR) has entered into application as a consequence of the Cambridge Analytica scandal—a consulting and data analysis company has obtained from Facebook Inc. the data of over 50 million people, further used for political campaigns, which created mass outrage for all individuals. The economic environment will be riskier and more uncertain than in previous periods and could redefine the way performance is measured at the company level.

5 Conclusions

The paper approaches the driving factors behind the high-tech knowledge-intensive services' productivity and profitability because it aims at understanding if the geographical location is a determinant for the sector's performance. The paper offers a continuation and a reinterpretation of the research on high-tech sectors, as it combines similar methodologies from the literature and brings a novel view of the high-tech sector by focusing only on service activities. We believe that this differentiation will be able to generate patterns that are not only available for services. This speculation comes from the shift the economy made towards intangibles because of the intense digital and technological advancement in the last twenty decades and propelled by the coronavirus pandemic. Macroeconomic aspects and theories were taken into consideration when analysing the data obtained because we acknowledge the importance of the economic environment in the performance of the industries.

The results obtained suggest an improvement of the high-tech services in the European Union in terms of performance. Economic wellbeing at the national level has proved to be relevant in assessing labour productivity, affecting each industry on a different level. Moreover, there is a positive connection between turnover and productivity, the number of persons employed and personnel cost negatively affecting it. An interesting note is on the negative link between investment rate and profitability that could be connected to the productivity paradox. The panel estimations do not show a very conclusive result for country characteristics, yet we can deduce that if the geographical position does influence a company's performance, it is most probably not definitory.

The empirical analysis was based on a methodology that could be applied to any sector of activity and that provides extensive statistics to analyse patterns and make inferences. However, the paper did not take into consideration a wider range of variables that could have better described the characteristics used to measure performance, but this is not necessarily a deficiency since identifying good parsimonious models is always envisaged. Despite this aspect, it did establish the theoretical framework at length with which many of the observations can be better understood. For further research, the indicators and variables could be slightly modified to check for other performance trends. More country attributes could be taken into consideration and the results could be discussed with regard to specific concepts mentioned above, such as the location advantage from the OLI paradigm or the Solow paradox. Overall, the paper offers a detailed analysis of the data and insights into a field that deserves more considerations as it could have significant developments and become an important sector of the economy.

References

Audretsch, D.B., Feldman, M.P.: R&D spillovers and the geography of innovation and production. Am. Econ. Rev. **86**(3), 630–640 (1996)

Baesu, V., Albulescu, C.T., Farkas, Z.-B., Draghici, A.: Determinants of the high-tech sector innovation performance in the European Union: a review. Proc. Technol. 371–378 (2015)

Capello, R., Caragliu, A., Lenzi, C.: Is innovation in cities a matter of knowledge-intensive services? An empirical investigation. Innov. Eur. J. Soc. Sci. Res. **25**(2), 151–174 (2012)

Child, J., Farmer, R., Smith, T. R., Tesvic, J.: As physical doors close, new digital doors swing open. https://www.mckinsey.com/industries/retail/our-insights/as-physical-doors-close-new-digital-doors-swing-open (2020). Accessed 19 June 2020

CIA Library—The world factbook https://www.cia.gov/the-world-factbook/countries/european-union/ (2020). Accessed 19 June 2020

Dunning, J.: Toward an eclectic theory of international production: some empirical tests. J. Int. Bus. Stud. **11**(1), 9–31 (1979)

Dunning, J.H.: The eclectic (OLI) paradigm of international production: past, present and future. Int. J. Econ. Bus. **8**(2), 173–190 (2001)

Evans, P.B., Timberlake, M.: Dependence, inequality, and the growth of the tertiary: a comparative analysis of less developed countries. Am. Sociol. Rev. **45**(4), 531–552 (1980)

Fischer, M.M., Scherngell, T., Jansenberger, E.: Geographic localisation of knowledge spillovers: evidence from high-tech patent citations in Europe. Ann. Reg. Sci. **43**(4), 839–858 (2009)

Gil, P.M., Afonso, O., Brito, P.: Economic growth, the high-tech sector, and high-skilled: theory and quantitative implications. Struct. Chang. Econ. Dyn. **51**, 89–105 (2019)

Gujarati, D.N.: Basic econometrics, 4th edn. McGraw-Hill Companies, Boston (2004)

Hofstede, G.: Culture consequences, 2nd edn. Sage Publications (2001)

Horobet, A., Popovici, O.: On technological intensity and performance gaps between EU Foreign and locally-owned companies. Working paper, Bucharest University of Economic Studies (2018)
Horobet, A., Popovici, O.C., Calin, A.C., Belascu, L: Industry versus location-driven competitiveness for the high-tech sector: a European analysis. Budapest (2018)
Horobet, A., Popovici, O., Belascu, L.: Drivers of competitiveness in European high-tech industries. In: Sliwinski, A., Polychronidou, P., Karasavvoglou, A. economic development and financial markets: latest research and policy insights from Central and Southeastern Europe, pp. 53–79. Springer (2020)
Jenks, G. F., Caspall, F. C.: Error on choroplethic maps: definition, measurement, reduction. Annals of the Association of American Geographers, 61(2), 217–244 (1971)
Kerr, W.R., Robert-Nicoud, F.: Tech clusters. Harvard Business School (2019)
Krishnan, M., Mischke, J., Remes, J.: Is the solow paradox back? The McKinsey Quarterly (2018)
Lanz, R., Maurer, A.: Services and global value chains: servicification of manufacturing and services networks. J. Int. Econ. Commer. Policy **6**(03), 1550014 (2015)
Lee, J., Jung, S.: Industrial land use planning and the growth of knowledge industry: location pattern of knowledge-intensive services and their determinants in the Seoul metropolitan area. Land Use Policy (2020)
Lu, X., Chen, D., Kuang, B., Zhang, C., Cheng, C.: Is high-tech zone a policy trap or a growth drive? Insights from the perspective of urban land use efficiency. Land Use Policy **95**, 104583 (2020)
Maurseth, P.B., Verspagen, B.: Knowledge spillovers in Europe: a patent citations analysis. Scand. J. Econ. 531–545 (2002)
Mol, M.J., Brandl, K.: Bridging what we know: the effect of cognitive distance on knowledge intensive business services produced offshore. Int. Bus. Rev. **27**(3), 669–677 (2018)
Porter, M.E.: The competitive advantage of nations. Free Press, New York (1990)
Powell, W.W., Snellman, K.: The knowledge economy. Ann. Rev. Sociol. **30**, 199–220 (2004)
Rainer, L., Andreas, M.: Services and global value chains: some evidence on servicification of manufacturing and services networks. World Trade Organization, Geneva (2015)
Schmidt, S.: Balancing the spatial localisation "Tilt": knowledge spillovers in processes of knowledge-intensive services. Geoforum **65**, 374–386 (2015)
Schwab, K.: The fourth industrial revolution. World Economic Forum, Geneva (2016)
Shapiro, C., Varian, H.R.: Information rules: a strategic guide to the network economy. Harvard Business School Press, Boston (1999)
Solow, R.: Technical change and the aggregate production function. Rev. Econ. Stat. **39**(3), 312–320 (1957)
Thompson, P., Fox-Kean, M.: Patent citations and the geography of knowledge spillovers: a reassessment. Am. Econ. Rev. 450–460 (2005)
Wang, C.-H., Chang, C.-H., Shen, G.C.: The effect of inbound open innovation on firm performance: evidence from high-tech industry. Technol. Forecast. Soc. Chang. **99**, 222–230 (2015)
Wang, J., Zhang, X., Yeh, A.G.: Spatial proximity and location dynamics of knowledge-intensive business service in the Pearl River Delta, China. Hab. Int. **53**, 390–402 (2016)
Zulfikar, R.: Estimation model and selection method of panel data regression: an overview of common effect, fixed effect and random effect model (2018)

Analysis of Fluctuations of Aggregate Indicators and Persistence of Business Cycles in the Caspian Countries

Musetescu Radu-Cristian and Grigore George-Eduard

Abstract The global macroeconomic context is increasingly prone to the emergence and prevalence of situations of uncertainty and risk. Starting from the theoretical particularities of economic cycles, this paper aims to analyse the dynamics of aggregate indicators in the Caspian countries. We have proposed to investigate the extent to which the existence of business cycles produces a series of disturbances at the level of each analysed state, as well as how their persistence contributes to a series of implications that may affect their performance at the macroeconomic level. The novelty of the study consists in the particular analysis of the countries of the Caspian region, as they present certain advantages in terms of competitiveness, mainly due to international transactions with petroleum products. From a methodological point of view, we used the Hodrick-Prescott filtering method in extracting and isolating the cyclical component of each macroeconomic variable (production, private and public consumption, investment, exports, imports, and the real price of oil) in the period 1990–2019. We showed the dynamic evolution of the analysed indicators, the degree of persistence of fluctuations, as well as the measurement of the volatility of each variable for each state, by calculating standard deviations and correlations in relation to production. At the same time, we showed the impact of the real price of oil on the dynamics of business cycles. The results showed increased volatility of production in Azerbaijan, and that production and real oil price are strongly positively correlated in Azerbaijan, Kazakhstan, and Russia, being over 35%.

Keywords Business cycles · Real oil price · Volatility

M. Radu-Cristian (✉) · G. George-Eduard
Bucharest University of Economic Studies, Bucharest, Romania
e-mail: radu.musetescu@rei.ase.ro

A. M. Dima and M. Kelemen (eds.), *Digitalization and Big Data for Resilience and Economic Intelligence*, Springer Proceedings in Business and Economics, https://doi.org/10.1007/978-3-030-93286-2_2

1 Introduction

Currently, oil is considered one of the most valuable natural resources, which propels the popularity of various states of the world, and through proactive attitudes and decisions, it continues to represent that piece of dominoes in the economic world dominated by constant competition to create value and welfare.

This paper aims to analyse the impact and influence of fluctuations in aggregate macroeconomic variables (production, private consumption, government consumption, investment, imports, exports, and real global oil prices) in the Caspian oil-exporting and producing countries (Azerbaijan, Kazakhstan, Iran, Russia, Turkmenistan, and Uzbekistan) in terms of volatility and business cycle characteristics.

Since the onset of the Great Financial Crisis of 2008, which continues to persist in recent times, concerns in the field of economic science research are outlined and directed towards the analysis, measurement, and understanding of fluctuations specific to the main macroeconomic indicators (Angeletos et al. 2020; Dosi et al. 2010; Polbin 2021). Attending a series of current episodes of turbulence, exacerbated by the effects produced by the Covid-19 pandemic, the global macroeconomic context is in a continuous cyclicality and change, the terms of instability and fragility being characteristic of the current state.

The objective of this paper consists in the following aspects: (i) analysis of empirical evidence that can measure the periods of cyclicality in the Caspian countries; (ii) quantification of the degree of identification and understanding of fluctuating trends, and the similarity of the shocks affecting the states under analysis, respectively. The proposed methodology is based on the analysis of time series of aggregate macroeconomic variables, being built around the Hodrick-Prescott filtering tool (Hodrick and Prescott 1997), which is designed to isolate trend components of each macroeconomic variable and focuses on the impact that the cyclical component has and how it propagates on the economic evolution of the states, and to quantify the volatility and fluctuating tendencies specific to the current state of the economy of the Caspian countries, respectively.

Focusing on these cyclical components specific to the macroeconomic indicators studied in the period 1990–2019, we could also show the evidence by determining the dependency relations and calculating those ratios to the volatility of production and the real global price of oil persistence of the business cycle (Drechsel and Tenreyro 2017; Giordani and Kwan 2019) and achieve a better understanding of how in which fluctuating sequence there is an increasing concern of government authorities to implement monetary and fiscal policies to counteract these macroeconomic turbulences (Mișa and Kagitci 2019).

Regarding the structure of the paper, it is divided into several sections. Section 2 highlights the review of the literature in the analysis of the business cycle theory. Section 3 presents the proposed methodological process. Section 4 describes and presents the main results obtained from the analysis of business cycles in the Caspian countries and Sect. 5 contains the main conclusions, followed by possible directions to be followed in future research.

2 Literature Review

Within the scientific economic context, a careful concern is directed towards the analysis of fluctuations in macroeconomic indicators. An important feature of these derives from the understanding and measurement of sensitivity movements and fluctuations, which is why academics and practitioners in economics are constantly looking for explanations and solutions from information extracted from the analysis of time series of aggregate variables (Bobeica and Manu 2013).

At the same time, the study of the cyclical component (Drechsel and Tenreyro 2017) at the level of each aggregate variable leads to the establishment of a framework oriented on its volatility and degree of persistence, outlining in this sense a new direction of research based on the study and characterization of economic cycles or business cycles (Isaic et al. 2019).

Therefore, the theory of economic cycles tries to answer a series of questions meant to determine the volatility recorded for each indicator, measuring the trend of persistence and fluctuation for each aggregate variable compared to production, and specifying the pro-cyclicality and/or anti-cyclicality by calculating the degree of correlation or autocorrelation of these variables over time.

In this respect, there has been a whole debate and a prolific theoretical framework that revolves around everything that is specific to business cycles, where finding practical solutions is an important aspect especially in terms of financial or economic stability (Jordà et al. 2015). Given the imminent characteristics and forces specific to today's society, in which uncertainty and imbalance tend to intensify, affecting the current state of a state's economic system, the literature is increasingly focused on the close customization of everything as it involves analysing the fluctuations of macroeconomic indicators, showing the role and efforts of policymakers in adopting the policy instrument, who are perceived as levers in the management of business cycles and macroeconomic disruptions.

Thus, it is worth mentioning the study conducted by Giordani and Kwan (2019), highlighting the beneficial effects of monetary policy, as well as the adoption of macro-prudential instruments used in managing and reducing the instability felt in the US financial sector. The same study (Giordani and Kwan 2019) showed that the fragility of the US financial system has persisted since 2008, with the outbreak of the Great Global Financial Crisis being the trigger.

Through the application of the Hodrick-Prescott filter (Hodrick and Prescott 1997), the results of the study materialized in determining an index that measures and shows the level of fragility over time, suggesting that a high level of leverage is always accompanied by overvaluations of financial assets. In the same direction, studies conducted by Jorda et al. (2015) and Dosi et al. (2010) have shown that macroeconomic fluctuations deepen as the trend of expansion of accreditation among financial institutions and overvaluation persists assets (housing commercial property, stocks, and corporate bonds). A solution is to design models that incorporate those indicators that increase the level of confidence in measuring the fragility and volatility of aggregate variables.

On the other hand, according to other research in the field (Busu et al. 2020; Angeletos et al. 2020; Polbin 2021), the analysis of macroeconomic fluctuations is based on the use of methods and tools to extract the trend component, which allows a specific focus in measuring the volatility associated with the cyclical component. In this sense, HP filtering, moving average filter, or first differentiation are the most commonly used methods in business cycle analysis (Bobeica and Manu 2013; Jorda et al. 2015). This is reinforced by the study conducted by Drechsel and Tenreyro (2017) showing that fluctuations in developing countries are different from those in developed countries. In particular, according to the results obtained in the same study, as well as by applying the proposed econometric model (SVAR), it was concluded that in terms of international trade, the analysed state (Argentina) is strongly affected by changes in global commodity prices with high production volatility. Also, by applying Bayesian-type calibration models, the resulting predictions showed a degree of persistence in business cycles in Argentina, generating strong effects on production, consumption, investment, and a negative effect on the trade balance.

Other recent studies focusing on business cycle issues have highlighted the key role that government authorities play in formulating, adopting, and implementing policies designed to control fluctuations specific to aggregate components. We mention the work done by Dosi et al. (2010), according to which technological changes and the intensification of the evolutionary process of globalization are factors that lead to short-term fluctuating episodes, affecting the long-term growth of a state.

The same study built around the two main theoretical approaches based on Keynes and Schumpeter, brings to the fore the structural model, according to which the authors (Dosi et al. 2010), showed that demand shocks are mainly caused by applied public policies and that macroeconomic fluctuations result from the effects of information and behavioural frictions of economic agents.

In the same direction, the study developed by Angeletos et al. (2020) shows that business cycles can lead to a positive impetus and reaction among economic agents to change their strategic decisions in accordance with the correct management of the application of public policies.

In addition, stability in the financial sector becomes an important condition, as fiscal and monetary policies can be directed and focused on analysing and reducing the volatility specific to each macroeconomic indicator. In another direction, the study carried out by Horvath and Rothman (2021) intended to explain the impact of changes in the global financial risk on macroeconomic variables specific to emerging countries.

This notified link is demonstrated following the application of the autoregressive model (VAR) at the level of the US mortgage sector in the period 1999–2019. The results showed that fluctuations in this sector are spreading to the automotive sectors in emerging countries, culminating in significant declines in production, consumption, and investment in these countries. The study (Horvath and Rothman 2021) also highlighted that the adoption of macro-prudential policies in emerging countries to control persistent fluctuations in macroeconomic variables is a necessary condition, especially in terms of monitoring capital flows or lending external conditions.

Studies by Kim and Shim (2020) and Hang and Xue (2020) focus on monetary policy transmission channels, examining their asymmetric effects in controlling the volatility of the main macroeconomic indicators, by applying an extended quantum regression model across the interval 2005–2016.

In the context of business cycle theory, the study conducted by Gong and Kim (2018) examines a number of implications and effects of the main types of integration on business cycles in developing countries in East Asia, Latin America, and Eastern Europe, demonstrating that the effects of integration are strongly positively correlated with the characterization of economic cycles.

Another remark, according to the same study, is that the conclusion of regional trade agreements between emerging countries and, implicitly, cooperation are the main conditions in controlling and managing the volatility of macroeconomic indicators. Regarding the relationship between the financial cycle, the exchange rate, and the real interest rate, according to Yan and Huang (2020), the interaction between the financial sector and real economic activity remains a relevant condition, especially in the control of imbalances found more and more often in the current period.

Through the application of the HP filter and the autoregressive vector model, (Yan and Huang 2020) showed that business cycle volatility can be explained by the presence of shocks felt in the financial sector, being able to anticipate the likelihood of future episodes of economic recession in the US. The same approach is present in the paper by Arčabić and Škrinjarić (2021), where the persistence of business cycles is explained between 50 and 90% of production variation.

By establishing a propagation index, (Arčabić and Škrinjarić 2021) investigated the effects of the business cycle in countries of the European Union, concluding that smaller countries are more prone to fluctuating sequences and/or exogenous systemic shocks (variations in business cycles can be explained by the effects of transnational trade).

As compared to other studies (Arčabić and Škrinjarić 2021), (Gong and Kim 2018), the study by Papageorgiou et al. (2016) demonstrated that financial integration, economic cooperation along with appropriate monetary policies can reduce the magnitude of macroeconomic fluctuations. Another study (Doytch 2021) followed the impact of foreign direct investment flows in relation to the fluctuations specific to the aggregate variables. Following the application in 19 countries of Europe and Central Asia, the results showed that FDI flows in the services sector are countercyclical, increasing during contractions and decreasing during expansions, culminating in the fact that the onset of the global crisis in 2008 remains a significant factor in decreasing the flows of foreign direct investment.

In this section, we highlighted the main theoretical benchmarks, given that our study aims to analyse the fluctuations of macroeconomic indicators and the persistence of the business cycle among the Caspian countries, which are considered important countries producing energy resources.

3 Methodology

Theoretical models produce predictions on consumer income, expenditure, and savings on firms' investments and production decisions. These decisions are then aggregated at the agent level to obtain predictions on macroeconomic indicators. To compare these predictions of theoretical models with real data it is necessary to use time series and cross-country data on per-capita measures for aggregate expenditure and trade in goods and assets.

This study investigates the impact of volatility on the persistence of business cycles in Caspian countries: Azerbaijan, Iran, Kazakhstan, Russia, Turkmenistan, and Uzbekistan. The specialized literature has highlighted an increasing emphasis on understanding the dynamics of the main macroeconomic indicators and measuring the degree of fluctuation recorded in each state under investigation.

The main concerns of the researchers were to closely monitor the fragility of the activity economic, and implicitly of the financial sector, by creating specific indicators (i.e., the local level filter, Giordani and Kwan 2019); analysis of cyclicality and behaviour of economic agents in situations of vulnerability (Polbin 2021) and formulation of monetary policies in such situations (Li et al. 2021, Angeletos et al. 2020).

Other research in the field has analysed the main features of business cycles and their dynamics (Arčabić and Škrinjarić, 2021, Kim and Shim 2020), as well as the development of econometrics aimed at measuring and estimating the level of volatility of production and how it interacts with other macroeconomic aggregates (in particular, individual consumption and investments), suggesting its pro-cyclical or counter-cyclical nature (Doytch 2021, Horvath and Rothman 2021, Yan and Huang 2020).

By formulating research questions: (i) How volatile is production? (ii) How is the movement of aggregate demand and supply components? (iii) How persistent are the movements of macroeconomic aggregates?, we turned to the analysis of business cycles in the countries of the Caspian region, by describing and analysing the dynamics of evolution and fluctuations of aggregate indicators, according to Tables 1 and 2.

On the other hand, in order to be able to achieve the proposed objective of this study, we used macroeconomic indicators, i.e., those statistical data which indicate the current situation of a state's economy, to apply the calculation of relevant business cycle statistics in the Caspian region in the period 1990–2019, such as: standard deviations, correlations with production, serial correlations.

Economic activity does not, as a rule, have a linear evolution, perfectly predictable, but a fluctuating one. Therefore, based on the use of macroeconomic aggregates, cyclical fluctuations can be captured with a certain degree of repeatability, related to the functioning of economic activity and interdependencies of its components. Cyclic fluctuations are considered to be a form of the normal evolution of activity, which ensures continuity and qualitative change in the economy. In the end, highlighting the cyclical evolution is possible based on the analysis of data expressing the activity

Table 1 Description of macroeconomic indicators

Macroeconomic indicators	Notation	Definition	Measurement unit	Data source	Sample size	Analysed period
GDP per capita	y	GDP per capita is gross domestic product divided by mid-year population	Constant LCU	World Bank	Azerbaijan Iran Kazakhstan Russia Turkmenistan Uzbekistan	1990–2019
Gross capital formation	i	Gross capital formation consists of outlays on additions to the fixed assets of the economy plus net changes in the level of inventories	% of GDP	World Bank		
General government final consumption expenditure	g	General government final consumption expenditure includes all government current expenditures for purchases of goods and services	% of GDP	World Bank		
Imports of goods and services	m	Imports of goods and services represent the value of all goods and other market services received from the rest of the world	% of GDP	World Bank		

(continued)

Table 1 (continued)

Macroeconomic indicators	Notation	Definition	Measurement unit	Data source	Sample size	Analysed period
Exports of goods and services	x	Exports of goods and services represent the value of all goods and other market services provided to the rest of the world	% of GDP	World Bank		
Household final consumption expenditure	c	Household final consumption expenditure is the market value of all goods and services, including durable products, purchased by households	% of GDP	World Bank		
Global oil price	p	Global price of Brent Crude adjusted to CPI	U.S. Dollars per Barrel	FRED		

Source Authors' contribution

at a macroeconomic level. What is certain is that, beyond explanations, cyclicality is a reality that cannot be denied, occurring both in the medium term, as is the case of the business cycle, and in the short and long term.

Also, as the analysis is performed in producing and net exporting countries of energy products (especially natural gas and oil), the global real oil price represents a relevant macroeconomic variable. The analysis of its dynamics has a direct impact on GPD per capita, exports, imports, or investments. It was used in the analysis by adjusting it to the inflation rate (using the consumer price index).

The quantitative approach of the data series of macroeconomic indicators consisted in applying logarithm to each data series, applying the HP cyclic component isolation tool, calculating relevant statistics for the business cycles, as well as using different graphs of the cyclical component of GDP per capita and global real oil price. The software programs used were Microsoft Excel, EViews, and Python.

Table 2 Descriptive statistics of the data series

Variable	Azerbaijan		Iran		Kazakhstan		Russia		Turkmenistan		Uzbekistan	
	Mean	Standard deviation	Mean	Standard deviation	Mean	Standard deviation	Mean	Standard deviation	Mean	Standard deviation	Mean	Standard deviation
y	7.360	0.6057	18.060	0.1615	13.053	0.3960	13.011	0.2715	8.439	0.4562	14.564	0.3458
c	3.996	0.2787	3.884	0.1252	4.038	0.1929	3.920	0.0763	3.179	0.8418	3.923	0.3241
g	2.551	0.2841	2.450	0.1302	2.460	0.1681	2.884	0.0959	2.327	0.3966	2.956	0.3833
i	3.058	0.8118	3.604	0.1350	3.215	0.2151	3.129	0.1898	3.6420	0.3041	3.243	0.2524
x	3.807	0.3225	3.104	0.2538	3.769	0.2284	3.404	0.2698	3.722	0.4143	3.289	0.2741
m	3.667	0.3561	3.061	0.2396	3.634	0.3021	3.1063	0.2031	3.663	0.4979	3.2710	0.2785
p	Mean	3.029										
	Standard deviation	0.5316										

Source Authors' contribution

At the same time, we used time series with the annual frequency, both the logarithm of each indicator and the stationary data series. At the same time, the formation of the variable real oil price was determined based on a ratio composed of the global Brent crude oil price and the US seasonally adjusted CPI.

Referring to the central objective of the paper, which is to understand the aggregate fluctuation in business cycles, in the quantitative research methodology we applied the Hodrick-Prescott Filter tool (Hodrick and Prescott 1997) according to Eq. 1, in order to obtain the cyclic component extracted from the raw time series for each indicator.

$$\min_{\tau}\left(\sum_{t=1}^{T}(y_t-\tau_t)^2+\lambda\sum_{t=2}^{T-1}\left[(\tau_{t+1}-\tau_t)-(\tau_t-\tau_{t-1})\right]^2\right) \tag{1}$$

where:

- T is the sample size;
- y_t is the observed time series;
- τ_t is the trend component;
- c_t is the cyclical component (determined as a difference between yt and τt);
- λ is the smoothing parameter (in this case it is 100 because we used yearly data).

From a scientific point of view, most academics and practitioners (Dosi et al. 2010) have struggled over time to obtain standardized and filtered time series. Although other methods of isolating the trend component are presented in the literature (Angeletos et al. 2020; Drechsel and Tenreyro 2017; Jorda et al. 2015), the HP filter tool is preferred and often used, having as objective the elimination of the independent and identically distributed noise that is shown in the Figs. 1 and 2.

The next step was to quantify volatility by determining standard deviations from production and the real price of oil, and then we calculated several types of correlations (correlation Pearson, serial correlations) to show and explain the degree of connection, dependence, and persistence of business cycles for each country in the sample.

4 Analysis

Following the applied methodological process, this section is intended to present, analyse, and interpret the main results related to the highlighted research question. Thus, the main records obtained following the application of the HP filter and the determination of volatility ratios are presented in Table 3.

Regarding the output/production variable, in the period 1990–2019, its volatility is different in each state. For example, in the case of Azerbaijan, it is 2.31 times higher than in Iran, 95% higher than in the case of Turkmenistan, or 2.60 times higher than in Uzbekistan. In the case of Russia, the situation is different, the volatility being

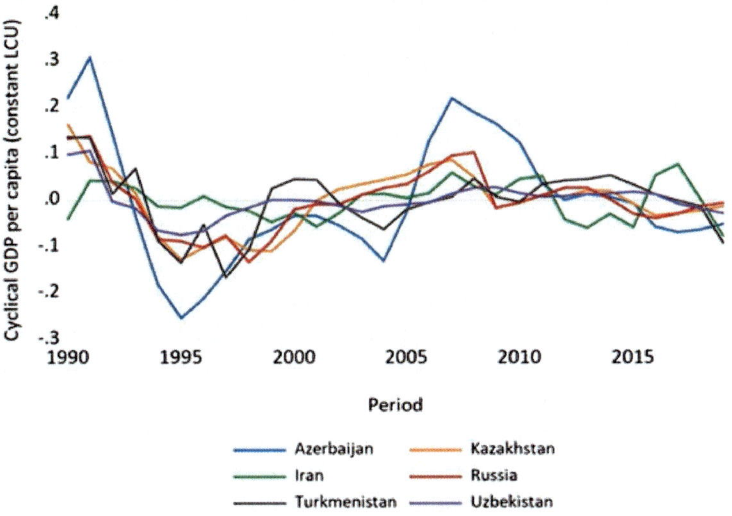

Fig. 1 Cyclical GDP per capita (Output) for each country. *Source* World bank open data and authors' representation (EViews)

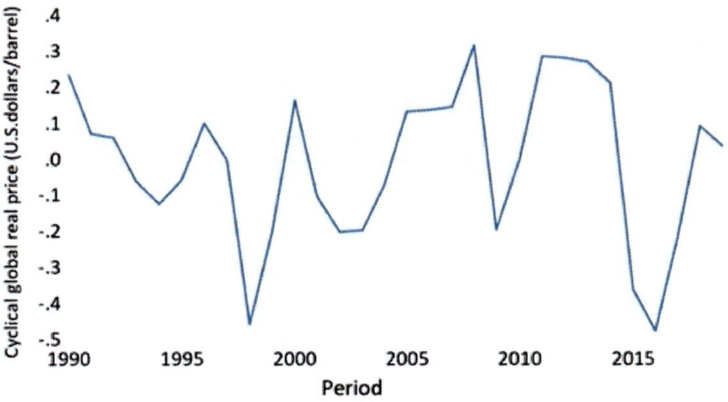

Fig. 2 Cyclical global real oil price. *Source* FRED data and authors' representation (EViews)

Table 3 Volatility of the main macroeconomic variables per output

Standard deviations	Azerbaijan	Iran	Kazakhstan	Russia	Turkmenistan	Uzbekistan
σ_y	0.13	0.04	0.07	0.06	0.07	0.04
σ_c/σ_y	0.85	1.31	0.77	0.95	8.62	5.63
σ_g/σ_y	1.18	2.42	1.32	1.37	3.07	2.00
σ_i/σ_y	4.71	2.69	2.26	1.67	2.60	4.68
σ_x/σ_y	1.65	4.39	2.30	3.50	3.69	4.83
σ_m/σ_y	1.76	3.89	1.74	2.78	4.62	5.77

Source Authors' contribution

higher compared to Iran and Uzbekistan (values of 61.03 and 72.83%, respectively) and lower compared to Turkmenistan (5.24%) and Kazakhstan (2.34%).

Thus, it can be stated that Azerbaijan is the state with the most volatile trend of production, compared to Kazakhstan and Uzbekistan, where volatility is on average 1.30 times higher than in other states.

Referring to the degree of investment volatility compared to the level of production, in the case of Russia there are values lower by 65% compared to Azerbaijan and Uzbekistan, by 38, 36, and 26%, respectively, compared to Iran, Turkmenistan, and Kazakhstan, noting that, on average, gross capital formation is much less volatile compared to that of production. The situation is different in the case of Uzbekistan, where the values obtained are higher than in other states, suggesting a sharp decline in its volatility, i.e., 2 times higher than Russia, 80% higher than Iran, and Turkmenistan. The situation is similar in the case of the state of Azerbaijan, showing an average volatility higher by 74.77% compared to the rest of the analysed states.

Similarly, government consumption is much more volatile in Turkmenistan by 53.86% higher than Uzbekistan, 1.59 times higher than Azerbaijan, or 1.25 times higher than Russia and Kazakhstan. The same situation is specific in Iran, where volatility is on average 44% higher compared to other states. Azerbaijan is the state with the lowest values of government consumption volatility, being 61.54% less volatile than Turkmenistan or 40.89% compared to Uzbekistan. Analysing the relationship between imports and production, Uzbekistan was shown to have the highest volatility values compared to the rest of the states.

Thus, imports from Uzbekistan are 1.08 more volatile than those from Russia, 25.08% more pronounced than Turkmenistan, and 2.30 times higher compared to Azerbaijan and Kazakhstan. The same situation is present in Turkmenistan, where on average imports are 64% more volatile than in the rest of the countries. However, Kazakhstan is the state with the lowest recorded volatility values, i.e., 62.25% compared to Turkmenistan or 70% compared to Uzbekistan.

Referring to the analysis of export volatility, the results showed that Azerbaijan is the least volatile compared to the other countries analysed, averaging 44% lower volatility. Regarding the situation in other states, Uzbekistan is the state with the highest volatility (on average 63.75%), followed by Iran with an average volatility value of 48.58% and Turkmenistan, with a value of 25%. In terms of private consumption, the results showed that in the case of Turkmenistan, it is 5 times more volatile than Iran, 8 times more volatile than Russia and Azerbaijan and only 53% higher compared to Uzbekistan. Thus, Turkmenistan is the most volatile state in terms of the ratio between private consumption and production, identifying significant differences compared to other states. Kazakhstan also has the lowest values of private consumption, on average 41% lower compared to the other countries analysed.

On the other hand, the paper allowed the study of the impact of the global real oil price on the main macroeconomic variables specific to each state. Thus, following the determination of the level of oil price volatility of 21.24%, the results were directed to the analysis of various ratios that could be determined at the level of each macroeconomic indicator. These results are presented in Table 4.

Table 4 Volatility of the main macroeconomic variables per global real oil price

Standard deviations	Azerbaijan	Iran	Kazakhstan	Russia	Turkmenistan	Uzbekistan
σ_p	0.21	0.21	0.21	0.21	0.21	0.21
σ_y / σ_p	0.63	0.19	0.31	0.30	0.32	0.18
σ_c / σ_p	0.54	0.25	0.24	0.29	2.77	0.99
σ_g / σ_p	0.74	0.46	0,41	0.42	0.99	0.35
σ_i / σ_p	2.96	0.51	0.70	0.51	0.84	0.83
σ_x / σ_p	1.04	0.83	0.72	1.07	1.19	0.85
σ_m / σ_p	1.10	0.74	0.54	0.85	1.48	1.02

Source Authors' contribution

Referring to the degree of volatility of production, it was observed that in the case of Azerbaijan the impact is quite high, i.e., 2.3 times more pronounced compared to Iran and 95% higher compared to Turkmenistan. The values obtained at the level of investments showed in the case of Azerbaijan that it is about 5 times higher than Iran and Russia and 3 times higher compared to the volatilities obtained in Turkmenistan, Uzbekistan. It was found that changes in oil prices are felt quite strongly in relation to investments.

Analysing the impact of oil prices on government consumption, the results showed that the highest volatility is in the state of Turkmenistan, about 2 times higher than Uzbekistan and 1.4 times higher compared to Russia and Kazakhstan, which confirms the high impact of the price of oil on the level of government consumption in this state. At the same time, this is changing in the case of Uzbekistan, where the values indicated lower volatility, i.e., 52% compared to Azerbaijan or 16% lower than Russia. The price of oil also plays an important role in the level of imports and exports from these countries. Specifically, in the case of imports, the results showed that we find higher volatility in the case of Turkmenistan, i.e., 1.73 times higher than Kazakhstan and 75.5% compared to Russia.

A similar situation was highlighted for exports, where Turkmenistan recorded on average 29% higher volatility compared to the rest of the countries. The values obtained in terms of private consumption have revealed the impact and the degree to which it reacts and is influenced in relation to the volatility of the global oil price. Also in the case of Turkmenistan, the results showed volatility 4 times higher than Azerbaijan or about 2 times higher than Uzbekistan.

According to other studies (Dosi et al. 2010; Drechsel and Tenreyro 2017; Polbin 2021), the values obtained allowed the study and characterization of business cycles in the countries of the Caspian region, where the understanding of aggregate fluctuations, the measurement, and analysis of the volatility of each macroeconomic variable are relevant issues and allowed us to study their persistence. Because the movement of macroeconomic variables is quite relevant according to studies developed by Arčabić and Skrinjaric (2021), Bobeica and Manu (2013), Drechsel and Tenreyro (2017), we could show, on the one hand, the degree of intensity of the dependency links, and on the other hand, the description of the fluctuating movements of the macroeconomic indicators.

The character of pro-cyclicality and anti-cyclicality was suggested to determine the various types of correlations (Pearson correlations, serial correlations in relation to the production for each country), as shown in Tables 5 and 6.

In this respect, the global price of oil compared to production has a countercyclical character (negative correlation) for investments, imports, and consumption. In the case of Iran, exports are pro-cyclical and private consumption is counter-cyclical, with a negative correlation of average intensity of −0.38.

The data from the analysis showed that the price of oil is pro-cyclical (positive intensity correlation of 0.58) in the case of Russia, in the case of Turkmenistan (0.33) and Kazakhstan (0.44), which demonstrates the role and position of net oil-exporting states and decision-making impact in energy policy-making. At the other end of the spectrum is the countercyclical consumption in the case of Russia (−0.37) and Kazakhstan (−0.55). Imports from Caspian countries with a different countercyclical

Table 5 Correlations with output (y)

	Azerbaijan	Iran	Kazakhstan	Russia	Turkmenistan	Uzbekistan
y	1.00	1.00	1.00	1.00	1.00	1.00
c	−0.77**	−0.38*	−0.55**	−0.37*	0.17**	−0.12
g	−0.11	0.07	0.20	−0.19	0.05	−0.16
i	−0.37*	0.11	0.45**	0.48**	0.01*	0.19
x	0.42*	0.14	0.48**	−0.11	0.08**	−0.16
m	−0.35*	0.10	0.50**	−0.18	−0.17**	−0.22
p	0.37*	−0.10	0.44*	0.58**	0.33*	0.22

* and ** indicate statistical significance at least at 1% and 5% level, respectively. *Source* Authors' calculations (Python and EViews)

Table 6 Serial correlations

Variables	Azerbaijan	Iran	Kazakhstan	Russia	Turkmenistan	Uzbekistan
y	0.795**	0.36*	0.752	0.733**	0.531**	0.658**
c	0.594**	0.456**	0.434*	0.261	0.291	−0.342
g	0.309*	0.317*	−0.373*	0.193*	0.341*	0.143
i	0.06	0.286	0.395*	0.298*	0.65**	0.11
x	0.365*	0.373*	0.282	−0.320	0.477*	0.659**
m	0.397*	0.596**	0.410*	−0.133	0.552**	0.607**
p	0.405*	0.405*	0.405*	0.405*	0.405*	0.405*

* and ** indicate statistical significance at least at 1 and 5% level, respectively, at the 1 lag. *Source* Authors' calculations (Python and EViews)

intensity, from −0.17 in Russia and Turkmenistan to −0.22 in the case of Uzbekistan, are also moving in the same direction.

At the same time, by determining the serial correlations at the first lag, it was shown that the production is positively correlated with strong intensity in the analysed states, i.e., 0.795 in Azerbaijan, 0.75 in Kazakhstan, or 0.73 in Russia. This is also similar in terms of individual consumption, noting the persistence of a positive correlation of average intensity for Iran of 0.456, 0.434 for Kazakhstan, or 0.594 for Azerbaijan. Strong positive correlations of exports and imports are suggested in the Caspian countries, which confirms that they are important oil-producing and the main net exporting countries.

After testing the significance of these correlations, it was observed that production, private consumption, exports, and the global price of oil continue to be the variables that describe the sequences of fluctuations and dynamics at the macroeconomic level, stating that their analysis over time is the main condition for measurement and quantification of the degree of volatility and persistence of business cycles, which was noted in the studies developed by Bobeica and Manu (2013), Özbilgin (2010), Munoz-Guillermo (2021), or Jorda et al. (2015).

Consequently, the results showed that analysing the dynamics of macroeconomic indicators determines a better understanding of how these fluctuating trends describe business cycles in the Caspian countries, given that the global price of oil is a determining factor in the description of persistent movements and of the degree of evolution of the aggregate variables.

5 Conclusions

The central objective of the present study was the analysis of the dynamics and fluctuations of the main macroeconomic variables (production, private and government consumption, investment, imports, exports, and the global price of oil) in order to measure the degree of volatility and to highlight the movement of persistence specific to business cycles in the Caspian countries.

Studying the dynamics of macroeconomic indicators is an important topic of attraction in the sphere of scientific research in the economic field, especially due to the way of analysing the specific evolution and the various types of correlations that are established between them. Consequently, the evolution of these macroeconomic indicators reflects the alternation of periods of growth, stagnation or reduction of economic activity, and even critical crisis situations. The study is positioned in this direction by Giordani and Kwan (2019). By establishing a composite index, it could be evaluated how the fragility of the US financial system can be corrected by adequacy corresponding to the macro-prudential instruments of fiscal and monetary policy. Using specific tools for studying and filtering data series, namely the Hodrick-Prescott filtering tool, we focused on extracting the cyclical component for each aggregate indicator, and we provided a statistical description of business cycles found in the analysed states. By determining the reports in which we have highlighted the degree of volatility of each macroeconomic variable depending on the volatility of production and the volatility of the global oil price, we found that the states in the Caspian region have a significant level of connection and reaction to the volatility of production.

Specifically, we resorted to determining correlations with production, and the analysis showed that the level of imports and private consumption is most likely to react to production in the context of the Caspian countries. At the same time, a significant average intensity link was observed in terms of investments, recording a value of 0.48 in Russia and 0.45 in Kazakhstan.

In line with our study is the research conducted by Polbin (2021). Thus, the results obtained regarding the evolution of GDP, individual consumption, and investments showed an increased nexus among the global real oil price, culminating in a significant slowdown of economic growth in Russia. The term cyclicality is understood as that form of motion/movement of economic activity that reflects the time repeatability of some states of the economy (phases of the business cycle), which was captured in the studies elaborated by Munoz-Guillermo (2021), Gong and Kim (2018), Yan and Huang (2020), according to which the state and aggregate performance have certain characteristics that differ from one phase to another.

Other studies (Papageorgiou et al. 2016; Kim and Shim 2020; Horvath and Rothman 2020; Angeletos et al. 2020) assess the impact that the countercyclical programs meant to promote the monetary measures (through price dynamics) and budgetary measures (through the volume of economic activity and coverage of the deficit budget) have over the economy. In this regard, measuring volatility, highlighting the procycle and anticycle character, as well as calculating various interdependence relations between macroeconomic variables (correlations with production, serial correlations) are the aspects that were addressed in our study. Thus, our paper is in line with other research that analyses business cycles and macroeconomic aggregates dynamics.

These results confirmed that most of the fluctuations and fluctuating movements at the level of macroeconomic variables represent the main characteristics of persistence of instability, affecting to the greatest extent the growth and development of the states on the Caspian Sea coast.

Another aspect brought by the present study was the analysis of volatility between aggregate variables and the global price of oil, materializing the idea that the instability felt at the macroeconomic level is an important determinant caused by persistent dynamic and fluctuating changes in each state. From another perspective, the impact of the oil price becomes a pattern, given that the states under analysis have the status of producing and net exporting states of petroleum products. Thus, it has been shown that in the case of Azerbaijan and Turkmenistan, the business cycle is still maintained due to the high degree of volatility in consumption, investment, and imports relative to production and the price of oil.

Another contribution was the determination of the different correlations and their evolution over time. In addition to varying degrees of dependence, they showed a description of the movements specific to macroeconomic variables. Thus, depending on the volatility of production, private consumption is countercyclical in most countries, and the price of oil is pro-cyclical in these countries, which is observed by testing the significance of correlations. In the same direction, serial correlations showed persistently high production, as well as an oil price correlation level of 0.405.

The limitations and risks that were noticed in the study came from the availability of data, the specificities of the research activity, the tools used, the limited access to some data processing, and the limitations of software programs used.

Consequently, the present study aimed to capture, understand, and quantify the persistent dynamics of each macroeconomic variable in the context of the Caspian countries, demonstrating how long these pro-cyclical and counter-cyclical movements persist. More intervention is needed to ensure stability for each state, especially in the current situation exacerbated by the implications of the pandemic crisis. Possible directions for research would be to link business cycles to the persistence of political risk in the Caspian countries or to correlate the analysis of the dynamics of aggregate variables and business cycles in terms of unconventional monetary policy.

References

Angeletos, G.M., Iovino, L., La'O, J.: Learning over the business cycle: policy implications. J. Econ. Theory **190**, 105–115 (2020)

Arčabić, V., Škrinjarić, T.: Sharing is caring: spillovers and synchronization of business cycles in the European Union. Econ. Model. **96**, 25–39 (2021)

Bobeica, E., Manu, A.S.: Empirical analysis of business cycle synchronization and shock similarity between Romania and the Eurozone. Emerg. Mark. Financ. Trade **49**(4), 74–97 (2013)

Busu, M., Vargas, M.V., Gherasim, I.: An analysis of the economic performances of the retail companies in Romania. Manag. Market. Chall. Knowl. Soc. **15**(1), 125–133 (2020). https://doi.org/10.2478/mmcks-2020-0008

Dosi, G., Fagiolo, G., Roventini, A.: Schumpeter meeting Keynes: a policy-friendly model of endogenous growth and business cycle. J. Econ. Dyn. Control **34**(9), 1748–1767 (2010)

Doytch, N.: Do FDI inflows to Eastern Europe and Central Asia respond to the business cycle? A sector level analysis. J. Econ. Asymmetr. **23**(C) (2021)

Drechsel, T., Tenreyro, S.: Commodity booms and busts in emerging countries. NBER Working paper 23716 (2017)

Giordani, P., Kwan, S.: Tracking financial fragility. Working paper, Federal Reserve Bank of San Francisco, pp. 1–35 (2019)

Gong, C., Kim, S.: Regional business cycle synchronization in emerging and developing countries: regional or global integration? Trade or financial integration? J. Int. Money Financ. **84**, 42–57 (2018)

Hang, Y., Xue, W.: The asymmetric effects of monetary policy on the business cycle: evidence from the panel smoothed quantile regression model. Econ. Lett. **195**, 109–450 (2020)

Hodrick, R.J., Prescott, E.C.: Postwar U.S. business cycles: an empirical investigation. J. Money Credit Bank. **29**(1), 1–16 (1997)

Horvath, J., Rothman, P.: Mortgage spreads, asset prices, and business cycles in emerging countries. J. Int. Money Finance 115 (2021)

Isaic, R., Smirna, T., Paun, C.: A critical view on the mainstream theory of economic cycles. Manag. Market. Chall. Knowl. Soc. **14**(1), 48–58. (2019). https://doi.org/10.2478/mmcks-2019-0004

Jorda, O., Schularick, M., Taylor, A.: Betting the house. J. Int. Econ. **96**(S1), S2–S18 (2015)
Kim, M., Shim, M.: Variable effort, business cycles, and economic welfare. Econ. Lett. **196** (2020)
Mişa, I., Kagitci, M.: An overview of the influence of some macroeconomic variables on public revenues. A panel approach for a sample of European countries. Manag. Market. Chall. Knowl. Soc. **14**(2), 249–265 (2019). https://doi.org/10.2478/mmcks-2019-0018
Munoz-Guillermo, M.: Revisiting the business cycle model with cubic nonlinear investment function. Chaos Solit. Fract. **142**, 110–510 (2021)
Özbilgin, H.M.: Financial market participation and the developing country business cycle. J. Dev. Econ. **92**, 125–137 (2010)
Papageorgiou, T., Michaelides, P.G., Tsionas, E.G.: Business cycle determinants and fiscal policy: a panel ARDL approach for EMU. J. Econ. Asymmetr. **13**, 57–68 (2016)
Polbin, A.: Multivariate unobserved component model for an oil-exporting economy: the case of Russia. Appl. Econ. Lett. **28**(8), 681–685 (2021)
Yan, C., Huang, K.X.: Financial cycle and business cycle: An empirical analysis based on the data from the U.S. Econ. Modell. **93**, 693–701 (2020)

E-Government and the General Population's Digital Skills in the European Union and OECD Member States

Paraschiv Dorel Mihai, Toader Liviu, and Nițu Maria

Abstract Technological progress has made it possible to change modern society, from the perspective of social interaction and of the interaction with local authorities and the government. The positive impact of digital technologies can be seen in the quality of the public services delivered by the government by increasing the efficiency and transparency of the public sector organizations. The e-government efforts were directed toward the use of technology to increase the efficiency and transparency of the public sector, for example, the digitalization of administrative procedures and the transition toward paperless administration. E-government depicts governments' use of the available technology and information in order to facilitate the administration and to supply better services to citizens and businesses, providing the citizens the opportunities to participate in democratic institutions and political processes. The spread and adoption of technology have generated an increased demand for digital and technology-related skills, which are extremely important in the professional and personal development. The purpose of this research article is to analyze the relationship between the Organisation for Economic Co-operation and Development (OECD) Digital Government Index (DGI) and the percentage of individuals who have basic or above basic digital skills in the European Union Member States that are also members of OECD.

Keywords E-government · Digital skills · Digital government Index (DGI) · European union · OECD member states

P. D. Mihai (✉) · T. Liviu · N. Maria
Bucharest University of Economic Studies, Bucharest, Romania
e-mail: dorel.paraschiv@ase.ro

N. Maria
e-mail: maria.nitu@rei.ase.ro

A. M. Dima and M. Kelemen (eds.), *Digitalization and Big Data for Resilience and Economic Intelligence*, Springer Proceedings in Business and Economics, https://doi.org/10.1007/978-3-030-93286-2_3

1 Introduction

The evolution of digital technologies has changed the modern societies, both in terms of how people interact with each other, as well as how they interact with the government or local authorities. The changes in technology can have a positive impact on the quality of the public services delivered by the governments (Gavurova et al. 2020) by increasing the efficiency and transparency of the public sector organizations through the digitalization of governments' processes. The adoption of digital technologies has the potential to transform how the government manages its core functions and, consequently, how citizens consume public services and interact with the public sector organizations. Early e-government efforts used technology to increase the efficiency and transparency of the public sector, like digitalization of administrative procedures and transition toward paperless administration. Despite having considerable advantages, these approaches often inserted technology into existing analogue processes, creating a hybrid system with certain limitations (OECD 2020a). Over time, a more integrated approach has aimed to achieve goals beyond efficiency and productivity, leading to the idea of a fully digitalized public sector. This implies a higher level of digital maturity enabling governments to "better meet citizen's needs, increase well-being and strengthen public satisfaction" (OECD 2020a).

2 Literature Review

Considered the third stage in the process of technological evolution (Knudsen 2020), digitalization represents the changes that have occurred in human society through the adoption and application of digital technology (Stolterman and Fors 2004) in daily and professional activities. The degree of digitalization is constantly expanding, which is associated with changes in the field of big data and their analysis (Milićević et al. 2020), as well as the implementation of digital technologies (Satalkina and Steiner 2020). Digitalization or digital transformation (Viduni 2020) is the implementation or high use by a company, sector, industry, or even by a country, of information or digital technology (Brennen and Kreiss 2014; Chayomchai, 2020), it stores or tracks data and information regarding different activities or tasks, which can be studied and analyzed in order to provide opportunities that can optimize the future process and also predict subsequent events (Ciarli et al. 2021; Agrawal et al. 2018). The advantages of digitalization are increased, with positive impacts on improving the quality of life, increasing individuals' access to public services, as well as streamlining the activity of governments and increasing transparency (Parviainen et al. 2017), through the process of implementing information and communication technology in public administration.

E-government, from the point of view of the information revolution, has transformed into a trend adopted by almost every state worldwide (Taylor et al. 2007).

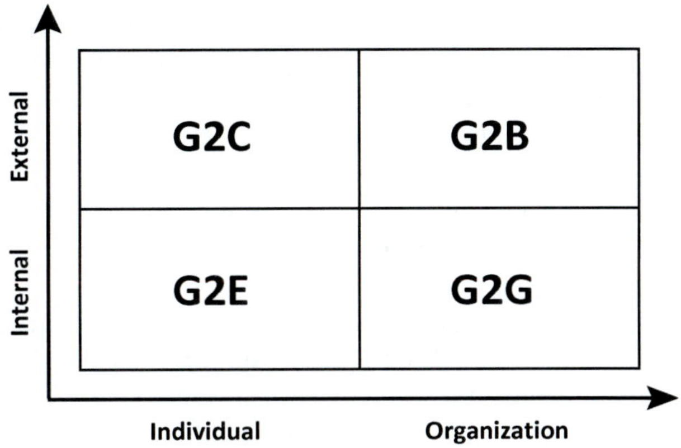

Fig. 1 E-government portfolio. *Source* Adapted from Siau and Long (2004), p. 222

Being a very important domain of information system innovation and IT, there has been an endeavor to encapsulate e-government in the actual information system (Alshehri and Drew 2010a, b).

It describes how governments utilize the information and technology available to facilitate the administration and provide better services to citizens and businesses, therefore providing extensive opportunities for citizens to participate in democratic institutions and political processes (Siau and Long 2004), and comprising four stakeholders: business, citizens, employees, and governments (Twizeyimana and Andersson 2019). E-government connects governments with individuals, businesses, and other parties, building a relationship among them (Davison et al. 2005) by facilitating electronic services and transactions. Services differ according to each party's needs, therefore generating four main categories of e-government functions: government-to-citizen (G2C), government-to-business (G2B), government-to-government (G2G), and government-to-employee (G2E) (Alshehri and Drew 2010a, b). Also, it contains digital applications that can be introduced by e-government as online services with external target groups or internal objectives as their main focus (Seljan et al. 2010) (Fig. 1).

The majority of government services, like social services, taxes, access to benefits, and so on, come under the G2C (government-to-consumers) category. The primary objective of these services is to improve the relationship between the government and its citizens by facilitating the interaction and making public information more accessible through the use of digital platforms, as well as by reducing the time required to conduct a transaction (Alshehri and Drew 2010a, 2010b).

Government-to-business (G2B) includes services exchanged between governments and the private sector that play an important role in business development and lead to a better tax collection. G2B services increase the efficiency and quality of transactions and dialogue between the state and private companies, while providing a higher degree of transparency of government contracting. The opportunity to conduct online transactions with the government simplifies the regulatory process and helps businesses to become more competitive (Ndou 2004). Government-to-employees (G2E) services help improve the efficiency of government administration by reorganizing internal operations and adopting best practices and facilitating the digital interactions between the government and its employees (Siau and Long 2004). Government-to-Government (G2G) refers to online communications between government organizations and departments (Odat and Khazaaleh 2012) to enhance cooperation and collaboration on different levels and when situated in various locations.

Therefore, the implementation and development capability of the e-government can represent a huge opportunity, due to the fact that, on one hand, it can change the way information and services are delivered, as well as the interaction with the citizens, the public, and, on the other hand, it can become a constituent element of government strategies (Zhang et al. 2014). Also, the majority of countries have transformed and digitalized public services, where individuals have to interact with public institutions and government using online applications, the digital skills and their continuous development are becoming increasingly more important (Rodrigues-Hevia et al. 2020).

Digital technologies lead to a digital transformation that presents a growth opportunity for European economies in terms of productivity and improvement of work conditions. The widespread of technology generates higher demand for digital and technology-related skills (Morandini et al. 2020). Digital skills represent an important tool for professional development and social inclusion (Gui and Argentin 2011), but they especially enable citizens to use digital services and engage in different types of online activities, including digital interactions with the government and its services (Van Deursen and Dijk 2009). Having made available E-government services for citizens, companies and other groups can represent a challenge by generating two forms of the digital divide. Access to the internet and online tools make the first-order digital divide highly dependent on both technological infrastructure and costs of online access (Seljan et al. 2010). In this domain, there is a digital divide between indigent and wealthy nations regarding internet penetration. The progress made by digital capabilities and digital literacy, considering the usage of the internet, along with its online tools and digital environment, is related to the second-order digital divide (Seljan et al. 2010).

The private and public sectors have been transformed or improved by digitalization, which provided the opportunity to develop a more efficient, reliable, and fast traditional process.

Digital learning is becoming an important driver in the process of skill development in order to enhance the digital transformation within the company or public institutions (Sousa and Rocha 2019).

Therefore, as a result of globalization and the rapid transformation of technology, which can create uncertainty, a need arises for the improvement of digital skills in order to overcome future challenges.

The concept of skills "has two dimensions: the individual and the collective" (Sousa and Rocha 2019). From the perspective of digital skills in the twenty-first century, we find information, creative digital skills, and problem-solving (Van Laar et al. 2020):

- Information digital skills—The skills to search the information online, to select and evaluate it—are contained in information digital skills. When a task or question arises, one must be able to search the derived terms properly, furthermore, when accessing information a person should be able to limit the amount of search results by selecting only relevant websites and also to be able to identify false, biased, or subjective information (van Laar et al. 2020);
- Problem-solving digital skills represent the ability to resolve a difficult situation using ICTs knowledge (van Laar et al. 2020);
- Creative digital skills involve the appeal of creativity and its encouragement by analyzing activities or tasks from another perspective (van Laar et al. 2020).

3 Methodology

For the development of this article, the authors resorted to the literature review on the concepts of digitalization, e-governance, and digital skills, followed by a visual inspection and analytical method to determine the type and strengths of the correlation between the general populations' digital skills and the level of digitalization within governments. The Analysis ToolPak in Microsoft Excel was used to visualize, analyze, and process the data for 2019.

Therefore, in this article, both the visual inspection and analytical methods were used to determine whether there is any type of relationship between the Digital Government Index and the number of individuals who have basic or above basic digital skills in countries that are both members of OECD and the European Union.

The first indicator used in the research was the Digital Government Index (DGI), which is a measuring instrument according to the 6 dimensions (proactiveness, digital by design, data-driven, government as a platform, open by default, user-driven) and evaluates the way in which governments have adopted strategic approaches to digital technologies and the use of data, and it also presents, at the level of OECD member countries, but also of partner countries, the transition from e-government to digital (OECD 2020b).

The areas of communication, information, software skills, and problem-solving are performed by people with ages from 16 to74, who are presumed to possess the corresponding skills, who use the internet or software in certain activities related to the second indicator, i.e., individuals' level of digital skills.

4 Analysis/Results Interpretation

4.1 Digital Skills—The Foundation of the Digital Government a Subsection Sample

Digital skills among the general population can vary from basic internet and computer usage skills, which enable individuals to consume digital services and be an active part of the digital society, to advance skills that contribute to the creation and development of new digital services and ecosystems. In the European Union, the level of digital skills continued to grow slowly in the last years, reaching 58% of individuals having basic or above basic digital skills and 28% with low overall digital skills (European Commission 2020). According to Eurostat (2021), digital skills refer to composite indicators based on selected activities related to the internet or software use performed by individuals aged 16–74 in four specific areas: information, communication, problem-solving, and software skills (Table 1).

From the list of countries that are both EU and OECD members, according to Eurostat (2021), Italy, Latvia and Greece register the lowest percentage of individuals who have basic or above basic overall digital skills, while the United Kingdom, Finland, and the Netherlands have the highest values.

The lack of basic digital skills is a major challenge when implementing e-government initiatives. This is can pose a particular problem especially if there is a lack of qualified ITC specialists needed to design and implement the digital systems or inadequate human resources training. Technical skills for implementation, installation, and maintenance of ITC hardware and software infrastructure, as well as appropriate skills for using the digital systems, are required to successfully implement e-government initiatives. Training and education programs among the general population can accelerate the adoption of e-government programs in the long run. Human capability development requires lifelong learning and does not end with the acquisition and achievement of basic initial digital skills (Ndou 2004).

4.2 The OECD Digital Government Policy Framework (DGPF)

The adoption of digital technologies transformed the citizens' expectations about their governments, leading to a generalized need for openness, accessibility, and the creation of mechanisms that allow for a more flexible and dynamic interaction between the state and its citizens. Failure to adapt to this new paradigm can lead to policy failures and delivery of irrelevant or outdated public services with possible long-run effects of a decrease in tax collection capabilities, larger VAT gaps, and dissatisfaction regarding the public services rendered. An increased level of digital maturity allows the public sector to meet citizens' expectations, remain relevant, and improve policymaking and public services (OECD 2020a).

Table 1 Individuals who have basic or above basic overall digital skills (% of total population) in countries that are both EU and OECD members

Italy	Latvia	Greece	Porturgal	Ireland	Slovenia	Lithuania	France	Spain	Belgium	Czechia	Estonia	Luxembourg	Austria	Germany	Denmark	Sweden	United Kingdom	Finland	Netherlands
42%	**43%**	**51%**	**52%**	**53%**	**55%**	**56%**	**57%**	**57%**	**61%**	**62%**	**62%**	**65%**	**66%**	**70%**	**70%**	**72%**	**74%**	**76%**	**79%**

Source Adapted from Eurostat (2021), Dataset—Individuals' level of digital skills, 2019

According to OECD (2020b), the digital government is understood as "the use of digital technologies as an integrated part of government's modernization strategies, to create public value". The key to delivering quality governmental services is to understand that public services must be designed as a response to citizens' needs. A successful digital transformation will enable governments to operate more efficiently in the digital sector and provide public services that are more efficient, yet simpler to access. A digital government represents the next step of evolution from e-government, helping the public sector to shift from a digital technology efficiency-oriented approach to a collaborative, innovative, and more open government (OECD 2020a) (Fig. 2).

The OECD Digital Government Policy Framework (DGPF) consists of six dimensions that form a fully digital government: digital by design, data-driven public sector, government as a platform, open by default, user-driven, proactiveness (OECD 2020b). The DGPF is a policy instrument that supports quantitative and qualitative assessments across countries and the six-dimensional framework for the OECD Digital Government Index (DGI). A digital government will achieve higher scores in all six dimensions, therefore will be able to provide quality public services with high internal efficiency and transparency (Fig. 3).

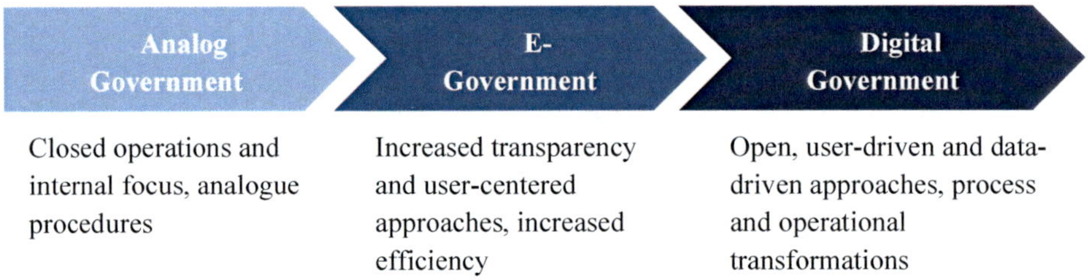

Fig. 2 Transition to Digital government. *Source* Adapted from OECD (2020a), p. 15

Fig. 3 OECD Digital Government Index Components. *Source* Adapted from OECD (2020b), p. 17

Dimension 1: Digital by Design. This dimension refers to the process of rooting the digital transformation in government structure and redesigning the relationship between governments and human interaction via technology. It rates whether a government exploits the full potential of digital technologies and instruments when designing public policies and services, while assessing the level of institutional capacity to develop and implement programs aimed at developing digital skills among its workforce.

Dimension 2: Data-Driven Public Sector. Data-driven public sector refers to the development of government data structures and the corresponding infrastructure needed to deliver better services and policies, promote data access, sharing and integration across the public sector (OECD 2020a). A data-driven public sector encourages the use of innovative and alternate data sources in order to deliver better public services and respond to the needs of its citizens. Higher scores in this dimension suggest that governments make strategic use of data by exploiting its potential to deliver value and create a digitally skilled public sector.

Dimension 3: Government as a Platform. Government as a platform dimension describes how governments use available technologies and data to improve the quality of services while facilitating collaboration for an ecosystem that equips governments' employees to design policies and deliver services coherently. According to OECD (2020b), the "Government as a platform" dimension also incorporates the digital tools required to leverage existing resources, promote coherence, sustain implementation of digital government solutions, and optimize public IT expenditures.

Dimension 4: Open by Default. The open by default dimension evaluates the existence of an open government data policy, strategy and implementation plan. It measures government openness in a broad sense, including the use of data and technologies to communicate with different actors to create a collective and knowledge-based public sector (OECD 2020a).

Dimension 5: User-Driven. A user-driven approach places the citizens at the core of government policies and service design by recognizing their needs and expectations as the main drivers to the transition toward a digital government.

Dimension 6: Proactiveness. This dimension measures the capacity of a government to anticipate the citizens' needs and economic and social developments by using predictive models and real-time data, therefore creating and implementing services and policies without waiting for formal requests by different actors.

The Digital Government Index (DGI) is a measurement tool based on the six dimensions of the OECD Digital Government Policy Framework that benchmarks the digital transformation of the public sector as a transition from e-government to digital government, across OECD Member and partner countries.

Figure 4 displays the OECD Digital Government Index composite score results by county, taking into consideration the average results registered for each of the six dimensions mentioned above. Sweden, Greece, and Finland scored the lowest

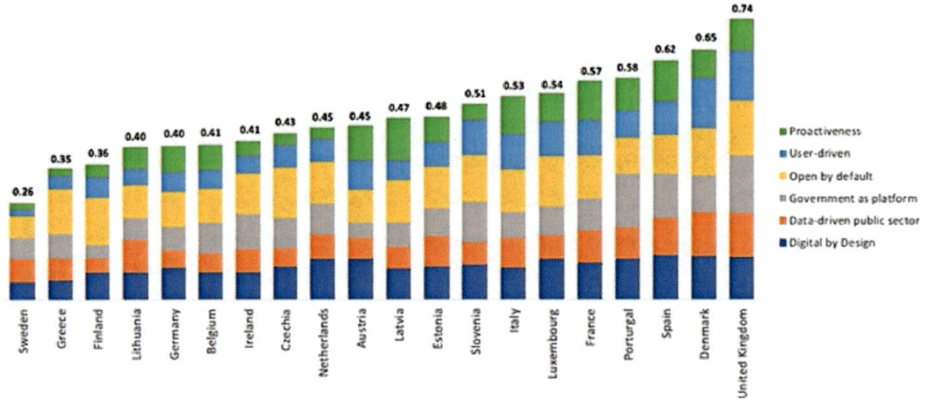

Fig. 4 OECD Digital Government Index Components countries that are both EU and OECD members—2019 results. *Source* Adapted from OECD (2020b), p. 54

values of the Digital Government Index, among the countries that are both EU and OECD Members (data from 2019), while Spain, Denmark, and the United Kingdom registered the highest values.

In order to determine whether there is any relationship between the OECD Digital Government Index and the overall digital skills of the general population, measured by Eurostat (2021) as a percentage of individuals who have basic or above basic overall digital skills, the datasets for both variables were combined into a single visual representation, depicted in Fig. 5.

A visual inspection of the two datasets does not appear to suggest the existence of any pattern that might describe a linear relationship between the Digital Government Index and the number of individuals who have basic or above basic digital skills. Also, the associated scatter diagram depicted in Fig. 6, along with the calculated correlation coefficient of R = −0.058, supports the hypothesis of a non-existing correlation between the two variables.

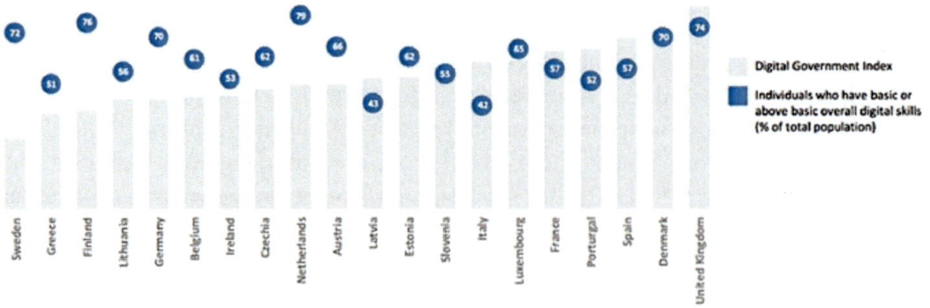

Fig. 5 OECD Digital Government Index and Individuals who have basic or above basic overall digital skills (% of total population), for countries that are both EU and OECD members – 2019 results. *Source* Adapted from OECD (2020b), p. 54 and adapted from Eurostat (2021), Dataset—Individuals' level of digital skills, 2019

Fig. 6 Scatter Diagram: Correlation between OECD Digital Government Index and Individuals who have basic or above basic overall digital skills (% of total population), for countries that are both EU and OECD members—2019 results. *Source* Own calculations from 2019 data by OECD (2020b), p. 54 and Eurostat (2021), Dataset–Individuals' level of digital skills

5 Conclusions

The potential of technological developments on companies, society, and governments is enormous, but generates a number of obligations and challenges that require a continuous adaptation to the evolution in technology and their application in local authorities, government as well as improving digital skills.

According to Rodriguez-Hevia et al. (2020), digital skills are an important determinant of the adoption of e-government services among citizens, as one's ability to effectively use the internet has a major impact on the intentions to use the e-government services and digital platforms. The lack of digital skills can limit the citizens' ability to interact with governments' digital platforms or retrieve data and information.

The present research focuses on finding a correlation between the populations' digital skills and the level of digitalization within the governments in a specific timeframe. The aggregated findings suggest that there is no correlation between the two variables, meaning that an improvement in the general population's digital skills does not appear to have any impact on the degree of government digitalization, at least not in the short run or in the same timeframe. Although, according to the analysed data, there is no linear significant relationship between the two variables in the same unit of time, there is no sufficient evidence to exclude a deterministic relationship that might occur over a longer period. In the medium or long run, it is reasonable to assume that a highly digitally educated population might ask for a more complex government digital ecosystem, or vice versa, a digitally oriented government can constraint the citizens to adopt digital technologies faster. Nevertheless, digital government efforts might not have the desired outcome if they do not take into consideration the preferences, expectations, and needs of the users when designing and implementing digitally enabled public services.

The lack of digital-savvy government employees can slow down the process of implementing correct and coherent digital government policies. Further efforts are needed for the Member States to fill the digital gaps and increase the overall level of civil servants' digital performance and competencies through comprehensive training programs.

The government digital transformation is generally a long-term effort and must be sustained and resistant to political change. The lack of strategic vision and continuity in formal roles and responsibilities throughout political regime changes represents a major challenge for coherent design and implementation of public digital services, regardless of the general population's digital competencies.

Further research might focus on determining the impact of specific digital competencies of the public sector employees on the level of government digitalization of public services. Governments with a solid track record of digital governance were better prepared to leverage digital technologies during the Covid-19 outbreak. Further research might evaluate governments' agility in designing and implementing digital public services as a response to the Covid-19 pandemic lockdowns.

References

Agrawal, A., Gans, J., Goldfarb, A.: Prediction machines: the simple economics of artificial intelligence. Harvard Business Press, Boston (2018)

Alshehri, M., Drew, S.: Challenges of e-government services adoption in Saudi Arabia from an e-ready citizen perspective. World Acad. Sci. Eng. Technol. **42**, 1039–1045 (2010a). http://citeseerx.ist.psu.edu/viewdoc/download?doi=10.1.1.294.1099&rep=rep1&type=pdf Accessed 15 July 2021

Alshehri, M., Drew, S.: E-government fundamentals. In: IADIS International Conference ICT, Society and Human Beings, pp. 35–40 (2010b). https://research-repository.griffith.edu.au/bitstream/handle/10072/37709/67525_1.pdf Accessed 30 March 2021

Brennen, S., Kreiss, D.: Digitalization and digitization. (2014). https://culturedigitally.org/2014/09/digitalization-and-digitization/ Accessed 02 April 2021

Chayomchai, A.: "The online technology acceptance model of generation-Z people in Thailand during COVID-19 crisis. Manag. Market. Challeng. Knowl. Soc. **15**, 496–513 (2020). https://doi.org/10.2478/mmcks-2020-0029

Ciarli, T., Kenney, M., Massini, S., Piscitello, L.: Digital technologies, innovation, and skills: emerging trajectories and challenges. Res. Policy **50**(7), 1–14 (2021)

Davison, R.M., Wagner, C., Louis, C.K.M.: From government to e-government: a transition model. Inf. Technol. People **18**(3), 280–299 (2005)

European Commission: Digital economy and society index (DESI). (2020). https://ec.europa.eu/newsroom/dae/document.cfm?doc_id=67086 Accessed 09 April 2021

Eurostat: Individuals' level of digital skills. (2021). https://ec.europa.eu/eurostat/databrowser/view/isoc_sk_dskl_i/default/table?lang=en Accessed 15 April 2021

Gavurova, B., Cepel, M., Belas, J., Dvorsky, J.: Strategic management in SMEs and its significance for enhancing the competitiveness in the V4 Countries—a comparative analysis. Manag. Martket. Challen. Knowl. Soc. **15**(4), 557–569 (2020). https://doi.org/10.2478/mmcks-2020-0032

Gui, M., Argentin, G.: Digital skills of internet natives: different forms of digital literacy in a random sample of Northern Italian high school students. New Media Soc. **13**(6), 963–980 (2011)

Knudsen, D.-R.: Elusive boundaries, power relations, and knowledge production: a systematic review of the literature on digitalization in accounting. Int. J. Account. Inform. Syst. **36**, 1–22 (2020). https://www.sciencedirect.com/science/article/pii/S1467089518301350 Accessed 05 April 2021

Milićević, S., Petrović, J., Đorđević, N.: ICT as a factor of destination competitiveness: The case of the republics of former Yugoslavia. Manag. Market. Challen. Knowl. Soc. **15**(3), 381–392 (2020). https://doi.org/10.2478/mmcks-2020-0022

Morandini, M.C., Thum-Thysen, A., Vandeplas, A.: Facing the digital transformation: are digital skills enough? Econ. Brief **54**, 1–15 (2020). https://ec.europa.eu/info/sites/default/files/economy-finance/eb054_en.pdf Accessed 17 April 2021
Ndou, V.: E-Government for developing countries: opportunities and challenges. Electron. J. Inform. Syst. Dev. Countr. **18**(1), 1–24 (2004)
Odat, A., Khazaaleh, M.: E-government challenges and opportunities: a case study of Jordan. Int. J. Comp. Sci. Issues **9**(5), 361–367 (2012)
OECD: Digital Government Index: 2019 results. OECD Public Governance Policy Papers, OECD Publishing, Paris, No. 03, (2020a). https://doi.org/10.1787/4de9f5bb-en Accessed 13 April 2021
OECD: The OECD digital government policy framework: six dimensions of a digital government. OECD Public Governance Policy Papers, OECD Publishing, Paris, No. 02 (2020b). https://doi.org/10.1787/f64fed2a-en Accessed 13 April 2021
Parviainen, P., Tihinen, M., Kaariainen, J., Teppola, S.: Tackling the digitalization challenge: how to benefit from digitalization in practice. Int. J. Inf. Syst. Proj. Manag. **5**(1), 63–77 (2017)
Rodrigues-Hevia, L.F., Navio-Marco, J., Ruiz-Gomez, M.L.: Citizens' Involvement in E-government in the European Union: the rising importance of the digital skills. MDPI Sustain. **12**, 1–19 (2020)
Satalkina, L., Steiner, G.: Digital entrepreneurship and its role in innovation systems: a systematic Literature review as a basis for future research avenues for sustainable transitions. Sustainability **12**(7), 1–27 (2020)
Seljan, S., Miloloza, I., Pejic Bach, M.: E-government in the European countries: gender and ageing digital divide. In: Conference: Interdisciplinary Management Research XVI, Croatia, pp. 1563–1584 (2010). https://www.researchgate.net/publication/341277764_e-Government_in_European_Countries_Gender_and_Ageing_Digital_Divide Accessed 15 July 2021
Siau, K., Long, Y.: Factors impacting E-government development. In: ICIS 2004 Proceedings, vol. 18, pp. 221–233 (2004). http://aisel.aisnet.org/icis2004/18 Accessed 25 April 2021
Sousa, M.J., Rocha, A.: Digital learning: developing skills for digital transformation of organization. Futur. Gener. Comput. Syst. **91**, 327–332 (2019)
Stolterman, E., Fors, A.C.: Information technology and the good life. Inf. Syst. Res. **143**, 687–692 (2004)
Taylor, J., Miriam, L., Organ, J.: Information- intensive government and the layering and sorting of citizenship. Publ. Money Manag. **27**(2), 161–164 (2007)
Twizeyimana, J.D., Andersson, A.: Public value of E-Government—a literature review. Govern. Inform. Quart. **26**, 167–178 (2019)
Van Deursen, A.J.A.M., Van Dijk, J.A.G.M.: Improving digital skills for the use of online public information and services. Govern. Inform. Quart. **26**(2), 333–340 (2009)
Van Laar, E., Van Deursen, J.A., van Dijk, J., de Haan, J.: Measuring the levels of 21st-century digital skills among professionals working with creative industries: a performance-based approach. Poetic **81**, 1–14 (2020)
Viduni, P.V.M.V.D.: Conceptual review of dimensions of digital transformation in modern Era. Int. J. Sci. Res. Publ. **10**(2), 520–529 (2020)
Zhang, H., Xu, X., Xiao, J.: Diffusion of e-government: a literature review and directions for future directions. Govern. Inform. Quart. **31**, 631–636 (2014)

Risk Management of Agri-Food Value Chains—Exploring Research Trends from the Web of Science

Irina-Elena Petrescu, Raluca Ignat, Marius Constantin, and Mihai Istudor

Abstract Risk management has always been considered of high importance when approaching the topic of agri-food value chains. By design, the management of agricultural and food systems is challenging. This is due to the high degree of uncertainty involving the success of making profit from carrying out small-scale agricultural activities with less performance of innovative technologies compared to multinational corporations. In this field, the literature is broad—there are numerous risk management studies focused on methods designed to prevent and mitigate the negative effects of threats that could significantly affect activities carried out with the aim of adding value along the agri-food chains. The aim of this research was to explore emerging research trends concerning risk management approaches in the literature related to agri-food value chains. In this regard, a comparative bibliometric analysis was carried out based on the research papers indexed in the Web of Science before and after the year 2015. Results show a paradigm shift caused not only by the need for a sustainable approach of risk management in the case of the global agri-food value chain but results also show a paradigm shift concerning the management of creating and co-creating value along the agri-food chains.

Keywords Risk management · Agri-food value chains · Value creation · Research trend · Bibliometrics · Competitiveness

I.-E. Petrescu · R. Ignat · M. Constantin (✉) · M. Istudor
Bucharest University of Economic Studies, Bucharest, Romania
e-mail: marius.constantin@eam.ase.ro

I.-E. Petrescu
e-mail: irina.petrescu@eam.ase.ro

R. Ignat
e-mail: raluca.ignat@ase.ro

M. Istudor
e-mail: istudormihai14@stud.ase.ro

A. M. Dima and M. Kelemen (eds.), *Digitalization and Big Data for Resilience and Economic Intelligence*, Springer Proceedings in Business and Economics, https://doi.org/10.1007/978-3-030-93286-2_4

1 Introduction

In the global agri-food value chain, risk has always been a constant. With the intensification of the open global market, food safety issues emerged at many levels: inside and outside Europe, referring to regulation, management; food quality being oftentimes doubted (Houghton et al. 2008). Managing agri-food supply chains is certainly challenging and consumer safety should always be a priority.

The proper functionality of agri-food supply chains is influenced by many factors: raw material availability, land use (Chivu et al. 2021), energy—referring to the associated environmental and economic costs, climate change (Istudor et al. 2019; Petrariu et al. 2021), exchange rates and many others factors (Stone and Rahimifard 2018), starting from the first production steps, continuing with manufacturing and distribution of food until the final step—consumption (Ignat and Constantin 2020). In such a complex and dynamic global chain, there are various risks associated with specific product vulnerabilities, e.g., food perishability (Wang et al. 2019).

The beginning of the third decade of the twenty-first century is marked by the interest intensification in the field of blockchain technology and its application in the agri-food chain (Shahid et al. 2020; Tian 2017), especially if considering the rapid growth of internet-based information technologies and their utility in constructing traceability systems—instruments that can help manage and mitigate food chain risks, as well as consolidate resilience throughout various layers (Min 2019).

In this paper, risk management of agri-food value chains was placed in the spotlight of research. Risk management involves a process of carefully considering alternatives through the lens of the result of evaluations or risks assessment(s), as well as selecting and even implementing and monitoring activities carried out in the direction considered appropriate for a particular issue. The literature is rich on papers based on risk assessment methodologies in the agri-food sector, at many levels: analysis on the impact of heavy metals in the soil-vegetable system on human health (Liu et al. 2013); dietary exposure to copper (Sadhra et al. 2007); soil and groundwater contamination (Fan et al. 2010); genetically modified foods (Varzakas et al. 2007) and many other types of risk assessment.

Yet, this particular research is much rather focused on the quantitative aspect of the scientific interest regarding the topic of risk management of agri-food value chains, especially in connection with the ardent need for action in accordance with United Nations' 2030 Agenda for Sustainable Development. Published in September 2015, this document aims to efficiently harmonize socio-economic progress and environmental protection (United Nations 2015). As far as the agri-food sector is concerned, the goals of the 2030 Agenda converge with other European strategies and policies with respect to agriculture and rural development (Constantin et al. 2021; Dinu et al. 2020; Stoian and Caprita 2019; Orîndaru et al. 2021). The reason why the topic of risk management of agri-food value chains was analyzed while taking the 2030 Agenda for Sustainable Development as the main reference point is because the aim of this research was to assess the impact of the need of a paradigm shift in the approach of the supply chain: switching from the traditional vision to a modern and sustainable vision of the agri-food supply chain.

Genovese et al. (2017) explained that risk management becomes "cleaner" in the case of the desirable agri-food supply chains grounded in the principles of circularity. By reducing the negative consequences on the natural capital and the use of the environment "as a sink" for managing residuals, the nature of risk itself is different and much more complex than the one specific to a linear type of food supply chain.

1.1 Problem Statement

Expressing risk management questions and concerns is one of the many managerial responsibilities aiming to ensure that goals are met under maximized odds for success. These questions aim to help transpose the utility of risk assessment(s) into practice through relevant actions designed to mitigate risks.

Risks assessments are intended for practical use, as their purpose is to spot and fully define a risk, in order to establish the foundation for a managerial decision regarding the actions needed with respect to the identified risk: Does it need to be contained, eliminated, avoided? Or is the risk small enough to be considered acceptable, insignificant and ignored? However, risk comparison and ranking are much more complex and require a solid framework of analysis. Figure 1 contains the main components of any risk analysis.

The risk cycle encompasses minimum interdependent stages of any risk analysis, relevant no matter the nature of the risk. As suggested by the caption of Fig. 1, the process is phased and iterative—additional revision is always welcome with the aim of a better mitigation of identified risks.

1.2 Research Questions and Research Aims

This paper answers the following research questions: (a) Which are the emerging research interests concerning the topic of risk management of agri-food value chains?; (b) How did the paradigm shift with respect to agri-food value chains risk management after the 2030 Agenda for Sustainable Development was published in 2015?; (c) Did researchers focus more on the sustainability factor of solutions?

Therefore, the objective of this research was to comparatively study the scientific papers published on the topic of risk management of agri-food value chains and indexed in the Web of Science database before and after the year 2015, focusing on exploring emerging research, as well as tapping into research interest convergence and divergence points in the specialized literature.

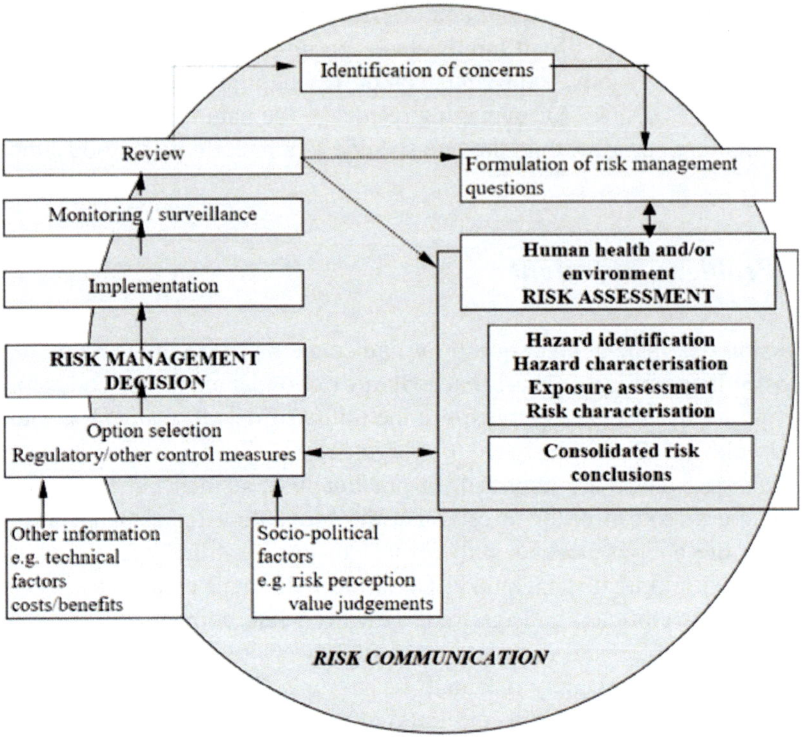

Fig. 1 The visual representation of a "risk cycle". *Source* European Commission (2000)

2 Methodology

Taking the aim of this research into account, the need for a quantitative method was implicit: the bibliometric analysis, which was considered optimal for developing this study on the scientific papers in which the topic of risk management of agri-food value chains was treated. As a science, bibliometrics involves resorting to a set of various quantitative techniques designed to monitor and assess scientific resources (Hood and Wilson 2001), thus making it a perfect tool for carrying out a comparative analysis based on the research papers published before and after the year 2015 (due to taking the 2030 Agenda for Sustainable Development as the point of reference).

Bibliometrics has become a popular tool for exploring research trends (Ignat et al. 2020; Pătărlăgeanu et al. 2020; Popescu 2020). This research was conducted by resorting to the VOSviewer 1.16.16 software tool, designed by Ness Jan van Eck and Ludo Waltman. Widely used in the bibliometric analysis (van Eck and Waltman 2010), VOSviewer facilitates the construction of networks, maps, heatmaps, and other relevant graphical representations that express the density and connection between keywords and word structures associated with the results (publications) identified based on querying specific databases. Publication metadata acts as the "raw materials" needed to design, construct and project bibliometric networks and maps.

This particular bibliometric analysis was carried out based on the Web of Science database. Consequently, the Web of Science database provides the necessary "raw materials" for the proper development of bibliometrics analysis of the papers elaborated on the topic of risk management of agri-food value chains. Therefore, the Web of Science database was queried in the following manner: TOPIC: ("risk management") AND TOPIC: (food chain) Timespan: All years. Indexes: SCI-EXPANDED, SSCI, A&HCI, CPCI-S, CPCI-SSH, BKCI-S, BKCI-SSH, ESCI, CCR-EXPANDED, IC. Performed in May 2021, this query led to the identification of 415 publications indexed in the Web of Science database at that time. The identified 415 publications contained the "risk management", "food" and "chain" word structures in their title, abstract or keywords. Mixing these three structures in the same query represented the premises for identifying and analyzing only the scientific publications specific to the topic of risk management of agri-food value chains.

3 Results Findings

Early studies published on the topic of agri-food value chains risk management were identified at the end of the second millennium: 21 papers were published starting from the year 1992, up to the year 2000, as displayed in Fig. 2. Regarding the nature of work, Van Leeuwen et al. (1996) developed a risk assessment of chemicals in European Communities with respect to consumer implications; Miles and Ross (1999)

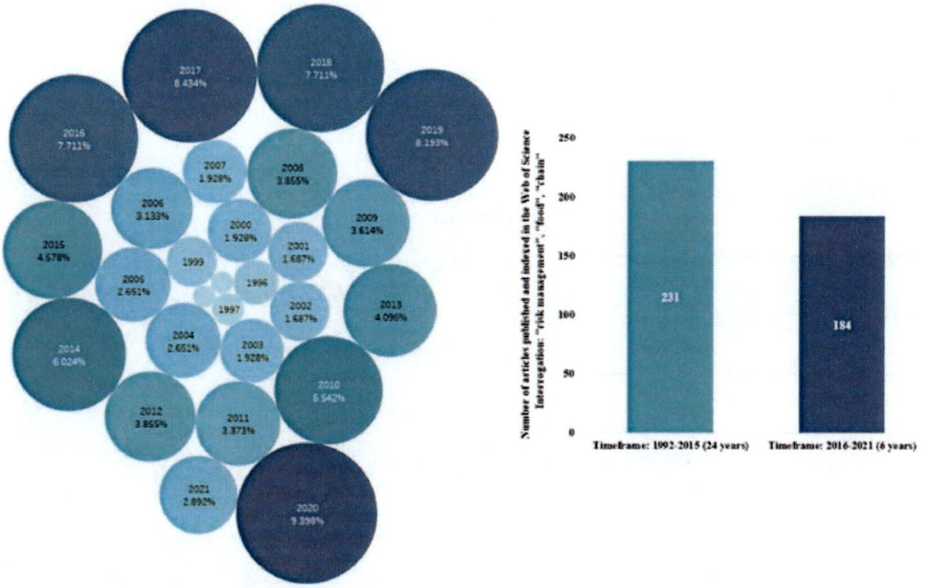

Fig. 2 The number of scientific papers identified by publication year. *Source* Authors' processing in Table 2021.1, based on the Web of Science results

proposed improving risk evaluation by bringing forward the concept of "quantitative microbial risk assessment" in the context of quantifying risks in a food production chain; Kruse (1999) argued that regional differences in the prevalence of food-borne pathogens need be considered in the risk management process of international food trading, in the context of intensified globalization.

From a quantitative perspective, before the 2030 Agenda for Sustainable Development was published (1992–2015), 231 papers were published and identified based on the performed query (55.66% from the total of 415 papers). After 2015, the scientific interest has intensified and has shifted toward the necessity of tackling the topic of risk management of agri-food value chains by placing the sustainability factor into the spotlight of research. In this regard, recent studies were focused on: overcoming the challenges specific to global food security (Andrei et al. 2021; Constantin et al. 2021) through research and solidarity in a sustainable manner (Barrett 2021); the impact of the agri-food sector on meeting the Sustainable Development Goals (McElwee et al. 2020; Pătărlăgeanu et al. 2021); strengthening climate-resilient and sustainable food supply systems (Ebi et al. 2020).

As displayed in Fig. 3, most of the identified papers were published under the Food Science Technology (128), Environmental Sciences (47), and Management (47) Web of Science categories, whereas the top 10 publishers were analyzed in Table 1.

Figure 4 was built based on the identified 251 publications during 1992–2015 and the authors' computation of the Web of Science-extracted metadata, whereas Fig. 5 is based on the 184 publications during 2016–May 2021. Specific VOSviewer restrictions and filters were applied to the metadata: (i) type of analysis: co-occurrence, (ii) unit of analysis: all keywords, (iii) counting method: full counting, (iv) the minimum number of occurrences of a keyword in order to be displayed in Figs. 4 and 5: 3 occurrences in both cases.

Fig. 3 The Web of Science categories associated with the identified papers treating the topic of risk management of agri-food value chains. *Source* Web of Science, May 2021

Table 1 Top 10 publishers of research papers treating the topic of risk management of agri-food value chains

Top publisher	Journal	Published papers	Percentage of total (415) (%)	Cumulative share (%)
1	Food Control	13	3.13	3.13
2	British Food Journal	12	2.89	6.02
3	International Journal of Food Microbiology	8	1.93	7.95
4	International Journal of Production Research	8	1.93	9.88
5	Supply Chain Management. An International Journal	8	1.93	11.81
6	Acta Horticulturae	7	1.69	13.49
7	International Journal of Logistics Management	6	1.45	14.94
8	Journal of Cleaner Production	6	1.45	16.39
9	Risk Analysis	6	1.45	17.83
10	Food Policy	5	1.20	19.04

Source Authors' processing, based on the Web of Science results

Regarding Fig. 4, out of the 1,356 total keywords associated with the 251 publications, 113 keywords met the threshold (8.33%), and in the case of Fig. 5, out of the 1,258 total keywords associated with the 184 publications, 115 keywords met the threshold (9.14%).

Based on VOSviewer computation (Figs. 4, 5, and 6), results confirm a paradigm shift starting from 2016 as far as risk management of agri-food value chains is concerned. Research interests, quantified through the lens of the published and indexed scientific papers in the Web of Science database, converge in the direction of meeting risk management and economic performance in a sustainable manner, by fostering resilience, as well as the potential of bioenergy and traceability through information technology. Early papers elaborated on this topic did not include such approaches, as one can notice by comparing Fig. 5 with Fig. 4.

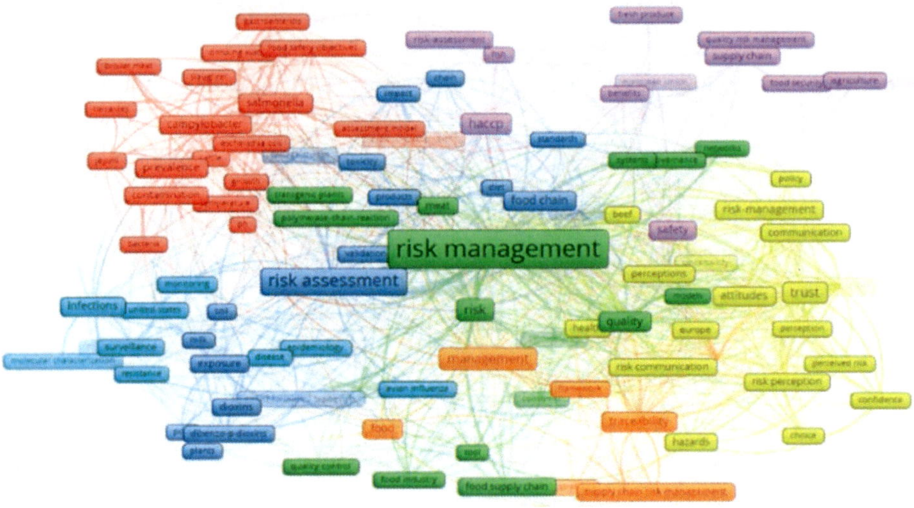

Fig. 4 Keyword cluster analysis (publications: 1992–2015). *Source* Authors' processing in VOSviewer 1.16.16, based on the Web of Science results

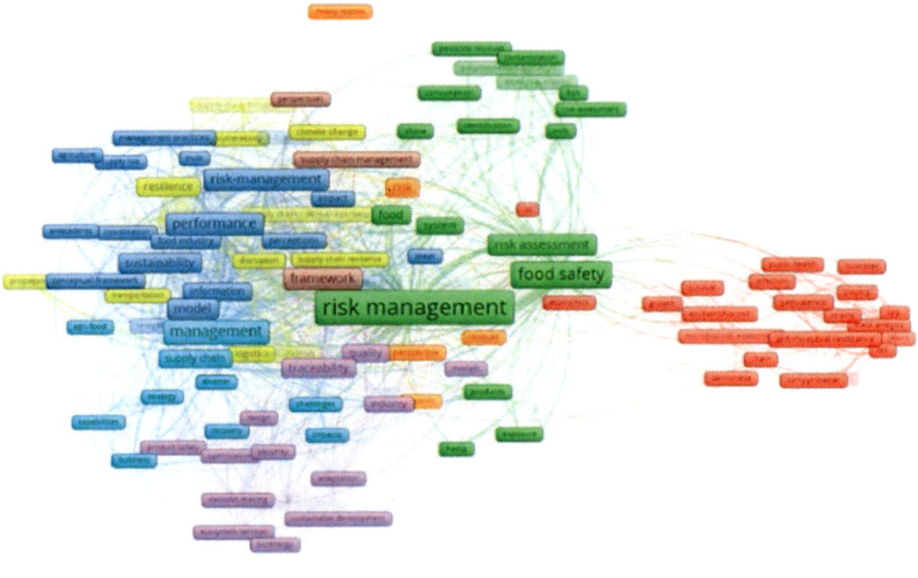

Fig. 5 Keyword cluster analysis (publications: 2016-May 2021). *Source* Authors' processing in VOSviewer 1.16.16, based on the Web of Science results

4 Conclusions

Agri-food supply chain risk management is increasingly calling for more efficient and intensified collaboration among various actors in both private and public sectors in order to be able to provide "real-time" adaptive responses to constantly changing

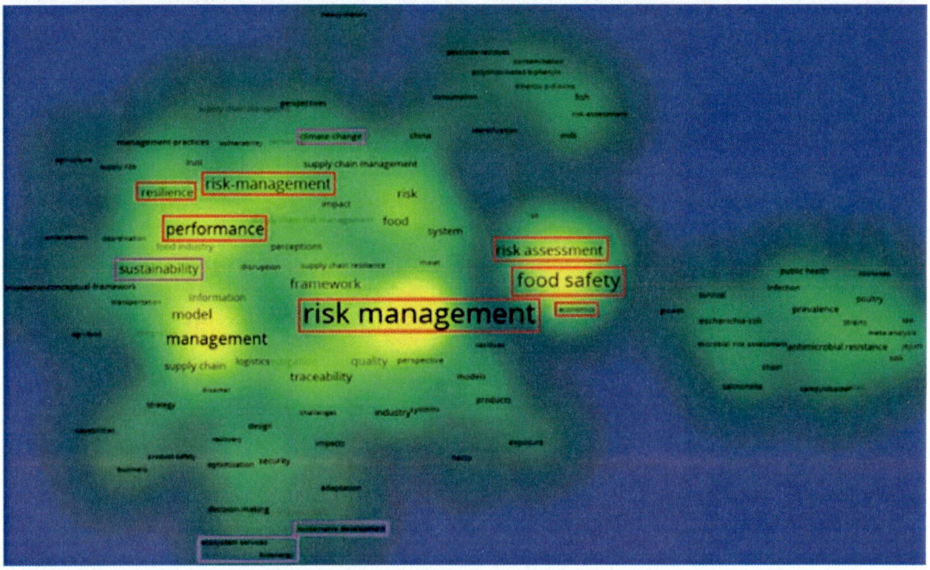

Fig. 6 The density analysis of keywords (publications: 2016-May 2021). *Source* Authors' processing in VOSviewer 1.16.16, based on the Web of Science results

market demands. In this context, risk management of agri-food supply chains is pushed on its path to a more resilient system, especially by the leaps of information technology. In this regard, modern challenges facilitate improving the transparency and traceability of raw agri-food materials in such a way that allows consumers to actively monitor food flows and information—digitally accessible only a tap away on smartphones or other similar devices, therefore reinforcing consumer confidence in the chain and mitigating the risks for both consumer and producer.

Results confirm that the necessity of approaching the global agri-food value chain in a holistic and sustainable manner has a direct impact on risk assessment and management. The 2030 Agenda for Sustainable Development has significantly contributed to changing the perspective of researchers when carrying out studies regarding the agri-food sector as an integrated part of a larger system that needs to be shaped on its path to sustainability and performance through resilience.

This research is subject to several minor limitations. Given the objective to quantitatively study the scientific literature published on the topic of risk management of agri-food value chains during different periods, paradigm shifts were identified in this paper by taking 2015 as a point of reference in carrying out the bibliometric analysis. However, more potential paradigm shifts could have been identified if the perspective was switched to a different publishing year, 2019 for example, when the European Green Deal, a set of policy initiatives with major implications for many sectors, including the agri-food sector, was initially signed off by the EU leaders.

Future research directions regarding this bibliometric analysis include expanding the Web of Science database query *TOPIC: ("risk management") AND TOPIC: (food chain)* to a much larger degree in order to cover more of the scientific literature specific to risk management of agri-food value chains. Additionally, the VOSviewer processing can also be improved by including relevant papers indexed in Scopus into the bibliometric computation. This would provide a more in-depth analysis of the scientific literature specific to the topic of risk management of agri-food value chains and would make paradigm shifts easier to be identified, by performing comparative bibliometric studies based on different publishing periods.

Acknowledgements This paper was developed through the institutional project entitled "Necesitate și posibilități de creare și dezvoltare a centrelor de achiziții, prelucrare, ambalare și livrare a produselor agroalimentare" ["Need and possibilities for the creation and development of centers for the acquisition, processing, packaging and delivery of agri-food products"], financed by Bucharest University of Economic Studies.

References

Andrei, J.V., Chivu, L., Constantin, M., Subić, J.: Economic aspects of international agricultural trade and possible threats to food security in the EU-27: a systematic statistical approach. In: Erokhin V., Tianming G., Andrei, J.V. (eds.) Shifting Patterns of Agricultural Trade. Springer, Singapore (2021). https://doi.org/10.1007/978-981-16-3260-0_10

Barrett, C.B.: Overcoming global food security challenges through science and solidarity. Am. J. Agr. Econ. **103**(2), 422–447 (2021)

Chivu, L., Constantin, M., Privitera, D., Andrei, J.: Land grabbing, land use, and food export competitiveness: bibliometric study of a paradigm shift. In: Erokhin V., Tianming G., Andrei J.V. (eds.) Shifting Patterns of Agricultural Trade. Springer, Singapore (2021). https://doi.org/10.1007/978-981-16-3260-0_6

Constantin, M., Radulescu, I. D., Andrei, J. V., Chivu, L., Erokhin, V. & Gao, T.: A perspective on agricultural labor productivity and greenhouse gas emissions in the Context of the Common Agricultural Policy exigencies. Econ. Agric. **68**(1), 53–67 (2021). https://doi.org/10.5937/ekoPolj2101053C

Constantin, M., Strat, G., Deaconu, M.E., Pătărlăgeanu, S.R.: Innovative agri-food value chain management through a unique urban ecosystem. Manag. Res. Pract. **13**(3), 5–22 (2021). http://www.mrp.ase.ro/no133/f1.pdf

Dinu, M., Pătărlăgeanu, S.R., Chiripuci, B., Constantin, M.: Accessing the European funds for agriculture and rural development in Romania for the 2014–2020 period. In: Proceedings of the International Conference on Business Excellence, vol. 14, no. 1, pp. 717–727 (2020). https://doi.org/10.2478/picbe-2020-0068

Ebi, K.L., Harris, F., Sioen, G.B., Wannous, C., Anyamba, A., Bi, P., Boeckmann, M., Bowen, K., Cissé, G., Dasgupta, P., Dida, G.O., Gasparatos, A., Gatzweiler, F., Javadi, F., Kanbara, S., Kone, B., Maycock, B., Morse, A., Murakami, T., Capon, A.: Transdisciplinary research priorities for human and planetary health in the context of the 2030 Agenda for sustainable development. Int. J. Environ. Res. Public Health **17**(23), 8890 (2020)

European Commission: First Report on the Harmonisation of Risk Assessment Procedures. Part 1: The Report of the Scientific Steering Committee's Working Group on Harmonisation of Risk Assessment Procedures in the Scientific Committees advising the European Commission in the area of human and environmental health, pp. 24 (October 2000)

Fan, C., Chen, Y., Ma, H., Wang, G.: Comparative study of multimedia models applied to the risk assessment of soil and groundwater contamination sites in Taiwan. Journal of Hazardous Materials **182**(1), 778–786 (2010)

Genovese, A., Acquaye, A.A., Figueroa, A., Koh, S.C.L.: Sustainable supply chain management and the transition towards a circular economy: Evidence and some applications. Omega **66**, 344–357 (2017)

Hood, W.W., Wilson, C.S.: The literature of bibliometrics, scientometrics, and informetrics. Scientometrics **52**(2), 291 (2001)

Houghton, J.R., Rowe, G., Frewer, L.J., Van Kleef, E., Chryssochoidis, G., Kehagia, O., Korzen-Bohr, S., Lassen, J., Pfenning, U., Strada, A.: The quality of food risk management in Europe: perspectives and priorities. Food Policy **33**(1), 13–26 (2008)

Ignat, R., Constantin, M.: Short-term effects of COVID-19 pandemic on agri-food value chains in Romania. In: Innovative Models to Revive the Global Economy, pp. 578–588, Sciendo (2020). https://doi.org/10.2478/9788395815072-058

Ignat, R., Lazăr, V., Costea, A.P.: Economic resilience: a bibliometric analysis of the concept. "Ovidius" Univ. Ann. Econ. **XX**(2), 355–361 (2020)

Istudor, N., Ion, R.A., Petrescu, I.E., Hrebenciuc, A.: Agriculture and the twofold relationship between food security and climate change. Ecidence from Romania. Amfiteatru Econ. **21**(51), 285–293 (2019)

Kruse, H.: Globalization of the food supply–food safety implications: Special regional requirements: future concerns. Food Control **10**(4), 315–320 (1999)

Liu, X., Song, Q., Tang, Y., Li, W., Xu, J., Wu, J., Wang, F., Brookes, P.C.: Human health risk assessment of heavy metals in soil-vegetable system: a multi-medium analysis. Sci. Total Environ. pp. 463–464, pp. 530–540 (2013)

McElwee, P., Calvin, K., Campbell, D., Cherubini, F., Grassi, G., Korotkov, V., Hoang, A.L., Lwasa, S., Nkem, J., Nkonya, E., Saigusa, N., Soussana, J.-F., Taboada, M.A., Manning, F., Nampanzira, D., Smith, P.: The impact of interventions in the global land and agri-food sectors on Nature's Contributions to People and the UN Sustainable Development Goals. Glob. Change Biol. **26**(9), 4691–4721 (2020)

Miles, D.W., Ross, T.: Identifying and quantifying risks in the food production chain. Food Aust. **51**(7), 298–303 (1999)

Min, H.: Blockchain technology for enhancing supply chain resilience. Business Horizons **62**(1), 35–45 (2019). https://doi.org/10.1016/j.bushor.2018.08.012

Orîndaru, A., Popescu, M.-F., Căescu, Ștefan-C., Botezatu, F., Florescu, M.S., Runceanu-Albu, C.-C.: Leveraging COVID-19 outbreak for shaping a more sustainable consumer behavior. Sustainability **13**(11), 5762 (2021). https://doi.org/10.3390/su13115762

Pătărlăgeanu, S.R., Dinu, M., Constantin, M.: Bibliometric analysis of the field of Green Public Procurement. Amfiteatru Econ. **22**(53), 71–81 (2020)

Pătărlăgeanu, S.R., Constantin, M., Strat, G., Deaconu, M.E.: Best Practices of Circular Activities in the Agri-Food Sector from the Netherlands and Romania, Editura ASE: Bucharest, Romania, (2021). ISBN 978-606-34-0375-0. https://www.ceeol.com/search/book-detail?id=949510

Petrariu, R., Constantin, M., Dinu, M., Pătărlăgeanu, S.R., Deaconu, M.E.: Water, energy, food, waste nexus: Between synergy and trade-offs in Romania based on entrepreneurship and economic performance. Energies **14**(16), 5172 (2021). https://doi.org/10.3390/en14165172

Popescu, M.-F.: The link between innovation, digitalization and the energy sector. A bibliometric analysis. J. Emerg. Trends Mark. Manag. **1**(1), 306–318 (2020)

Sadhra, S.S., Wheatley, A.D., Cross, H.J.: Dietary exposure to copper in the European Union and its assessment for EU regulatory risk assessment. Science of the Total Environment **374**(2), 223–234 (2007)

Shahid, A., Almogren, A., Javaid, N., Al-Zahrani, F.A., Zuair, M., Alam, M.: Blockchain-based agri-food supply chain: a complete solution. IEEE Access **8**, 69230–69243 (2020). https://doi.org/10.1109/ACCESS.2020.2986257

Stoian, M., Caprita, D.: Organic agriculture: opportunities and trends. In: Popescu, G. (ed.), Agrifood Economics and Sustainable Development in Contemporary Society, pp. 275–293, IGI Global (2019). https://doi.org/10.4018/978-1-5225-5739-5.ch013

Stone, J., Rahimifard, S.: Resilience in agri-food supply chains: a critical analysis of the literature and synthesis of a novel framework. Supply Chain Manag. Int. J. **23**(3), 207–238 (2018)

Tian, F.: A supply chain traceability system for food safety based on HACCP, blockchain Internet of things. In: 2017 International Conference on Service Systems and Service Management, pp. 1–6 (2017). https://doi.org/10.1109/ICSSSM.2017.7996119

United Nations: Transforming our World: The 2030 Agenda for Sustainable Development A/RES/70/1 (2015).

van Eck, N.J., Waltman, L.: Software survey: VOSviewer, a computer program for bibliometric mapping. Scientometrics **84**(2), 523–538 (2010)

Van Leeuwen, C.J., Bro-Rasmussen, F., Feijtel, T.C.J., Arndt, R., Bussian, B.M., Calamari, D., Glynn, P., Grandy, N.J., Hansen, B., Van Hemmen, J.J., Hurst, P., King, N., Koch, R., Müller, M., Solbé, J.F., Speijers, G.A.B., Vermeire, T.: Risk assessment and management of new and existing chemicals. Environmental Toxicology and Pharmacology **2**(4), 243–299 (1996)

Varzakas, T.H., Chryssochoidis, G., Argyropoulos, D.: Approaches in the risk assessment of genetically modified foods by the Hellenic Food Safety Authority. Food Chem. Toxicol. Int. J. Publ. Br. Ind. Biol. Res. Assoc. **45**(4), 530–542 (2007)

Wang, Y., Yang, C., Hou, H.: Risk management in perishable food distribution operations: a distribution route selection model and whale optimization algorithm. Industrial Management & Data Systems **120**(2), 291–311 (2019)

Civic University Challenges in Romanian Higher Education; Students' Perceptions of Civic Engagement

Iordache Platis Magdalena

Abstract The contemporary context defined by the current pandemic effects has generated several challenges to individuals, institutions, and organizations across all sectors and industries. Higher education institutions also had to rapidly adapt the teaching and learning processes, the research activity, and the programs for the society development to the virtual or remote context, being a permanent reflection of the institutional missions. The current challenges of the civic university have determined several strategic decisions in Romanian universities due to the international alliances and European framework on civic engagement institutional networking. The paper aims to reveal how Romanian universities have adapted to the civic university approach and if and how student civic engagement is related to their academic results and their extracurricular activities. The study focuses on the civic university concept and characteristics and promotes institutional practices based on leadership initiatives and a survey related to students' perception of their civic engagement. The research is based on a literature review, on a comparative analysis of institutional academic leadership decisions, and on a questionnaire-based study in one university that has integrated the civic orientation in its institutional mission; the research includes a case study and the use of statistical support. The main findings reveal clarifications on the civic university concept and the Romanian university's challenges in this context; they also prove that students' perception of civic engagement is dependent on their extracurricular experience and that the civic engagement level is not exhaustively dependent on the academic results of students.

Keywords Civic university · Civic engagement · Academic leadership

I. P. Magdalena (✉)
University of Bucharest, Bucharest, Romania
e-mail: magdalena.platis@unibuc.ro

A. M. Dima and M. Kelemen (eds.), *Digitalization and Big Data for Resilience and Economic Intelligence*, Springer Proceedings in Business and Economics, https://doi.org/10.1007/978-3-030-93286-2_5

1 Introduction

Higher education institutions have always played an important role in society. Over time, their capacity of educating future generations of employees and entrepreneurs has been followed by the innovative contribution of higher education institutions in a variety of research areas and later by a significant role in shaping the city and contributing to social development.

In 2017, under the Erasmus + framework, a new focus was put on active citizenship defined by getting involved in the society; universities were therefore promoted as main actors capable to equip students with proper skills to become actively engaged in the society, to become European citizens (Erasmus+ 2017). Moreover, at UNICA, which is a network of universities located in capital cities throughout Europe, a working group was established to deal with the relationship among institutions, organizations, including universities, and the urban ecosystem, which they all interact with; in this context, universities become leaders in societal impact and get students engaged (UNICA and The City 2021 and Activity Report 2016–2019 (2021)).

Therefore, universities are no longer simple knowledge providers, but they are being actively engaged in civic actions. Unfortunately, a simple declarative sentence, or even a proper mission statement, is not enough if the academic community does not get involved, especially students. This paper aims to explain and demonstrate the capacity of the Romanian higher education of becoming compliant with civic university characteristics. The main objectives of the study are the following: to explain the civic university concept and characteristics, to describe the Romanian context of change specific to higher education university, and to present a case study based on leadership initiatives and on research related to students' perception of their civic engagement to demonstrate how their civic engagement is related with it.

2 Literature Review

The main concepts that need clarifications are civic engagement and civic university. Although they are explained separately, they remain interconnected, as a civic university must prove its community civic engagement and, at the same time, civic engagement of individuals and groups must be institutionally supported and developed.

2.1 Civic Engagement in Universities—Conceptual Analysis

Different research papers state that in order to develop, both universities and regions must collaborate, which is the reason why leadership in both areas faces new challenges by considering territorial development as possible under a holistic approach; this is possible for a civic university, which means there are new roles and responsibilities for current universities to act outside their own campuses (Goddard and

Vallance 2012; Goddard 2014). In other studies, civic engagement is related to a variety of behaviors, attitudes, and knowledge, which create effective citizenship (Dee 2020). Therefore, specialists consider that the main forms of civic engagement are volunteering and giving; while the former is promoted by the community, the latter is related to personal resources (Jones 2006). Civic engagement can also be understood as a diverse multi-causal phenomenon, which can be present in three forms: individual actions, contacts with authority, and collective action; in order to see the effectiveness of the civic engagement and to increase people's involvement, they need to see that their actions have an impact (Pattie et al. 2003).

students is revealed as activist movementsIn addition, civic engagement of students is revealed as activist movements or integrated into institutional practices like creating a learning community focusing on how society might be better organized or deep learning through creativity and discomfort (Bălan et al. 2019; Corrente et al. 2018; Reiff and Keene 2012). Moreover, higher education contributes to citizenship and helps students to become more engaged by providing them opportunities for specific courses and extracurricular experiences (Perrin and Gillis 2019). Civic engagement has become a priority for many higher education institutions, and it is also linked to experiential education and service-learning, as some indicators have been considered in the process of evaluation within the efforts for civic engagement (Bowen 2010; Foerster-Pastor et al. 2019).

Similar examples can be furthermore recently identified: at the European University Association a thematic group on environmental sustainability in connection to learning and teaching published in 2021 the so-called formula for sustainability education with integrated impact where the authors, apart from commitment, time, and resources, consider important other three components—a common cause, proper knowledge and skills, and authenticity of actions (Gwilliam 2021). In addition to this, research has demonstrated that civic engagement is directly connected to student success, as it generates greater learning and different learning of the academic context when students become equipped not only with skills such as critical thinking and communication (Onea 2020) but also with higher emotional intelligence and motivation; additionally, another interesting skill that is provided to students through their civic engagement is the ability for moral reasoning (Cress 2012; Bernacki and Jaeger 2008). Another study demonstrates that between civic engagement and leadership, education is a direct and strong link revealing the need for some service hours; apart from the curricular description, this involves the need for meaningful experiences, effective community partnerships, a certain design of the components of the civic engagement, and curriculum diversity (Johnson and Woodard 2014).

Starting from this, different universities have established offices for civic engagement, such as the Office for Student Engagement at Stanford University where students are invited to take part in a fair to find how to get involved in a student organization, or the Civic Engagement at Georgia State University, where students get involved as volunteers in service-learning projects getting recognition for their service, or the Community Engagement Office at Central European University, which supports civic activities of the entire university community (Civic Engagement 2021;

Community Engagement Office 2021; Office for Student Engagement 2021). Therefore, the most important role in institutional actions toward the academic community civic engagement touches upon academic leadership. Decision-making processes, resources allocation, explanatory materials, examples of events, and projects are efforts to make universities effective actors in the society and the city through civic engagement. Current studies do not cover practices in the Romanian higher education, as this civic engagement as a strategic determinant of the new university is currently shaping the institutional transformative processes gradually. This paper intends to fill the gap between what a civic university means from a theoretical approach and the current needs of Romanian universities by providing institutional practices and integrating the student perceptions on civic engagement in this transformative process. Best practices have always been considered useful for similar development in other institutions and therefore, in the end, findings will be a good start for other Romanian universities to move in the direction of the civic university approach.

2.2 *Civic University and Its Characteristics*

It has been promoted as part of theThe civic university is not a new concept. It has been promoted as part of the new citizen-centered quadruple helix model where universities support activities based on innovation that are initiated by and relevant for citizens (Arnkill et al. 2010). A civic university can be characterized by several items, such as (Goddard et al. 2016):

- Provides different opportunities for the society;
- Gets involved in community areas;
- Establishes partnerships with other universities;
- Becomes active in the development process of other entities in the region (individuals, companies, etc.).

At the same time, QS (Quacquarelly Symonds—a provider of services and analytics and insights on higher education, including different academic rankings) published in 2018 simple advice on the benefits of universities becoming civically engaged and ways to better communicate their civic involvement; therefore, in this context, a civic university is at least an institution:

- With a strategy to connect its actions to the local community;
- Which analyses the influences in the community;
- Which explores ways of generating positive change in the region (QS: What Does it Mean to be a Civic University 2021).

To maximize the university contribution to the local community and society, institutions face challenges to embedding civic engagement in the institutional strategy; this means fostering cooperation between university leadership and city leaders to develop the right programs and also to develop an internal system of structures and mechanisms to support the civic engagement of the university of high societal impact (Goddard et al. 2016). Moreover, it is very important for universities to learn from other institutional experiences and lessons, to address their local community issues, and maximize the impact of their efforts. Among the future challenges of the civic university of 2040, the same authors claim the importance of teaching and learning through resolving societal needs in a transformative and innovative university where the holistic approach will be predominant, more impactful than all the activities summarized.

2.3 *Civic University in Romanian Higher Education*

Under the Erasmus + framework, two calls for applications were managed in 2019 and 2020 to invite universities to develop in the context of different alliances to strengthen cooperation between universities and their staff and students (Erasmus+ 2019, 2020). The calls revealed a huge interest of universities to submit applications:

- First call: 54 applications, 17 alliances selected consisting in 114 higher education institutions; among these, 3 universities from Romania got involved in 3 different alliances.
- Second call: 52 new applications were received, 24 alliances were selected including 165 higher education institutions; among these, 7 universities from Romania got involved in European alliances.

This context provided the opportunity for 10 Romanian universities to cooperate with other universities in the direction of becoming the European University as observed in Fig. 1. Moreover, the transformation of the higher education processes started being governed by the following keywords: active citizens, active Europe, solidarity, engagement, community, and responsibility.

Therefore, most of the universities decided to work together within the alliances toward a new type of education and research that shares European values, considering social need as a starting point to develop programs and find effective responses to

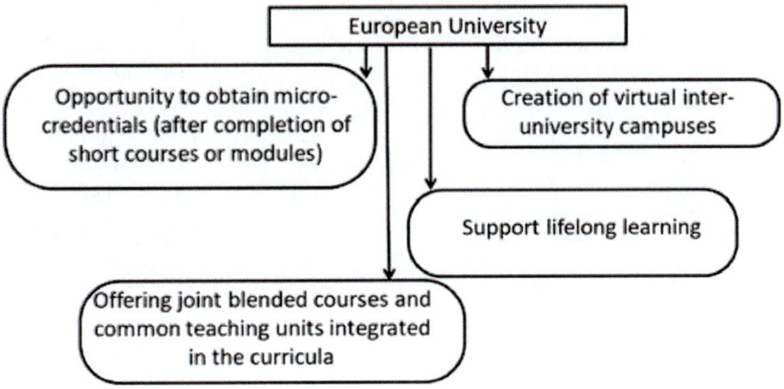

Fig. 1 European University Challenges. *Source* Author's own research, adapted from the European Commission (2020)

address it. In the following section, the University of Bucharest has been identified as a case study in this direction, with actions generating community impact.

A simple analysis of the alliances in which Romanian universities take part will reveal the efforts they make to adapt the civic approach in their current activity (Table 1). The examples provided include the universities that were selected in the first call and three others from the second call. The selection of the three universities out of seven in the second call is based on the availability of data.

The alliances have specific features due to local challenges, but they all have the main purpose of educating young generations according to cooperation principles, innovative trends, and social values.

Table 1 Romanian universities and European alliances

University	Alliance (no. of universities)	Short description
University of Bucharest	CIVIS (8 + 1)	· Transnational cooperation · Addressing major global challenges · Innovative and responsible teaching and research
National University of Political Studies and Public Administration	CIVICA (8)	· Knowledge is a public good · Civic responsibility is facilitated Advice is provided to policymakers on society challenges
Technical University of Civil Engineering Bucharest	EU- CONEXUS (6)	· Urbanized coastal areas · Cross-disciplinary approach Innovative education and research
Alexandru Ioan Cuza University of Iasi	EC2U (6)	· Smart higher education eco-system · Pan-European campus Model of joint governance
Technical University of Cluj Napoca	EUT (7)	· Long term strategy based on sustainability and European values · Student mobility based on curriculum Trans-disciplinarity teams
West University of Timisoara	UNITA	· Innovative education and research in renewable energy, cultural heritage, circular economy · Share common European values

Source Authors' own research (adapted from university websites) (UNIBUC website 2021; SNSPA website 2021; UAIC website 2021; UTCB website 2021; UTCLUJ website 2021; UVT website 2021)

3 Methodology

The current research includes both qualitative and quantitative research consisting of a case study of one civic university and a questionnaire addressed to students to identify their perceptions on civic engagement. The case study shows the leadership support provided for institutional civic development, while the students' perceptions reveal their current and future levels of engagement. The research design is presented in Fig. 2.

3.1 The University of Bucharest as a Civic University—The Leadership Approach

be narrative, while in the last case, theyThe University of Bucharest (UB) has become a member of a European alliance in the first call under the ERASMUS + framework. Many strategic changes have taken place since CIVIS. A qualitative case study is an exploration of a complex phenomenon in a specific context and includes four phases—foundation (a clear understanding of the research), prefield (design of the research question and research logic), field (contact analysis, if so decided), and reporting (description of the case) (Rashid et al. 2019). Other authors claim that the case study is useful in the process of gaining contextual and concrete knowledge on particular subjects and present the case study phases in the following order—selection, theoretical framework, data collection, description, and analysis (McCombes 2019). Considering the categories of the case studies, they can be exploratory, descriptive, or explanatory; in the first category, the studied phenomenon is explored, in the second one, the data describe the phenomenon, and the case can be narrative, while in the last case, they represent a causal analysis providing an explanation of the phenomenon (Zainal 2007). Table 2 includes the case study elements.

At an institutional level, leadership commitment to developing strategies toward the civic university approach generated internal transformations and lessons learned in this complex process.

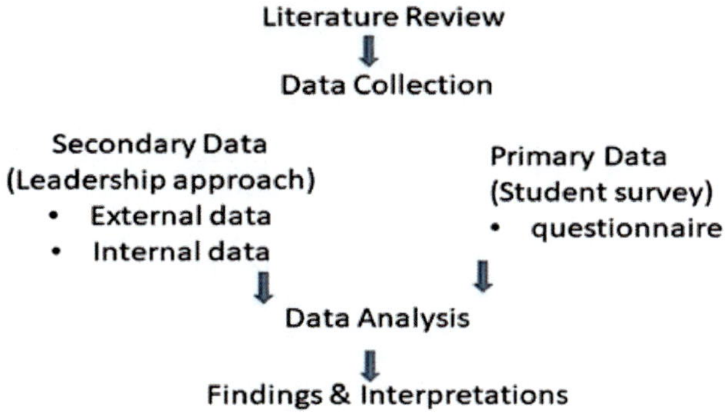

Fig. 2 Research design. *Source* Author's own research

Table 2 Case study phases

Phase	Description
Selection	Case study of the University of Bucharest that promotes civic engagement
Category	Descriptive case study
Research question	How can academic leadership implement civic engagement actions/strategies?
Research sub-questions	1. What are the sources/motives that generate academic leadership support for civic engagement? 2. What are the main civic initiatives at an institutional level? 3. What are the best practices that were generated from the institutional initiatives?
Sources	Official records (reports, statements, website)

Source Author's own research (adapted from the university website)

3.2 Students' Perceptions of Civic Engagement

A questionnaire was sent to all students in the first year of their undergraduate studies at the Faculty of Business and Administration (University of Bucharest) during December 2020 to April 2021, and it was designed as a Google forms document. The reason for which only the first year of study was chosen was the premise that civic engagement takes time and some of the community-based actions require more than one year of student engagement. Table 3 reflects the respondents' distribution among the study programs and subjects where they were invited to act as part of their evaluation.

Therefore, no specific sampling was needed, as all students at the Faculty of Business and Administration in the first year were chosen as respondents. The author decided to send the questionnaire to this faculty as it was a significant academic unit of the university, with a high number of students and an active student union which implemented several projects on a voluntary basis for their student community benefit. In other words, these students were already aware of the engagement issues.

Table 3 Distribution of respondents

Study program	Subject	Number of students/respondents
Public administration	Macroeconomics	195/72
Business administration	Marketing	225/98
Marketing	Marketing	122/67
Total number of students/respondents		542/237

Source Author's own research

Therefore, the respondents' rate was almost 44% of the total number of students studying at the abovementioned programs. This rate was obtained after several invitations were addressed to the students attending their Macroeconomics and Marketing class. These subjects were chosen as the most pertinent disciplines where the professor could explain the purpose of the research. In fact, Macroeconomics deals with the economic or domestic territory among other issues, such as flow, factor income, stock, while Marketing also applies to non-profit organizations and is linked to a societal activity (Sastry CBSE 2019, Kotler and Levy 1969). One month after the questionnaire was launched, the response rate was less than 10% and therefore, the decision was to keep the answering possibility still open until April, by which point the response rate will have increased to 44%. This result is based on convenience sampling, which is often used when respondents are students (Peterson and Merunka 2014). This is a non-probability sampling based on the judgement that students in the first year of studies are more available that others to get involved in civic actions; students were simply asked to fill in the survey; moreover, the sources of data are convenient and the researcher did not select the sample of respondents like in the purposive sampling (Lavrakas 2008). Calculating the confidence interval based on the mean and the standard deviation, the 237 samples, is relevant for a 95% confidence level and a significance level of 0.05; the margin of error is 0.0992. As for the response rate, it is considered that a rate of 10%-15% for external surveys and a rate of 30%-40% for internal surveys would be a proper target; therefore, 44% is reasonable in the case of online data collection (Pandya 2019, Nulty 2008). The confidence interval describes the degree of confidence in the estimation of the population (Allen 2017).

The questionnaire consisted of 20 questions: 4 open, 4 closed (multiple-choice), and 8 questions based on a Likert construction of 5 levels of agreement (5 was the highest level of agreement), apart from group characteristics questions.

In addition to the student perception, the study correlates the civic engagement level with the academic score and the extracurricular experience students achieved. Two hypotheses and their alternate hypotheses were formulated:

H1 0. There is no association between civic engagement level and the academic score of students ($p = 0$).

H1 a. A correlation could exist between civic engagement level and the academic score of students.

H2 0. There is no association between civic engagement level and extracurricular experience ($p = 0$).

H2 a. A correlation could exist between civic engagement level and extracurricular experience.

Pearson correlation will be used to obtain the correlation of the abovementioned variables (Social Science Statistics 2021). All the variables were considered as high, moderate, or low, with the civic engagement level being the independent variable, while the academic score and the extracurricular experience-dependent variables.

Correlation is a way of measuring the association between variables, and Pearson correlation is used for jointly normally distributed data (Schober 2018).

4 Analysis/Results Interpretation

The analysis conducted at the institutional level contributed to the identification of effective measures taken in the process of civic engagement enhancing. The results demonstrate the compliance of the UB leadership approaches with the civic university concept and characteristics and will correlate the students' perceptions to the academic leadership decisions that lead to institutional practices.

4.1 UB Case Study—Leadership Approach

Table 4 includes the most important challenges leadership had to face and support under the international civic context. The documents studied (the University Strategy and the Mission of the CIVIS Alliance) reveal that a leadership commitment at an institutional level is enough to generate proper results in terms of concrete actions or

Table 4 Institutional initiatives and best practices at UB

Institutional initiatives	Best practice	Short description
CIVIS—society needs identification	Open Lab Establishment	This is a network of different stakeholders that work together in identifying social needs, which then provides solutions to them
CIVIS—call for projects	Methodology of evaluation, projects approved, seed money allocated	14 applications in the first call, to address 3 challenges—Sustainability and urban resilience, Education and culture, Research and digital transformation
CIVIS—microprograms	Common offer for students of short courses	Two directions of certification after completion of several courses—Civic Engagement + Global Awareness
Current Strategic Plan	University Foundation establishment	A program was launched to support exceptional pupils from disadvantaged regions (called SEED educational support for disadvantaged pupils of high potential)

Source Author's own research (adapted from the university website)

initiatives (CIVIS Mission Statement 2021; Development Strategy of the University of Bucharest 2021).

The abovementioned initiatives reflect the leadership commitment to creating a civic university. The newly established Open Lab is a network of stakeholders that take part in different small projects dedicated to responses to the local needs; most important is the engagement of students in the implementation of all projects. At UB, in the first call for projects, three were selected and a new call was already set up and announced (Call for Open Lab projects 2020, 2021). Moreover, at an international level, short courses started to be delivered as a joint offer for students to get additional credits (microcredentials) under the Civic Engagement or Global Awareness certification (Call for students to enroll in microprograms 2021). Concrete answers to the research questions and main lessons learned are revealed in Fig. 3; therefore, UB has proved to be very open to transforming the university development toward becoming a civic university, due to the following features: local community is integrated into the Open Lab projects; projects have a local impact; positive change is generated at least for the beneficiaries of the projects.

As a civic university, UB is committed to increasing the students' level of engagement in voluntary activities, besides professors and more experienced students. Their perception of civic engagement is very important for the institutional development strategy, in general, and for the future projects of local impact, in particular.

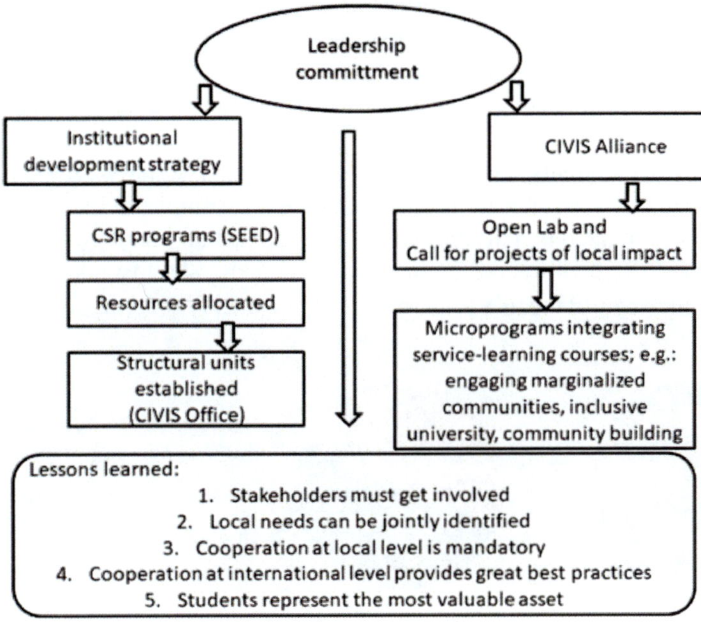

Fig. 3 Findings and Lessons Learned from the UB Experience. *Source* Author's own research

4.2 Students' Perceptions on Civic Engagement—Questionnaire Results

Students at the UB are involved in different civic actions: they are part of voluntary engagement in Open Lab projects, they take part in courses including service-learning, and they become mentors to young pupils selected in the supporting project. Therefore, the need to have open-minded students who are willing to offer volunteer in different extracurricular activities such as Open Lab projects, microprograms, and SEED program, generated a survey among students in the first year of studies to find out their level of interest in such programs and projects. The main answers generated the following findings:

- Among other questions, students were asked to declare in one word what civic engagement means to them and most answers consisted in the following words: people, unity, responsibility, community, passion, kindness, empathy, communications, solidarity, team, society, dedication, model citizen, and doing good;
- A better community means that people help each other, people care about the environment, a different governance, more respect, more openness to innovation, no place for selfishness, thinking of others first, better civilization, rules followed by everybody, safety, happier people, honest community, and no conflict;
- 92.3% of the respondents consider that any student can become an active player in voluntary action with social impact (see Fig. 4a);
- 43.8% of the respondents consider that a voluntary activity has to generate societal impact (see Fig. 4b) as they had already experienced voluntary and extracurricular projects;
- 40.3% of the students consider that some voluntary activity can be of no impact to society. Later, in another question related to examples where they would like to become engaged in activities with a high impact on society or low impact, they mentioned the level of the community where the activity takes place—a large community would mean a high impact, while a small one, a low impact;

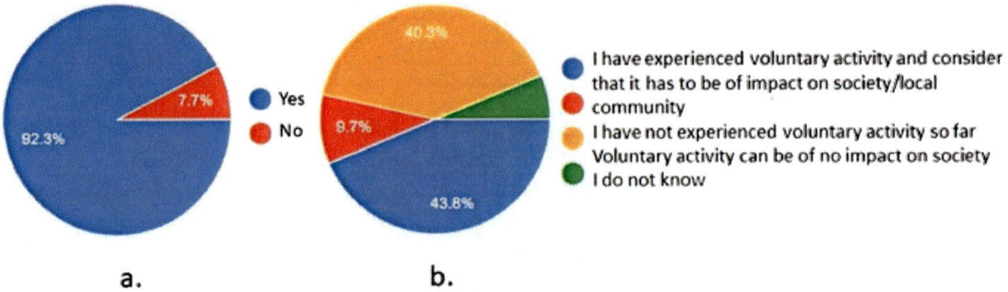

Fig. 4 Students' perception on becoming an active player (**a**) and their experience in voluntary activity (**b**). *Source* Authors' own research

Table 5 Students' perception on civic engagement

Crt. No	Question/sentence	Likert score
1	Civic engagement is about helping others	3.78
2	Civic engagement always generates social change in the community	2.81
3	Social change audience can be smaller than the place of living (city)	2.03
4	Civic engagement is always generating a positive change	3.49
5	Civic engagement is always of group activity	3.31
6	Civic engagement is based on voluntary activity	4.13
7	Individual engagement is also generating social impact	2.79
8	Civic engagement can increase the whole community participation	3.02

Source Author's own research

- Based on a Likert scale, the findings revealed that (see Table 5) students have in general a good understanding of what civic engagement means and implies, but they do not believe too much in its effectiveness in the community (sentences 2 + 7) or in the individual capacity of generating impact; they were somehow hesitating in answering regarding the level of the community and the characteristic of positive change;
- In addition to all these, an open question referring to the importance of cooperation between academic and student communities in civic engagement activities, most of the students (78.48%) mentioned the need of working together and of having institutional support from the top management;
- 64.8% of the respondents would like to get involved in a voluntary activity such as Open Lab or Foundation programs;
- 50.7% of the respondents have not been involved in voluntary activities yet, but would like to if they clearly understood their role.

In addition to these, to observe the correlation between the civic engagement level and the academic score, on the one hand, and extracurricular experience, on the other hand, the Pearson correlation was calculated and the results are reflected in Fig. 5.

Therefore, there is a positive correlation between the civic engagement level and the academic score, but the relationship between variables is weak (the value is close to zero); moreover, there is a moderate positive correlation between civic engagement level and extracurricular experience, which means there the two variables go up at the same time (or down).

In the first correlation, there is strong evidence for the null hypothesis, which means that the alternative hypothesis is rejected. In the second correlation, as p is s than 0.05, there is strong evidence against the null hypothesis, being less than 5% probability, the null is correct. In conclusion, the null hypothesis is rejected, and statistically, the alternative hypothesis is accepted. Therefore, the results show that there is no association between the civic engagement level and the academic score of students, but a correlation exists between the civic engagement level and extracurricular experience of students.

X and Y Combined
$N = 237$
$\Sigma(X - M_x)(Y - M_y) = 12.278$

R Calculation
$r = \Sigma((X - M_y)(Y - M_x)) / \sqrt{((SS_x)(SS_y))}$

$r = 12.278 / \sqrt{((109.629)(143.291))} = 0.098$

Meta Numerics (cross-check)
$r = 0.098$

The value of R is 0.098.

The P-Value is .132494.
The result is not significant at p < .05.

a).

X and Y Combined
$N = 237$
$\Sigma(X - M_x)(Y - M_y) = 86.962$

R Calculation
$r = \Sigma((X - M_y)(Y - M_x)) / \sqrt{((SS_x)(SS_y))}$

$r = 86.962 / \sqrt{((137.932)(143.291))} = 0.6186$

Meta Numerics (cross-check)
$r = 0.6186$

The value of R is 0.6186.

The P-Value is < .00001.
The result is significant at p < .05.

b).

Fig. 5 Pearson coefficient calculation. Correlation between civic engagement and academic scores (**a**) and extracurricular experience (**b**). *Source* Author's own research

The results are compliant with the study on the civic engagement scale that reveals that students' attitudes toward and behaviors of civic engagement can be assessed based on service learning experience (Doolittle and Faul 2013).

5 Conclusions

The paper explains the concept of the civic university under the ERASMUS + initiative when several higher education institutions decided to apply together with international partners for projects aiming to improve education and research in a common strategy based on European common values. The main characteristics of the civic university are described on a literature review basis and prove one general common issue: different stakeholders work together to identify the relevant societal need and then to find solutions to these.

The paper also reveals the interest of European universities in such an initiative, which demonstrates that the civic mission of universities is no longer a declarative feature of these institutions, but an engine to their institutional and regional development. Moreover, Romanian universities have applied to different alliances to change their governance into a European and joint approach. Therefore, based on the increasing number of Romanian universities that entered different European civic alliances, it is clear that these universities had to adapt their civic approach to a common approach at the level of the alliance. Moreover, the study shows that at an institutional level, academic leadership is prepared to take actions in two ways: actions generated from the alliance objectives and activities and actions decided beyond the alliance under a civic engagement framework.

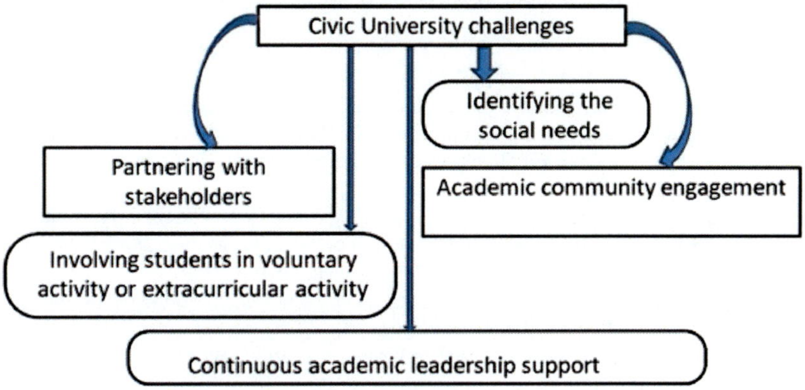

Fig. 6 Civic university challenges. *Source* Authors' own research

Students have demonstrated that they have a general understanding that civic engagement means voluntary participation for the community benefit and that they consider more effective a group rather than an individual activity. Students have a good understanding of what civic engagement and better community mean and see these as voluntary actions.

This leads to the need of developing the civic engagement approach through a new student-institution relationship where students are initiators and contributors along with other members of the academic community. Moreover, students with a high level of civic engagement are not necessarily the high academic scores students, but those with an interest in extracurricular development. Therefore, academic leadership should promote more activities outside or complementary activities to teaching and learning regular activities. These results are very important for the academic leadership to continue the efforts in promoting civic engagement student opportunities. These opportunities are addressed to all students, no matter their academic scores. These opportunities are more likely to be taken by students that are already experienced in extracurricular activities. Figure 6 synthetizes the civic university challenges, which can be also considered as leadership requirements for the civic development of the institution.

The main limitations of the study are respondents were students only at one faculty—Business and Administration—and an institutional pertinent view would be to consider also students from exact sciences and philological ones. In addition to this, an increasing number of respondents would be necessary to understand the willingness and openness of the student community for voluntary activity with social impact.

References

Allen, M.: The sage encyclopedia of communication research methods, vols. 1–4 (2017)

Arnkill, R., Järvensivu, A., Koski, P., Piirainen, T.: Exploring Quadruple Helix Outlining user-oriented innovation models. Final Report on Quadruple Helix Research for the CLIQ project. Work Research Centre (2010)

Bălan, M., Marin, S., Mitan, A., Pînzaru, F., Vătămănescu, E. & Zbuchea, A.: Leaders in focus: generational differences from a personality-centric perspective. Manag. Mark. Chall. Knowl. Soc. **14**(4), 372–385 (2019). https://doi.org/10.2478/mmcks-2019-0026

Bernacki, M., Jaeger, E.: Exploring the impact of service-learning on moral development and moral orientation. MJCSL **14**, 5–15 (2008)

Bowen, G.A.: Exploring civic engagement in higher education: an international context. Asian J. Educ. Res. Synerg **2**(2) (2010)

Civic Engagement: Georgia State University. https://service.gsu.edu/programs/. Accessed 16 Aug 2021

Call for Open Lab projects 2020. https://unibuc.ro/universitatea-din-bucuresti-lanseaza-primul-apel-de-propuneri-civis-open-lab-pentru-cofinantarea-unor-proiecte-de-responsabilitate-sociala/. Accessed 19 Aug 2021

Call for Open Lab projects 2021. https://unibuc.ro/universitatea-din-bucuresti-lanseaza-un-nou-apel-de-propuneri-civis-open-lab-pentru-cofinantarea-unor-proiecte-de-responsabilitate-sociala/. Accessed 19 Aug 2021

Call for students to enroll in microprograms 2021. https://unibuc.ro/universitatea-civica-europeana-civis-microprograme-dedicate-studentilor-ub-la-licenta/. Accessed 19 Aug 2021

CIVIS Mission Statement (2021). https://civis.eu/storage/files/mission-statement-en.pdf. Accessed 18 Aug 2021

Community Engagement Office: Central European University, Community Engagement Office (2021). Accessed 16 Aug 2021

Corrente, M., Hilsher, J., King, S., Tejada, M.L.: Effective strategies for supporting student civic engagement. NASPA (2018)

Cress, C.: Civic engagement and student success: leveraging multiple degrees of achievement. Diversity Democr. **15**(3) (2012)

Dee, T.S.: Education and civic engagement. In: Bradley, S., Green, C. (eds.) The Economics of Education (Second Edition). A Comprehensive Overview, pp. 103–108. Academic Press (2020)

Development Strategy of the University of Bucharest (2021). https://unibuc.ro/wp-content/uploads/2020/11/Strategia-de-dezvoltare-a-UB.pdf. Accessed 18 Aug 2021

Doolittle, A., Faul, A.C.: Civic engagement scale: a validation study. Sage Open 1–7 (2013)

Erasmus+: Erasmus+ shapes active citizens for an active Europe (2017). https://ec.europa.eu/programmes/erasmus-plus/news/erasmus-shapes-active-citizens-active-europe_en. Accessed 16 Aug 2021

Erasmus+: European Universities Initiative (2019 and 2020). https://ec.europa.eu/education/education-in-the-eu/european-education-area/european-universities-initiative_en. Accessed 16 Aug 2021

European Commission: Press Release. 24 new European Universities reinforce the European Education Area (2021). https://ec.europa.eu/commission/presscorner/detail/en/ip_20_1264. Accessed 16 Aug 2021

Foerster-Pastor, U., Foerster-Metz, U., Golowko, N., Hell, C., Marquardt, K.: Creating talent pools through coopetition: a case study on vocational training programs in Romania. Manag. Market. Chall. Knowl. Soc. **14**(2), 203–219 (2019). https://doi.org/10.2478/mmcks-2019-0014

Goddard, J., Vallance, P.: The civic university and the leadership of place (2012). https://www.researchgate.net/publication/266471508_The_civic_university_and_the_leadership_of_place. Accessed 16 Aug 2021

Goddard, J.: What do we mean by the "civic university"? Why is it important? What do we mean by the "civic university"? Presentation on the occasion of the EESC workshop on Universities for Europe (2014). https://www.slideshare.net/EESCsocsection/1-john-goddardcivicuniversities. Accessed 16 Aug 2021

Goddard, J., Hazelkorn, E., Kempton, L., Vallance, P.: Why the Civic University? (2016). https://www.researchgate.net/publication/311086324_Why_the_Civic_University. Accessed 16 Aug 2021

Goddard, J., Hazelkorn, E., Kempton, L., Vallance, P.: The Civic University. The Policy and the Leadership Challenges. Elgar online (2016)

Gwilliam, J. (Chair): Learning & Teaching Paper #14 Environmental sustainability of learning and teaching Thematic Peer Group Report. Publication licensed under the Creative Commons Attribution-NonCommercial CC BY-NC (2021). https://eua.eu/downloads/publications/eua%20tpg%20report_environmental%20sustainability%20of%20learning%20and%20teaching.pdf. Accessed 16 Aug 2021

Johnson, M., Woodard, J.: The role of civic engagement in undergraduate leadership courses. JOLE **13**(1) (2014)

Jones, K.S.: Giving and volunteering as distinct forms of civic engagement: the role of community integration and personal resources in formal helping. Nonprofit Volunt. Sect. q. **35**(2), 249–266 (2006)

Kotler, P., Levy, S.: Broadening the concept of marketing. J. Mark. **33**(1), 10–15 (1969)

Lavrakas, P.J.: Encyclopedia of survey research methods, vols. 1–0 (2008)

McCombes, S.: How to do a case study (2019). https://www.scribbr.com/methodology/case-study/. Accessed 18 Aug 2021

Nulty, D.D.: The adequacy of response rates to online and paper surveys: what can be done? Assess. Eval. Higher Educ. **33**(3) 301–314 (2008)

Office for Student Engagement: Stanford University, https://ose.stanford.edu/. Accessed 16 Aug 2021

Onea, I.A.: Innovation indicators and the innovation process-evidence from the European innovation scoreboard. Manag. Market. Chall. Knowl. Soc. **15**(4), 605–620 (2020). https://doi.org/10.2478/mmcks-2020-0035

Pandya, C.: What is an Acceptable Response Rate for Online Surveys? (2019). https://www.appjetty.com/blog/acceptable-response-rate-for-online-surveys/. Accessed 06 Sept 2021

Pattie, C., Seyd, P., Whiteley, P.: Citizenship and civic engagement: attitudes and behaviour in Britain. Polit. Stud. **51**, 443–468 (2003)

Perrin, A.J., Gillis, A.: How college makes citizens: higher education experiences and political engagement. Socius Sociol. Res. Dyn. World **5** (2019)

Peterson, R.A., Merunka, D.R.: Convenience samples of college students and research reproducibility. J. Bus. Res. **67**, 1035–1041 (2014)

QS: What Does it Mean to be a Civic University? https://www.qs.com/what-does-it-mean-to-be-civic-university/. Accessed 16 Aug 2021

Rashid, Y., Rashid, A., Warraich, M.A., Sabir, S.S., Waseem, A.: Case study method: a step-by-step guide for business researchers. Int. J. Qual. Methods (2019). (January)

Reiff, J., Keene, A.: Best practices for promoting student civic engagement: lessons from the citizen scholars program at the University of Massachusetts Amherst. J. High. Educ. Outreach Engagem. **16**(4), 105 (2012)

Sastry, CBSE: Introduction to Macroeconomics and its Concepts–CBSE Notes for Class 12 Macro Economics (2019). Accessed from https://www.learncbse.in/introduction-macroeconomics-concepts-cbse-notes-class-12-macro-economics/

Schober, P.M.D., Boer, C., Schwarte, L.A.: Correlation coefficients: appropriate use and interpretation. Anesth. Analg. **126**(5), 1763–1768 (2018)

SNSPA website (2021). http://snspa.ro/en/. Accessed 16 Aug 2021

Social Science Statistics (2021). https://www.socscistatistics.com/. Accessed 19 Aug 2021

UNICA & The City (2021). https://www.unica-network.eu/activity/working-groups/unica-the-city/. Accessed 16 Aug 2021

UNICA Activity Report (2021) https://www.unica-network.eu/publications/activity-report-2016-2019-2/. Accessed 16 Aug 2021

UAIC website (2021). https://www.uaic.ro/en/communique-on-the-submission-of-a-proposal-for-pilot-alliance-of-european-universities-by-the-ec2u-consortium/. Accessed 16 Aug 2021

UTCB website (2021). https://utcb.ro/en/eu-conexus/. Accessed 16 Aug 2021

UTCLUJ website (2021). https://www.utcluj.ro/media/documents/2019/EUT.pdf. Accessed 16 Aug 2021

UVT website (2021). http://www.univ-unita.eu/. Accessed 16 Aug 2021

Zainal, Z.: Case study as a research method. Kemanus. J. bil. 9 (2007)

The Impact of Data Science, Big Data, Forecasting, and Predictive Analytics on the Efficiency of Business System

Băcescu-Cărbunaru Angelica and Popovici Mariluzia

Abstract Facing the actual context and nowadays' challenges related to the new actions generated by pandemic factors, we will center the paper on the following areas: Data Science, Big Data, Big Data analytics, which are impacted by forecasting and predictive analytics thus generating improved results for organizations and business units. We will focus on practical implementations in banking and other technical-economical industries. The actual challenges, related to global problems, enforce companies to reshape their business model to current events. Only companies managing businesses optimally adjusted will resist. Organizations should synergistically correlate all their business components, internal units, and processes with the environment. The paper will present the latest methods and technologies used in Big Data analytics for an organization's efficiency and productivity increase. We will focus on the forecasting part, by making a correspondence with predictive analytics. Through forecasting, estimating future values of indicators, managerial Key Performance Indicators, based on specified forecasting algorithms, will show the value of this field, in parallel with predictive analytics for business strategies. Between these two areas, there are interdependencies, each of them having different approaches, providing methods and techniques for the goal of increasing outputs, measured by indicators, usually revealed in views, reports, dashboards, and other system outputs and layers. Pointing on these sections of predictions will reveal the impact of these fields on decision improvement and return enhancement for organizations. The current pandemic circumstances, correlated with afferent effects: teleworking / working from home, improved communications, increased medical actions and treatments etc., reveal the information and predictive' actions values for mankind future evolution.

Keywords Data science · Big data · Statistics · Economic intelligence · Forecasting · Support vector machine

B.-C. Angelica (✉)
Bucharest University of Economic Studies, Academy of Romanian Scientists, Bucharest, Romania
e-mail: mihaela.carbunaru@csie.ase.ro

P. Mariluzia
Vodafone Technologies, Bucharest, Romania

A. M. Dima and M. Kelemen (eds.), *Digitalization and Big Data for Resilience and Economic Intelligence*, Springer Proceedings in Business and Economics, https://doi.org/10.1007/978-3-030-93286-2_6

1 Introduction

In this paper we will present new domains: data-technologies—Data Science, Big Data, forecasting, predictive analytics, but also new concepts like: Continuous Intelligence, SMART Data, SMART Analytics, etc., and their impact on businesses efficiency.

The aim is to show how the novelty and actuality of informatics systems (targeting financial-banking systems) storing and processing data with Big Data platforms, using forecasting methods, particularly Machine Learning algorithms, from the predictive-analytics sub-domain, can increase efficiency in the financial-banking industry, achieving future benefit-growth.

One of the recent areas of knowledge is *Data Science*—exploring different concepts associated with data—methods, techniques, algorithms, processes, and systems, in order to extract information and mainly knowledge and insights from different data types, structured and unstructured data, in order to apply results and findings in a large number of industries and areas from real life, so as to increase benefits. As an interdisciplinary field, this domain is related to data analysis, modeling, informatics, statistics, machine learning—interconnecting theories and knowledge from many areas—like mathematics, information technology, predictive analysis, etc. The most actual concepts and technologies used to work with data are as follows: Databases, Economic Intelligence, Data Warehouse, Data Mining, Big Data, predictive analytics, forecasting, etc. Some of the concepts we will discuss and detail in the next paragraphs are Big Data and its techniques; predictive analytics, forecasting, but also M.L. and Artificial Intelligence (we will also mention and frame modern concepts like SMART Data, SMART Analytics, Continuous Intelligence, Strategic decisions, etc.). Referring to other technologies interconnected with Data Science—like Data Bases, Economic Intelligence, most recently studied: Continuous Intelligence, data processing, data analytics—we will mention the *Big Data* area, which deals with data collection mechanisms—analyzing, extracting information from datasets with high volumes or increased complexity, so huge that they cannot be operated with traditional methods and techniques through classic software platforms for data processing. So, the concept of Big Data points out the large data volumes, which hamper classical applications to achieve efficient time and cost results, by significant sizes. Some of the most important Big Data companies in 2021 are Google, VMware, Splunk, Amazon, Oracle, IBM, HP Enterprise, Teradata, Mu Sigma, SAP, EMC, etc. (Analytics Insight 2021). The most important advantages of Big Data are *Analytics* and *predictive analysis*. "Predictive analysis should be based on taking into account in the analytical methodology possible the most *modern prognostic models* and a large amount of data necessary to perform the most accurate predictive analysis. In this way, the result of the prediction analysis performed will be the least subject to the risk of analytical error, i.e., an incorrectly designed forecast" (Gwoździewicz et al. 2020).

Big Data analytics tools can predict outgrowth accurately; in this way, driving businesses and organizations to optimal decisions and strategies, while optimizing their processes and operations in an efficient manner, while also reducing risks. *Big Data Analytics* is the process of huge dataset investigations, structured or unstructured data, of various types, collected in different ways, aligned per variated models, the main objective being detecting hidden *patterns*, correlations—predicting customers behavior and preferences, trends in market movements. All of these elements are helpful aspects for decisional processes and organizational strategies. (Improving customers' experience, developing new products, enhancing innovation area, avoiding risks by identifying fraudulent activities, etc.) There are many actual platforms developed for the Big Data Analytics area. Several of them—strongly outlined on the market—are Storm, Cloudera, Apache Hadoop, Grid grain, Space Curve, SAS, Microsoft Azure, etc. "It is a further progression of Business Intelligence (BI) and data mining combined with statistical techniques. Business Intelligence processes help analysis of internal and external data to enable business executives to make intelligent decisions" (Jeble et al. 2016). Economic Intelligence is closely linked to BI.

The process of making predictions, anticipating future trends, based on historical and present data, usually by analyzing actual tendencies, is represented by ***forecasting.*** Bajari et al. have recently shown that "Clearly, data is used in many aspects of company decision-making, and our focus is on the application to demand forecasting. We believe that this is a particularly good area to study, as the success of forecasting models is relatively straightforward to assess" (Bajari et al. 2019).

Data analytics represents an area of raw data analysis, extracting information, knowledge, and conclusions from these data. Generally, associated techniques and processes are automated; revealing trends and metrics resulting from data investigated. Outputs and conclusions are used in processes optimization, efficiency enhancement for systems, or organizations. Strongly related to forecasting, there is the predictive analytics area, nowadays growing conjunctively with ITC and Data Science fields. ***Predictive analytics*** represents operations over data, using mathematical-statistical algorithms, lately machine learning techniques, in order to identify the expectations/probability for future outputs, taking into consideration influencing factors. Research on this area is based on historical events and data, providing the best estimation of what will happen in the future. "This analytics is concerned with forecasting and statistical modelling to determine the future possibilities based on supervised, unsupervised, and semi-supervised learning model" (Sivarajah et al. 2017).

We will focus our research on the forecasting area, taking into consideration techniques of forecasting. One of the forecasting areas, with the parallel growing domain, *Machine Learning*, is widely used together with Mathematics and computing, Probability and Statistics, and other connected domains.

2 Literature Review

The aim of this study is to present the area of modern data-technologies: Data Science, pointing to Big Data platforms newly utilized in companies, with forecasting algorithms, from the Machine Learning field (and other new technologies like digitalization, distant-communication, etc.). Many authors have addressed issues related to new data technologies, from different points of view, depending on the specificities of the activity.

In this regard, we will mention some of the most recent research papers. Jeble et al. (2016) published a study exploring the use of Big Data and predictive analytics, and Gwoździewicz et al. (2020) developed a study on the use of Data processing tools in a period of fast digitalization. Also, Bajari et al. (2015) studied and published an article on the evolution of Big Data in the modern economy and Big data impact on firm performance, and Sivarajah et al. (2017) elaborated a study that deals with critical analysis based on Big Data and analytical methods. Mikalef et al. (2019) examined also the relations between Big data and firm performance and the possibilities to meet future challenges. Bajari et al. (2015) studied how to use Machine Learning methods for demand estimation. Carbo-Valverde et al. (2020) published an extensive paper on the ML approach to the digitalization process inside the bank system, and Ampountolas et al. (2021) deal with the study of the ML approach for micro-credit scoring and have published a paper on this topic. He et al. (2014) wrote and presented a material at an international conference paper about the importance of the loss of customers' prediction of commercial banks, based on the Support Vector Machine model. Sabbeh (2018) was concerned with how the ML techniques are used for customer retention and publishes an article with a focus on SVM techniques, and Aydiner et al. (2019) conducted a study on what role plays business process performance in the relationship between the adoption of business analytics and firm performance.

The data used in the analysis within the article are taken from the statistical yearbook 2018 and other works of the National Institute of Statistics, the Romanian Association of Banks (ARB), and the official site of the National Bank of Romania. The final aim is to show how the novelty and actuality of ITC systems (we will focus on informatics financial-banking systems) and Big Data platforms can increase efficiency in the financial-banking industry, realizing future benefit-growth—we will also use forecasting methods and algorithms for this. This endeavor is realized in order to identify the impact of these new modern technologies on decisions and strategies influencing the efficiency of business systems. Using Machine Learning algorithm (in particular, SVM) we will point out the increased efficiency in business units after using modern data technologies (financial-banking units being one of the impacted areas).

Tudorel Andrei, the president of INS, recalled that "Big Data information is essential for the modernization of statistics in the globalized world." (CECAR Business Magazine 2021). Bajari et al. claim that there has been a high level of interest in modeling consumer behavior in the fields of computer science and statistics (Bajari et al. 2015). In a 2018 comparative study, Sabbeh says that customer retention has been increasingly investigated in many business domains including banking. In May 2019, Mikalef et al., who published in the Journal of Business Research, showed that big data analytics, when applied to problems of specific domains such as healthcare, service provision, supply chain management, and marketing, can offer substantial value.

3 Research Questions/Aims of the Research

3.1 Data

The current research uses annual time series data for the period 2018–2020 gathered from several sources, namely the Romanian Statistical Yearbook (2018), the Romanian Association of Banks (ARB)/the Romanian banking system (2021); Financial Magazine, 2021, the National Bank of Romania (2021) official sites, etc. Apart from the technological development (in particular digitalization using Big Data and other Data platforms), business sector development growth is also included in the model as a control variable.

3.2 Technological Development Impacted the Financial-Banking Sector

Several figures of the Romanian *banking systems* show that this sector holds *76.1%* of the assets of the Romanian financial system (Q1 2020). Credit institutions have invested substantial amounts in the development of *modern technologies and digital solutions* during the last years. In the COVID-19 pandemic context, the number of various banking operations realized remotely increased, the digitalization of this industry was promoted, so it improved and grew. The value and number of payment transactions with cards issued by resident payment service providers increased by almost 10% since the beginning of the COVID-19 pandemic, thus accelerating the digitization process in the banking system. With this process of digitization increase (using modern storage and operating systems) and optimization of operational expenses, in 2019, the network of banking units registered a *reduction of 6.4%*, up to 4,*758* banking branches, while the number of employees reached *53,106*. For the financial-banking sector, using modern systems, the above figures mean cost reductions so, *efficiency increase*." Understanding the digital jump of bank customers is key to design strategies to bring on board and keep online users, as well as to explain the increasing competition from new providers of financial services" (Carbo-Valverde et al. 2020).

Fig. 1 Access of householders to data-technologies and communication, 2014 and 2019. *Source* https://www.bancherul.ro/stire.php?id_stire=20262&titlu=[big-data-technologies-can-lead-to-anti-competitive-behaviors-warns-the-competition-council]

From a global perspective, the Romanian data market, including Big Data technologies, recorded an increase in the period 2013–2019, the average annual compound growth rate (CAGR) being 26.4%, well above the European average (CAGR 7.4%) (on data market, digital data is marketed as products or services). The above figures indicate an orientation of the economy toward the use of *Big Data technologies*, the introduction of *artificial intelligence,* and a continuous process of digital transformation. Thus, the number of data providers has increased significantly, from approximately 2,400 in 2013 to 5,750 in 2019 (Bancherul Homepage 2020).

Referring to technologies used by customers, especially those related to data and communication, according to the information from the official site of the European Union [https://ec.europa.eu/], and by comparing data from 2014 and 2019, we can see in the following figure (Fig. 1), for Romania, in 2014, that the percentage of ITC technologies utilization by householders was 61%; in 2019, the percentage was 84%, which appears as an average value comparing with the other countries studied.

According to the data provided by the Institute National of Statistics, in the second figure below (Fig. 2), we can see that for the period 2014–2019, the subjects using data technologies and communication for banking operations increased from 17.2% in 2014 to 29.4% in 2019. A significant increase: 5.1%, in 2017, compared to this previous year (only 18% from the total of users).

These figures indicate growth in using data and communication technologies and also banking services for transactions (based on new ITC technologies implementations on a business level in this case, the banking field).

Also, the figure below (Fig. 2), another source for our data input, shows the transactions in Romania, 2014–2019 (this means ITC technologies utilization increased last years due to the implementation of new communication and data technologies in business and organizations) (EUROSTAT Homepage 2021).

Based on the above data collected from different sources and processed, it was realized a first set of data sources for the application of the research methods and associated algorithm.

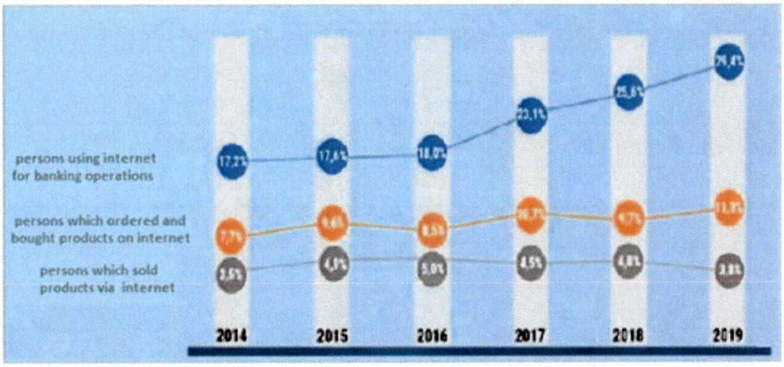

Fig. 2 Internet services utilization—online transactions, 2014–2019. *Source:* https://www.facebook.com/INSTATISTICA/videos/2927143920718411/

3.3 Applying Modern Forecasting with Machine Learning Algorithm—SVM

The research aims to apply Machine Learning forecasting algorithm (in particular—Support Vector Machine) in order to identify the impact of new data-technologies implemented (Big Data and digitalization) on online operations, increased transaction volumes in the banking sector, leading to business efficiency in units within the financial-banking area (this endeavor focuses on the identification of increased growth in efficiency for the next period for those units using new data-technologies (above-mentioned). "Increasing financial consumption demand of customers further intensifies the competition among commercial banks. To increase their profits for continuing operations and enhance the core competitiveness, commercial banks must avoid the loss of customers while acquiring new customers. We study commercial bank customer churn prediction based on the SVM model and use a random sampling method to improve the SVM model, considering the imbalanced characteristics of customer data sets. The results show that this method can effectively enhance the prediction accuracy of the selected model" (He et al. 2014). Using the Support Vector Machine algorithm, the purpose is to find the hidden impact of increased ITC technologies (Data based in particular), on predicted increased efficiency and better decisions and strategies on organization's management.

4 Research Methods

One of the data sets used in the study is described in the table below (Table 1). Data refers to financial-banking indicators from Romania, Dec. 2019–Dec. 2020.

The paragraphs below present the model specification and methodology applied in order to obtain the estimated results and prove efficiency increase.

Table 1 Aggregate indicators for credit institutions (Banks, branches of foreign banks, Credit coop)[a]

	Dec. 2019	Mar. 2020	Jun. 2020	Sep. 2020	Dec. 2020
Number of credit institution	34	34	33	34	34
of which foreign banks	7	7	7	8	8
Total net assets *(billion lei)*	495.2	518.4	518.5	533.1	560.2
ROA[b] *(%)*	1.34	1.27	1.08	1.17	0.98
ROE[c] *(%)*	12.21	11.70	9.81	10.48	8.86
Rate of return for base activity *(%)*	184.09	168.08	180.02	185.58	185.51

Source Adapted from BNR
[a]The indicators include only banks and Credit coop
[b]Return on assets (Annualized net profit/Total average assets)
[c]Return on equity (Annualized net profit/Average own capital)

4.1 Methodology and Specification of the Model

The current study, by applying Machine Learning algorithm: Support Vector Machine, in particular, will assess the impact of ITC development (particularly data technologies, Big Data, and digitalization) on financial-banking sector efficiency increase. Referring to the Support Vector Machine algorithm, the model applied is presented below. This is a supervised learning algorithm, generally used for classification tasks, but it is also suitable for regression tasks. SVM separates classes/clusters by drawing a decision boundary (therefore, to find the maximum margin hyper-planes it offers the best solution for generalization). For the present case, linearly separable, SVM aims to find a function, a hyper plane, which maximizes the margin between two opposite classes, and therefore, it optimally separates the data into two categories. An SVM classifier tries to maximize the next function (Lp), with respect to the vectors $\overrightarrow{w}$ and constant b, to ensure that it is the function with the maximum margin that will separate the two classes,

$$L_P = 1/2\|\vec{w}\|^2 - \sum_{i=1}^{t} \alpha_i y_i (\vec{w}\vec{x}_i + b) + \sum_{i=1}^{t} \alpha_i, \tag{1}$$

where t is the number of training examples;

- αi, (i = 1, …, t), are non-negative numbers such that the derivatives of Lp with respect to αi are zero and αi are the Lagrange multipliers;
- $\vec{w} = \sum_{i=1}^{t} \alpha_i y_i x_i$,
- Lp is called the Lagrangian.

"In this equation, the vectors w and constant b define the hyper plane (Popovici and Bacescu 2021)."

A graphical view of the meaning of the SVM algorithm applied is shown below (see Fig. 3).

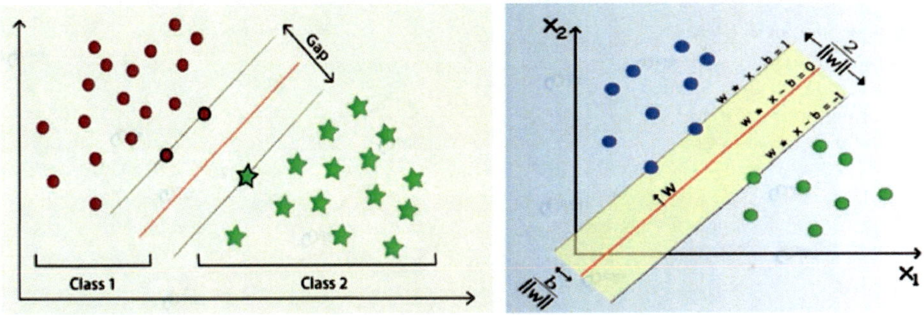

Fig. 3 SVM algorithm and limits graphical view. *Source* Top 10 algorithms in data mining—https://www.researchgate.net/publication/

Finally, the main goal is to classify units based on the IT data technologies applied (for financial-banking sector units) and to identify outputs resulting in efficiency growth, due to classification realized. Below, the SVM applied algorithm will identify these classes per labels applied ('Significant Efficiency Increase'—0, 'Not Significant Efficiency Increase'—1). Based on this information we will formulate conclusions at the end of this study.

4.2 *Applied Algorithm and Results*

Regarding the methods used, we will investigate classification for efficiency by SVM algorithm using Python programming language structures. In testing and Python coding writing, we use *Scikit-learn (Sklearn)*–one of the most useful libraries for machine learning from Python. The code below shows some of the pre-processing data as well as the matching data, results for the SVM classifier.

```
import matplotlib.pyplot as plt
import numpy as nm
import pandas as pd
data_set=pd.read_csv('test_data.csv')
x=data_set.iloc[:,[2,3]].values
y=data_set.iloc[:, 4].values
from sklearn.model_selection import train_test_data
x_train, x_test, y_train, y_test - train_test_data (x,y, test_size=0.25, random_state=0)
from sklearn.processing import StandardScaler
st_x=StandardScaler()
x_train=st_x.fit_transform(x_train)
x_test=st_x.transform(x_test)
from sklearn.svm import SVC # "Support vector classifier"
classifier = SVC (kernel='linear', random_state=0)
classifier.fit(x_train, y_train)
```

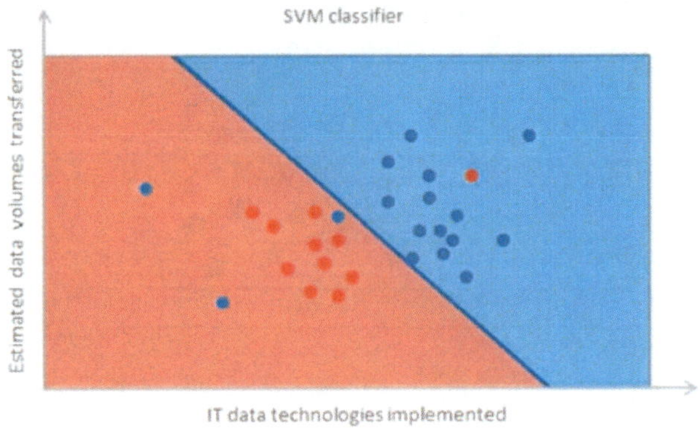

Fig. 4 Output of SVM classifier, dividing units into two regions. *Source* Studied information from https://www.analyticssteps.com

In order to predict output for tested data, we will use the vector: Using the previous

```
output_pred = classifier.predict (x_test)
```

code, we will get the output from the image below (Fig. 4), which will classify business units based on the IT Data technologies applied identifying efficiency growth, due to the classification realized. Classes could be ('Significant Efficiency Increase', 'Not Significant Efficiency Increase').

As we will see in the output image below, the SVM classifier divides the units into two regions with *increased efficiency* and slight *increase efficiency.* Units with *increased efficiency* are in the red area, with red scatter points and those with *slight increase efficiency* are in the blue area with blue points. As expected from our research, we estimated increased efficiency for business units applying modern data techniques (Big Data in particular).

The hyper-plane divided the above-mentioned classes into significant and not-significant efficiency increase variables, which is in line with our estimation.

5 Analysis/Results Interpretation

This paper evaluated the usefulness of machine learning models in assessing defaulting in a financial-banking businesses environment.

We measured increases provided by data-associated informatics systems (Big Data and Smart data platforms) for financial-banking units—referring to volumes of customer transactions, online transactions, digitalization, data platforms, etc. The present study is based on data for the period 2019–2020. The study provides the technique and analysis for the construction of a technological development index in order to trace its impact of data technologies over financial-banking sector growth.

The analysis is based on the Machine Learning model—Support Vector Machine—supervised learning algorithm.

Access to real data is usually not easy. Most articles currently use online datasets, already prepared in a certain format for the model to work well with most machine learning algorithms. In this paper, we confirmed that machine learning algorithms could implicitly predict a real data set in the financial-banking field. The available literature on the identification of outputs resulting in increasing the efficiency of the financial-banking sector did not pay special attention to the impact of ITC development by applying the ML algorithm and in particular SVM, which we did. These elements make this work have its own identity. Based on the findings of this paper, future studies will focus on how to achieve increases in the efficiency of the financial-banking system by implementing new data-related technologies and mass digitization. Big Data Analysis is the often difficult process of examining Big Data to uncover information—such as hidden patterns, correlations, market trends, and customer preferences—that can help financial-banking entities make informed business decisions. On the other hand, the algorithm used in this paper is static in nature and does not take into account the temporal aspects of increasing efficiency. So, we did not estimate how long the efficiency of the organizations will increase. If we can estimate the average time for its growth, the financial-banking unit can consider what other steps need to be taken in the implementation of new technologies and digitalization. Future studies will take macroeconomic variables, such as inflation and unemployment rates, into account in our models to estimate their impact.

These results are relevant to perceive the real transformations behind the digital evolution of consumers. While previous theories and studies have emphasized the importance of the technological components of service and consumer perceptions to explain the evolution of digitalization, other machine learning models demonstrate the phenomenon that customers become digital primarily for the needs of obtaining banking information and, later, for performing transactional services.

Although the models reported in several studies (Apostoulos et al., Sabeh et al.), have the three most accurate results, and the best performances (random forest, XGBoost, and Adaboost), respectively, these are all classifier sets and tree-based algorithms. We are sure that the performance metrics should not be limited to these tree-based algorithms, and the main argument is that SVM allows not only the best accuracy on the training data but leaves, at the same time, a lot of space for the correct classification of the future data. While such models are commonly used to obtain estimates with reasonable accuracy, these techniques were the prelude to the success of ML-SVM models that have been widely applied in many fields.

Numerous studies on the applicability of machine learning techniques have been implemented in various financial-banking fields due to their ability to recognize trends in data evolution (Carbo-Valverde et al. 2020). Other studies indicated that a combination of machine learning methods could provide high accuracy of estimates (Bajari et al. 2015). Our beliefs are that the model applied in the present study offers an appropriate solution in order to generalize the increase of efficiency for the business units that apply advanced data techniques. In ML applications, vector support machines, SVM, are considered one of the safest and most accurate methods of all study algorithms.

Overall, our study confirms the need to conduct research that covers the entire process of implementing new technologies on Big Data and digitization, rather than focusing on a single dimension. In addition, our research finds that applying machine learning techniques to consumer research provides more accurate results that increase business efficiency.

6 Conclusions

In our study, we intended to emphasize the impact of ITC data technologies (particularly Big Data and digitalization) on the efficiency of the business units (financial-banking businesses in particular).

Findings indicate that ITC data-technologies development (Data platforms like Big Data with specific techniques, digitalization, distant communication, and SMART data analytics), increase the efficiency of the financial-banking system (first of all by cost-reduction and also by implementing and increasing innovation in the IT area, applied on financial-banking products and services—like transactions, loans, etc.). Technological evolution in the IT area—databases, tools, and software applications and analysis and forecasting applications—had a major impact at the micro, but also macroeconomic level—driving the evolution and direction of each unit and organization from the financial-banking area.

Databases and DBMSs, Statistics, forecasting, predictive analytics represent important areas of study and practice of data, helping a lot to make business decisions, based on the information extracted from the stored data. Like any field, these domains are constantly evolving, with new systems, technologies, methods, and techniques developing constantly, systems that help to optimize and streamline business decisions.

The analytical results showed that machine learning algorithms are able to be used to model the efficiency of banking units. Like any other research activity, our study has certain limitations. Therefore, it would be interesting to examine whether emerging economies can face the same process of bank digitization as developed economies. Despite these limitations, we believe that the results of this study are valuable for other researchers and practitioners interested in understanding how digitalization is making its mark in people's lives and implicitly in the work of financial-banking units. Another limitation emerged from the sample selection (credit institution from Romania). Although our effort focused on using real data from profile institutions in Romania, we will base the experimental analysis on a more extensive data set in future works. While some broad qualitative conclusions can be drawn from our results about the importance of different SVM implementation techniques, it is possible that the particular choice of features, etc. may not be universally applicable in other countries and other institutions. Using an extensive data set could not only increase the performance of the model, but could also provide more accurate estimates. Similarly, we could better control the number of estimated values while understanding the limits of machine learning algorithms. The inclusion of temporal issues at the macroeconomic level is another area of interest for future research. The findings of the study suggest that financial-banking units could benefit from new Big Data technologies and the digitization process by providing services that better meet customer needs and respond more quickly. So, the classification of customers using techniques and data similar to SVM models would make it possible to offer some more personalized digital services. The method is not yet commonly used in the financial-banking field. We believe that practitioners will find arguments in favor of their immediate application (flexibility, ease of use, and scalability).

Our study has a modest contribution to the analytical analysis at the level of financial-banking institutions of the role that the SVM algorithm can play, proposing an efficiency estimation model that takes into account the identification of the results that led to its increase. Therefore, it is recommended that authorities in the business sector (particularly in the banking area) should implement innovative ITC and Data technologies in order to increase the business area and also the efficiency of organizations.

Based on the results of this paper, in future studies we will address ways to increase efficiency for units in the financial-banking sector, proposing the application of modern data techniques in identifying patterns on the one hand complex, and on the other hand non-obvious, hidden in a database with millions of data points. At the same time, we will consider the influences of economic shocks caused by extreme phenomena, such as global pandemics (for example COVID-19), on the growth rate of efficiency.

References

Ampountolas, A., Nde, T.N., Date, P., Constantinescu, C.: A machine learning approach for microcredit scoring. Risks **9**(3), 50 (2021). https://doi.org/10.3390/risks9030050. https://www.mdpi.com/2227-9091/9/3/50. Accessed 10 Mar 2021

Aydiner, A.S., Tatoglu, E., Bayraktar, E., Zaim, S., Delen, D.: Business analytics and firm performance: The mediating role of business process performance. J. Bus. Res. **96** 228–237 (2019)

Bajari, P., Nekipelov, D., Ryan, S., P., Yang, M.: Machine learning methods for demand estimation. Am. Econ. Rev. **105**(5), 481–485 (2015). https://doi.org/10.1257/aer.p20151021. Accessed 15 Apr 2021

Bajari, P., Chernozhukov, V., Hortaçsu, A., Suzuki, J.: The impact of big data on firm performance: an empirical investigation. AEA Papers and Proceedings, vol. 109, pp. 1–5 (2019). https://doi.org/10.1257/pandp.20191000. Accessed 10 Mar 2021

Bancherul Homepage (2020). https://www.bancherul.ro/stire.php?id_stire=20262&titlu=[big-data-technologies-can-lead-to-anti-competitive-behaviors-warns-the-competition-council. Accessed 20 Dec 2020

Carbo-Valverde, S., Cuadros-Solas, P., Rodríguez-Fernández, F.: A machine learning approach to the digitalization of bank customers: Evidence from random and causal forests. PLoS ONE **15**(10), e0240362 (2020). https://doi.org/10.1371/journal.pone.0240362. Accessed 17 May 2021

CECAR Business Magazine (2021). https://www.ceccarbusinessmagazine.ro/[president-ins-most-of-data-sources-are-owned-by-profit-oriented-private-companies]-a4883/

Gwoździewicz, S., Prokopowicz, D., Grzegorek, J.: The use of advanced data processing tools in the era of digitization; Chapter 4, pp. 93–128 (2020). https://www.researchgate.net/publication/344467694.Aaccessed 10 Apr 2021

He, B., Shi, Y., Wan, Q., Zhao, X.: Prediction of customer attrition of commercial banks based on SVM model. In: 2nd International Conference on Information Technology and Quantitative Management, ITQM, Procedia Computer Science, vol. 31, pp. 423–430 (2014). https://www.sciencedirect.com/science/article/pii/S1877050914004633. Accessed 12 May 2021

Jeble, S., Kumari, S., Patil, Y.: Role of big data and predictive analytics (2016). https://www.researchgate.net/profile/Yogesh-Patil-30/publication/309809606. Accessed 15 Apr 2021

Mikalef, P., Boura, M., Lekakos, G., Krogstie, J.: Big data analytics and firm performance: findings from a mixed-method approach. J. Bus. Res. **98**, 261–276 (2019)

National Bank of Romania (2021)

ORACLE Homepage (2021). https://www.oracle.com/ro/data-science/machine-learning/what-is-machine-learning/. Accessed 03 Mar 2021

Popovici, M., Bacescu-Carbunaru, A.: Data management and data governance. Correlations with the area of databases and statistics. Romanian Statistical Review–Supplement no. 2, pp. 121–138 (2021)

RG Homepage (2021). https://www.researchgate.net/publication/29467751_Top_10_algorithms_in_data_mining. Accessed 18 Feb 2021

Sabbeh, S.F.: Machine Learning techniques for customer retention–a comparative study, (IJACSA). Int. J. Adv. Comput. Sci. Appl. **9**(2), 273–281 (2018). https://thesai.org/Downloads/Volume9No2/Paper_38-Machine_Learning_Techniques_for_Customer_Retention.pdf

Sivarajah, U., Kamal, M.M., Irani, Z., Weerakkody, V.: Critical analysis of Big Data challenges and analytical methods. J. Bus. Res. **70**, 263–286 (2017). https://www.sciencedirect.com/journal/journal-of-business-research. Accessed 12 Apr 2021

Romanian Association of Banks (ARB)/Romanian banking system (2021). https://www.arb.ro/sistemul-bancar-din-romania. Accessed 03 Mar 2021

The Romanian Statistical Yearbook (2018)

Is Trust a Valid Indicator of Tax Compliance Behaviour? A Study on Taxpayers' Public Perception Using Sentiment Analysis Tools

Coita Ioana-Florina, Cioban Ştefana, and Mare Codruţa

Abstract Compliant behaviour in the field of taxes has a profound impact on the economic and social field. Tackling the tax evasion phenomenon is not an easy thing to do. That is why there are several public institutions that are preoccupied with discovering and punishing it. The discovery of the actions that rely on the sphere of tax evasion can come through the Tax Authority which in turn is able to punish it by a fine. Fraudsters in the tax field are using more sophisticated techniques and technological tools that make the discovery very difficult. Identifying and combating tax evasion is a complex process and knowledge from various fields is needed. Our study tries to identify those variables relating to taxpayers' behaviour that could be tackled by the Tax Authority in order to control this phenomenon. We achieved this objective by the use of NLP algorithms for analysing free speech answers on an online survey. In this sense, our research hypothesis is that trustworthiness in the State is positively correlated with an optimistic perception of the fiscal system. We analysed what is the structure of perception and which are the words that are most frequent. Results are in accordance with the literature review of the factors that impact compliant behaviour and confirm our hypothesis. The utility of results relies on the fact that in the context of smart governance, and Public Authorities should look at citizens' perception of tax policies and services in order to adapt its actions for an efficient collection of revenues to the State's budget.

Keywords Fiscal system perception · Tax compliance behaviour · Sentiment analysis · Bert algorithm · Tax evasion sentiment prediction

C. Ioana-Florina
University of Oradea, Oradea, Romania

C. Ştefana (✉) · M. Codruţa
Babeş-Bolyai University, Cluj-Napoca, Romania

A. M. Dima and M. Kelemen (eds.), *Digitalization and Big Data for Resilience and Economic Intelligence*, Springer Proceedings in Business and Economics, https://doi.org/10.1007/978-3-030-93286-2_7

1 Introduction

The phenomenon of tax evasion or tax avoidance is affecting societies across the globe. Inside public budgets' structure, tax revenues cover the majority of public revenues, therefore tax avoidance is of great interest for public authorities and the taxpayers. From the public policy perspective, efficient tax policies that target maximizing public revenues can be achieved through a complex understanding of the taxpayer's behaviour.

Predicting tax compliance behaviour by the use of a unique model requires using interdisciplinary knowledge due to its uncertain, non-linear, and dynamic nature. Being able to model tax compliant behaviour needs taking into account taxpayers' perception of quality of public services and fiscal policy efficiency, risk appetite or aversion regarding punishment, trust in the authority's way of spending the taxes collected, and internal motivations regarding notions like tax morale, cheating, social welfare, fairness of tax laws, fairness of fiscal incentives. The tax avoidance phenomenon has preoccupied scientists from various fields like legal, economics, financial, or others.

Taking into account the fact that measuring tax avoidance or the tax evasion phenomenon is not an easy thing to do, several mathematical, statistical or AI models have been developed. Each model focuses on a particular aspect, either qualitative or quantitative, depending on whether the purpose is either to understand the hidden pattern existing in order to explain the causes of this widespread "disease" of every economy or to be able to predict its evolution. The latter case is of greater interest for the public government preoccupied to collect from taxes the planned amount of revenues to the state budget.

The main objective of the current research refers to the fact that we searched for meaning in taxpayers' perceived aspects of fiscal policy and public authority that could reveal patterns driving tax compliant behaviour. This study aims at revealing certain variables that have a favourable impact on compliance behaviour. These in turn could be tackled accordingly by public authorities in order to prevent and combat tax evasion.

2 Literature Review

The first models that used to study tax compliance had been employed since the 1970s (Allingham and Sandmo 1972) and they were solely behavioural. In time, studies added new elements from sociology, psychology, legal studies, finance, system theory, agent-based models, or data mining tools. The first behavioural model revealed the underlying factors of taxpayers' decisions and how much revenue they could declare to the Tax Authority taking into account the possibility of being uncovered and punished (Allingham and Sandmo 1972). This model is based on the taxpayer's utility function taking into consideration their risk aversion of penalty. It is all about the classical choice to maximize expected utility under risk (Allingham and Sandmo 1972). Insights coming from other disciplines brought new meaning towards the complex nature of taxpayers' decisions, taking into account their internal motivation. In this sense, research points out the fact that the decision to pay taxes could be motivated by trust in the states' policies and services (Kirchler et al. 2008). On the contrary, some research showed a demotivating aspect, referring to the fear of punishment that comes along with low trust in public authorities (Hofmann et al. 2014). The negative impact of approaching citizens as being egoistic, outcome-oriented, and non-compliant has shown to push taxpayers' behaviour towards a non-compliant one (Iancu and Popovici-Coita 2019). Taxpayers' decision whether to cooperate or not is also based on their judgments about the fairness of government's policies, efficiency of fiscal measures, and the perceived value for the money they receive from public services based on the taxes they pay and a sense of social justice (Kirchler 1999; Kirchler et al. 2003). Transparency in fiscal legislation that is based on fair principles and is also welfare-oriented could support tax compliant taxpayer behaviour (Hofmann et al. 2014; Picciotto 2005). Building welfare for the society as a whole and offering quality public services act as an internal motivation for tax complaint behaviour (Dell'Anno 2009; Stankeviciusa and Leonas 2015; Coita and Mare 2021).

The utility of computational intelligence in detecting the probability of any individual to show intention for evading taxes refers to finding the most accurate empirical model that can be tested and validated on real-life data, in order to predict fraudulent behaviour. Predicting tax behaviour solely on tax filling or financial data reporting is not showing the whole picture about the tax avoidance phenomenon. In this sense, some research shows that people showing empathy and sympathy are more inclined to tax compliance (Christian and Alm 2014). A government that solely relies on its coercive force and looks only at public revenues surely is not adapting to the current technological landscape. Notions like interactive policy framing smart governance are more and more embraced by governments that want to adapt to this rapidly changing world. And this is done by looking at what your citizens are thinking and feeling about public authority measures and public services. In this regard, one study is analysing general opinion reflected on Twitter comments polarized into three categories: positive, negative, neutral, and draws several conclusions on improving government measures (Sharma and Shekhar 2020). In the same manner, another study found that the presence of strong moral values among taxpayers leads to improved rates of tax compliance (Antoci et al. 2014).

Finding what people feel about a subject is best seen in their opinion, revealed and analysed by real text data. One study showed that real text can reveal behavioural patterns in the financial field by testing several sentiment analysis methods (Kearney and Liu 2014; Kumar et al. 2020). Sentiment analysis can be done using various natural language processing models. Some that are mostly deployed in studies analysing opinions over text are transformers-based models, which are capable of understanding and modelling the context of the text. Several studies showed that, within the various transformers, BERT—Bidirectional Encoder Representations from Transformers—proves to be efficient in analysing semantic perception or feelings when using data as text (Arase and Tsujii 2021; Song et al. 2021; Gonzalez et al. 2020).

In our study, we perform a sentiment analysis on how taxation is perceived in Romania by using data collected from a questionnaire answered by 709 Romanian people, aged 22–35 years old, on how they perceive the national tax system. We tested a pre-trained sentiment analysis BERT model on the database in order to compute sentiment polarity scores, and we also calculated word frequencies to deliver a word cloud of the most frequent words for each question. This type of sentiment analysis performed on real text data in order to reveal semantic perception and feelings in the field of tax behaviour analysis has not been done yet, to be best of our knowledge.

The evolution of the tax evasion phenomenon at the international level has undergone a profound technological character due to the increasingly elaborated methods and innovative technologies, for collecting and manipulating information present in the virtual environment that is being used by criminals in developing increasingly complex tax fraud mechanisms. On the other hand, national governments and investigative bodies must keep up with this complexity of the tax evasion phenomenon in order to exercise control by preventing and combating fraud.

A valid tax compliance model gathers notions from various fields in order to clarify what tax compliance behaviour looks like today. Taxpayers' decision to pay taxes is complex and cannot be explained solely from a single perspective.

The hypothesis of current research is that the trustworthiness of the State's institutions impacts tax compliant behaviour and it is positively correlated with an optimistic perception of the taxpayers.

Our main objective was to reveal certain variables that have a favourable impact on tax compliance behaviour. Having this purpose in mind, we looked for meaning in taxpayers' perceived aspects of fiscal policy and the public authority that could reveal patterns, positive or negative, which could impact tax behaviour.

3 Methodology

The methodology we adhered to for answering the research questions is following the path of classical NLP (Natural Language Processing), from text and word frequencies to word clouds, and finally, sentiment classification based on a pre-trained model. As a data science tool for the text analysis, we have used Python (2014 version) and for visualization purposes, Tableau (2009 version). All steps in the methodology outlined in this paper, together with the initial and final dataset are published in our GitHub repository (Cioban et al. 2021).

The raw dataset consists of a corpus of questionnaire answers from 709 taxpayers to three questions related to the fiscal policies in Romania, during a timeframe of 5 years:

Q1. What is it that displeases you about the Romanian tax system?

Q2. If you were the Minister of Public Finance, what would you change about the Romanian tax system?

Q3. In your opinion, what does the current tax system offer you?

The questions were formulated in a manner that *would balance* the overall text sentiment such as the first question is implying a *negative polarity, while the second is neutral and the last, positive.* All questions and answers were written in Romanian; hence most resulting diagrams and graphs here consist of words and expressions in both English and Romanian language. Where not possible, we have interpreted the meaning of the most relevant text or word results to enable understanding.

First, full answers' frequencies were analysed to determine the recurrence of opinions for each question and to understand how the most prominent answers align with the theory behind taxpayers' behaviour. Basic pre-processing was computed on top of the answers' text to decode accents specific to the Romanian language, clean the text from special characters and extra spaces, convert all words to lower case and remove all non-word values (such as '-').

As a second step of the analysis, word frequencies were computed and displayed as a word cloud of uni-grams (the most frequent sequences of a word). The text was pre-processed in terms of removing any possible emoji, decoding the accents, cleaning the special characters and extra white spaces, lowering all letters, tokenizing (splitting the text into words), removal of stop words (frequently used words that do not add meaning to the sentence) and punctuation signs. Last, the words were stemmed or trimmed to a common root, or stemma such that, for example, from the initial word 'Ineficiența' (the inefficiency), after pre-processing and stemming, we got to the word 'inefficient'. All three answers were mixed in a single paragraph, for each respondent, as the purpose of this analysis step was to understand the overall tendency for words expressed by the people. We used the Bag of Words (Tache et al. 2021; Zhang et al. 2010) as a methodology to construct a dictionary of the topmost frequent 1000 words to structure the text and calculate frequencies for the visualization of the word cloud.

As our ultimate objective was to determine the patterns in the taxpayers' perceptions of the fiscal policy and authorities in Romania, sentiment polarities were predicted for each answer to all questions in the corpus. The model used for prediction is a BERT transformer pre-trained and tested on a balanced dataset of 38,210 positive and negative movie and product reviews in Romanian compiled from two sources (Kataknonst 2018; Arun 2020). The model was chosen from an accuracy evaluation procedure done between classical Machine Learning models, such as LR (Logistic Regression), DT (Decision Tree) and SVM (Support Vector Machine), and Perceptron-based models: RNN (Recurrent Neural Network) and BERT. Out of all models, BERT has proven to have the best performance, as even after only training for 5 epochs, it reached a constant loss of around 0.1 with an accuracy of 0.98. Due to training on a high volume of natural Romanian text—the training was done on 80% of the corpus, while the testing on the remaining 20%—and to the fact that the text was focused on various domains of interest, we considered the model as fitted for predicting the sentiment class for our dataset as well. The text was pre-processed using the implicit pre-processor module from ktrain (Arun 2020), the Python library used for training the BERT model and predicting new texts. The results consist of an enhanced dataset with the original text corresponding to the answers for each question in the questionnaire and its predicted sentiment score with 0 as a label for

Table 1 Descriptive statistics of the sentiment scores values for the answers to each question

	Q1	Q2	Q3
Count	710.000000	710.000000	710.000000
Mean	0.233803	0.409859	0.471831
std	0.423547	0.492154	0.499558
Min	0.000000	0.000000	0.000000
25%	0.000000	0.000000	0.000000
50%	0.000000	0.000000	0.000000
75%	0.000000	1.000000	1.000000
Max	1.000000	1.000000	1.000000

Source Authors modelling and calculations

negative texts and 1 for positive. The descriptive statistics corresponding to each sentiment score column are listed in Table 1. Moreover, we have used the same predictor to compute polarities for the words in the word cloud, to colorize the words according to their sentiments.

4 Results Interpretation

Now, are these answers of statistical importance for picturing the behaviour of taxpayers? To further answer this, we have computed sentiment scores for all words in the Bag of Words (BoW) dictionary computed from the corpus and visualized them using a word cloud (Fig. 1). To that extent, this BoW only implies that at a stemma-level, the attitude would seem balancing towards a more positive sentiment, hence the presence of more reddish words in the figure. This would, however, not answer the question, but rather highlight the positive specificity of single words in general without taking into consideration the entire semantics of an answer.

Fig. 1 Word cloud of the top-most frequent 50 words in the corpus coloured against the polarity of each word. *Source* Authors modelling and calculations

The answer frequency analysis can be viewed in Fig. 2 and consists of a top-15-words bar chart represented for each question. We have noticed that the most recurrent answers to all questions consist of the word 'nothing', hence many of the respondents in the dataset either were sincere, saying that nothing displeases them about the tax system, or there is anything to offer or improve, or maybe they were not interested

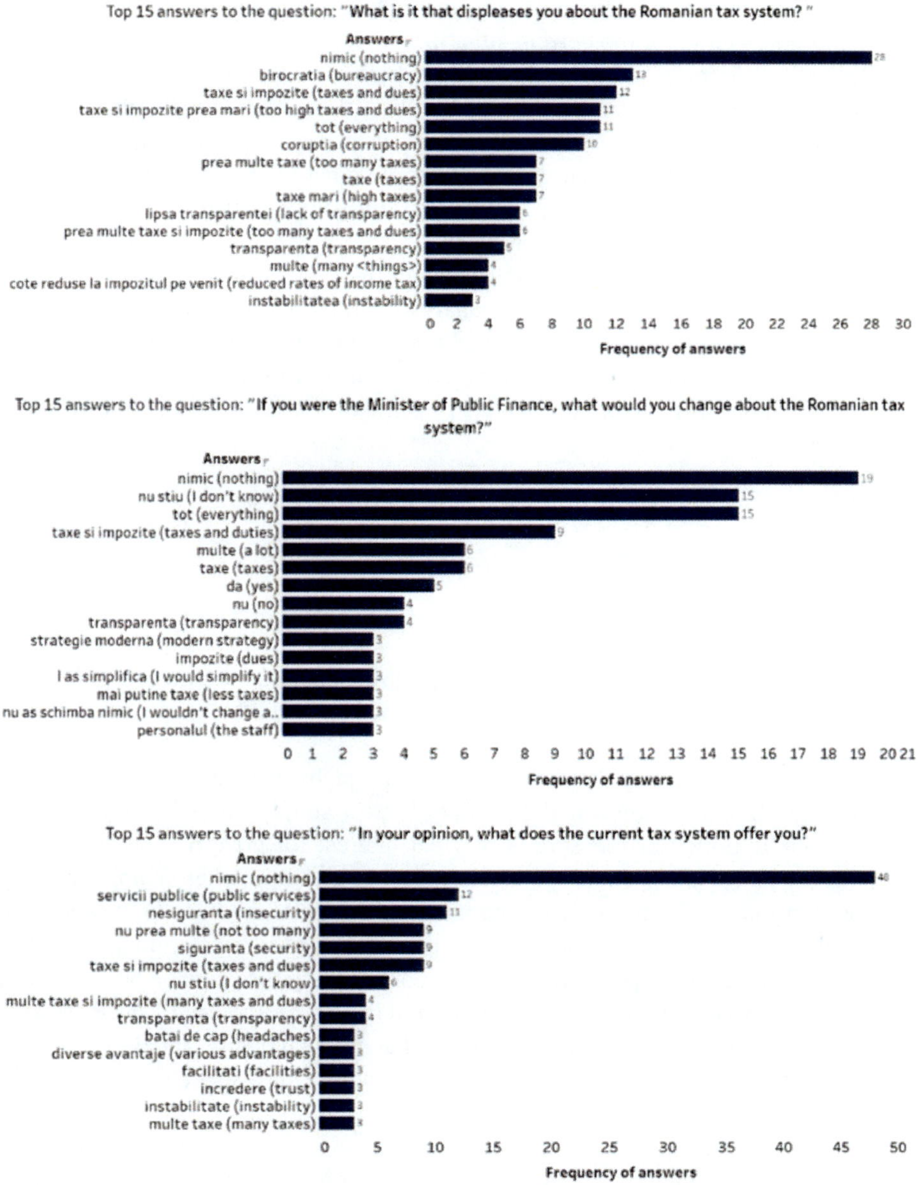

Fig. 2 Frequency bar charts of the top 10 answers for each question, from Q1 (top) to Q3 (bottom). *Source* Authors modelling and calculations

into answering such questions. Many of the remaining *answers seem to gravitate around issues like the high amount of taxes and dues, transparency of the fiscal system, security, and stability.* Meanwhile, even with the proven pessimistic sentiment towards the fiscal policy and public authority, there are answers of importance that show the positive aspects of the system as well or the several ways in which the system can be improved. While most of the top 15 answers for each question seem to have a common root, there are also some that step out of this pattern and enhance a broader knowledge of the current situation.

The most common words used with a negative nature were bureaucracy, taxes and dues, too high taxes, corruption, lack of transparency, and instability. The most frequent words with a positive nature were: public services, security, facilities, and trust. On the other hand, when we asked people what they would change, the most frequent answers were modernizing the system, more transparency, simplifying, administrative staff, fewer taxes, and dues.

Therefore, the need for a paragraph or sentence-level sentiment polarity prediction was materialised as a final step of the analysis using context-specialized algorithms for the task. The descriptive statistics in Table 1 and the results of the overall polarity scores for the answers to each question reveal an overall negative tendency within the corpus, implying, again, an overall pessimistic attitude towards the Romanian tax policies.

5 Conclusions

Preventing and combating the phenomenon of tax evasion are present concerns of national governments both due to the magnitude of this phenomenon and because of the increasingly sophisticated techniques used by the authors in carrying out tax frauds.

Understanding human behaviour can be done by various methods. Grasping knowledge of what people feel or think about a subject or how they perceive a certain public policy or measure is of great interest for governments who wish to stay updated on what technology offers today. It is a time when people share their perceptions and feelings freely on the internet, on social media, or other platforms. The Public Authority can implement a certain policy in the fiscal domain but only by analysing how citizens perceive and feel about could politicians be helped to make the best decisions. And this purpose is best achieved by the use of NLP modelling which, like in our case, analyses free speech that has no meaning and derives a certain conclusion. We used the BERT algorithm to analyse free speech answers to three questions that gave the opportunity to the respondent to answer freely. NLP models analyse this type of speech for deriving meaning. In this sense, we analysed people's answers in order to see their perception regarding the efficiency of the fiscal system, how they perceive it. We wanted to reveal what are the aspects that get negative feelings and, on the other hand, what are those which get more positive feedback. We had in mind the following research question:" What is the public perception of the taxpayer relating to tax policies and how does this impact trust in the State?". This in turn could be one of the questions that public authorities should have in mind when designing fiscal policies in this current context based on smart governance principles. Finding what people feel about a certain public policy could help politicians make better decisions. People leave comments on social media or other platforms and by using our employed model of NLP analysis, one could derive meaning in the form of a positive or negative feeling about it.

The goal of the current research was to assess the attitude of Romanian taxpayers in respect to the fiscal system. Results obtained through applying sentiment analysis emphasize a negative, pessimistic tendency. This result is a premise for improvement in the features of the Romanian fiscal system in both education and perception of taxpayers. The current study confirmed our hypothesis referring to the fact that a trust climate between the state and its citizens could encourage tax compliant behaviour. The negative, pessimistic attitude of Romanian citizens regarding the fiscal system is backed by a lack of transparency, quality of public services, and a higher tax burden that people perceive, and this, in turn, erodes trust in the State. Our study revealed those variables that negatively impact taxpayers' behaviour and the public authority could tackle to sustain compliant behaviour. Going further, we are going to analyse how people perceive the efficiency of the fiscal measures taken by authorities, by introducing more data into the analysis and with the help of other ML models we can predict people's trust in the State's policies. We are researching various models for using behavioural data in order to predict people's inclination to tax evasion.

Acknowledgements This paper is part of the project COST CA19130 FinAI—Fintech and Artificial Intelligence in Finance—Towards a Transparent Financial Industry.

References

Antoci, A., Russu, P., Zarri, L.: Tax evasion in a behaviorally heterogeneous society: an evolutionary analysis. Economic Modelling, vol. 42, pp. 106–115 (2014). ISSN 0264-9993

Allingham, M.G., Sandmo, A.: Income tax evasion: a theoretical analysis. J. Public Econ. **1** 323–338 (1972). (0. North-Holland Publishing Company)

Arase, Y., Tsujii, J.: Transfer fine-tuning of BERT with phrasal paraphrases. Comput. Speech Lang. **66**, 101164 (2021). ISSN 0885-2308

Arun, S.M.: ktrain: A low-code library for augmented machine learning (2020). Accessed from https://arxiv.org/abs/2004.10703

Christian, R., C., Alm, J.: Empathy, sympathy, and tax compliance. J. Econ. Psychol. **40**, 62–82 (2014). ISSN 0167-4870

Cioban, Ş., Coita, I., Mare, C.: Sentiment analysis on Taxation Perception in Romania, retrieved from Github repository (2021). https://github.com/stefanacioban/taxation_perception

Coita, I., Mare, C.: The utility of neural model in predicting tax avoidance behavior. In: Czarnowski, I., Howlett, R.J., Jain, L.C. (eds.) Intelligent Decision Technologies. Smart Innovation, Systems and Technologies, vol. 238. Springer, Singapore (2021). https://doi.org/10.1007/978-981-16-2765-1_6

Dell'Anno, R.: Tax evasion, tax morale and policy maker's effectiveness. J. Socio-Econ. **38**(6), 988–997 (2009). ISSN 1053-5357

Gonzalez, J.A., Hurtado, L.-F., Pla, F.: Transformer based contextualization of pre-trained word embeddings for irony detection in Twitter. Inf. Process. Manag. **57**(4), 102262 (2020). ISSN 0306-4573

Hofmann, E., Gangl, K., Kirchler, E., Stark, J.: Enhancing tax compliance through coercive and legitimate power of tax authorities by concurrently diminishing or facilitating trust in tax authorities. Law Policy **36**(3) (July 2014). ISSN 0265-8240, © 2014 Law & Policy published by University of Denver/Colorado Seminary and Wiley Periodicals, Inc. (2014)

Iancu (Nechita), E.-A., Popovici-Coita, I.F.: Rethinking economics-of-crime model of tax compliance from behavioral perspective applied to Romanian case. Ann. Univ. Oradea Econ. Sci. Ser. **25**(2), 372–381, 10p, (2019). Dec. 2016

Kataknonst: Sentiment Analysis with Tensorflow (2018). Accessed from https://github.com/katakonst/sentiment-analysis-tensorflow

Kearney, C., Liu, S.: Textual sentiment in finance: a survey of methods and models. Int. Rev. Financ. Anal. **33**, 171–185 (2014). ISSN 1057-5219

Kirchler, E., Hoelzl, E., Wahl, I.: Enforced versus voluntary tax compliance: The "slippery slope" framework, available online at www.sciencedirect.com, Journal of Economic Psychology 29, pp. 210–225 (2008).

Kirchler, E.: Reactance to Taxation: Employers' attitudes toward taxes. J. Socio-Econ. (July 1999). https://www.researchgate.net/publication/4931915

Kirchler, E., Maciejovsky, B., Schneider, F.: Everyday representations of tax avoidance, tax evasion, and tax flight: Do legal differences matter?. J. Econ. Psychol. **24**, 535–553 (2003). ScienceDirect (2003)

Kumar, R., Guha Deb, S., Mukherjee, S.: Do words reveal the latent truth? Identifying communication patterns of corporate losers. J. Behav. Exp. Financ. **26**, 100291 (2020). ISSN 2214-6350

Picciotto, S.: Constructing compliance: game-playing, tax law and the regulatory state?. Centre for Tax System Integrity (Working Paper No. 81), Australian National University, Canberra (2005)

Sharma, A., Shekhar, H.: Intelligent learning based opinion mining model for governmental decision making. Proc. Comput. Sci. **173**, 216–224 (2020). ISSN 1877-0509

Stankeviciusa, E., Leonas, L.: Hybrid approach model for prevention of tax evasion and fraud. In: 20th International Scientific Conference Economics and Management –2015 (ICEM-2015), Published by Elsevier, Procedia-Social and Behavioral Sciences, vol. 213, pp. 383–389 (2015)

Song, W., Wen, Z., Xiao, Z., Cheol Park, S.: Semantics perception and refinement network for aspect-based sentiment analysis. Knowledge-Based Syst. **214**, 106755 (2021). ISSN 0950-7051

Tache, A.M., Gaman, M., Ionescu, R.T.: Clustering word embeddings with self-organizing maps. application on LaRoSeDa–a large romanian sentiment data set (2021). arXiv:2101.04197

Zhang, Y., Jin, R., Zhou, Z.H.: Understanding bag-of-words model: a statistical framework. Int. J. Mach. Learn. Cybern. **1**, 43–52 (2010)

The Context of Digital Entrepreneurship. New Technologies Between Evolution and Revolution

Volkmann Christine and Gavrilescu Ileana

Abstract The world has changed a lot in the last few decades. Increasingly exhausted of its physical resources and assaulted by pollution beyond its endurance limit, the Earth is showing increasing signs of fatigue. At the same time, technology is moving from the third industrial revolution to the fourth industrial revolution. Already, digital technology has begun to invade our living environment. Correspondingly, entrepreneurship has also changed, embracing "on the fly" new digital technologies, as well as the big issues of e-commerce and the contemporary world. But do the new digital technologies really represent a genuine technological revolution for the economy or are they just a new stage in an automation that began at least two hundred years ago (when the steam engine and Jacquard's loom became iconic)? But are the new digital technologies just a much-needed and very useful placebo to inspire enthusiasm in a world facing other great impasses, or do they represent a reality with huge economic potential and, correspondingly, an essentially determining factor in the development of revolutionary digital entrepreneurship? But do the new technologies, historically speaking, fit Kondratieff's law of economic super-cycles (called by Joseph Schumpeter "Kondratieff waves") or are they just some kind of evolutionary economic process, of circumstance, specific to a particular historical moment and to a certain degree of world development? And, given the credibility with which the Sustainable Development Goals have been implemented by the UN, what will be the effects of digitisation and digital entrepreneurship on people and work? Drawing on scientific literature devoted on the one hand to digital entrepreneurship and on the other hand to the economic and cultural nature of digital technology, this study aims to provide theoretical answers to the above-mentioned economic philosophy questions, as well as to other questions related to the proposed topic.

V. Christine · G. Ileana (✉)
University of Wuppertal, Wuppertal, Germany
e-mail: gavrilescu@wiwi.uni-wuppertal.de

V. Christine
e-mail: volkmann@wiwi.uni-wuppertal.de

A. M. Dima and M. Kelemen (eds.), *Digitalization and Big Data for Resilience and Economic Intelligence*, Springer Proceedings in Business and Economics, https://doi.org/10.1007/978-3-030-93286-2_8

Keywords Economy · Entrepreneurship · Entrepreneur · Evolution · Revolution · Digitalization · Big-data · Internet · New technologies · Digital technology · Artificial intelligence · Sustainable development · Kondratieff cycles

1 Introduction

The transition between the Third Industrial Revolution and the Fourth seems to be so discrete and subtle that it makes it difficult to perceive and discern its chronological framing. Although the 'digital revolution' is on everyone's lips, seemingly ubiquitous in the life of the world today, it is very likely that, from a strictly economic point of view, it means nothing more than (another) extraordinary evolution of robotic electronisation and automation that began in the second half of the twentieth century and circumscribed by the third industrial revolution. A clarification in this sense would, on the one hand, has the honourable task of (re)placing things in their place in economic history and, on the other hand, would help entrepreneurs to distinguish strategically between a more comfortable functional continuity (the evolutionary variant) and a confusing inhibition that would affect their inspiration and decision-making (the revolutionary variant), even leading to a loss of company efficiency. Cases of entrepreneurs' reluctance towards any technological novelty have been reported over time (Atkeson and Kehoe 2001). In practice, this is also the stated purpose of this study. Specifically, the issue of digital technology is to discern between its evolutionary alternative and that of a genuinely new revolution so that digital entrepreneurship—which relies on digital technology—can make an informed approach to the most appropriate and timely business strategy. It is a hypothesis that needs to be delicately demonstrated theoretically, through logical artifices based on the evaluation of conclusions highlighted in the reference literature.

Digital entrepreneurship is a notion that describes how entrepreneurship will change as business and society continue to be transformed by digital technology (Milićević et al. 2020). Digital entrepreneurship highlights changes in entrepreneurial practice, theory, and education (Allen 2020).

From another point of view, the issues of the present study can also be assimilated to the contextualization of entrepreneurship research (e.g. Baker and Welter 2018), which helps a lot in understanding entrepreneurial coordinates such as "when", "how" and "who" has determination on entrepreneurship and business.

The first question is how economically genuine the revolutionary bill of the fourth industrial revolution is (Vrânceanu et al. 2020), i.e. "whether digitization, big-data analytics, and even artificial intelligence can be regarded economically as an essentially new technological revolution, or whether it should be regarded as a new stage in the classic technological evolution—possibly as a continuation of automation(?)". As a corollary-issue, answers/conclusions are sought for other related questions: "what are the genuine techno-economic moment and reason symbolically marking the beginning of the fourth industrial revolution?" and "what should be the optimal, appropriate and timely position of integrative digital entrepreneurship vis-à-vis a digital technology whose identity authenticity oscillates between evolution and revolution?".

But even before any problematization, there are five general cultural considerations related to the topic of industrial revolutions, which the authors of this study invoke as premises for the research of the relationship between digital entrepreneurship and new technologies, respectively as levers of logical reasoning in the demonstration of the hypothesis advanced in this study.

The four technical revolutions consecrated as "industrial"—which emerged in the history of culture and civilisation only since two hundred and some years ago—are similar in one respect, but also different. The classification of the first three industrial revolutions was historically based especially on the energy factor. But now that energy is no longer the most relevant criterion for the transition to the fourth industrial revolution, the authors of this study believe that the logic of the succession of industrial revolutions needs to be revised. This is why, in the present study, the authors raise the question "whether what is known as the 'fourth industrial revolution' or the 'digital revolution' can be regarded as a genuine stage in economic terms, or whether it is merely a form of continuation of the electronic revolution—which started more than half a century ago, if not a continuation of the automation process—as a techno-economic production process that began more than two centuries ago?".

From an economic point of view, the steam engine is a technical invention that marks the beginning of the first great industrial revolution and thus takes precedence for all industrial revolutions that followed. Although mining, metallurgy, the textile industry, the food industry, the printing industry, water, and rail transport, and many other more or less industrial fields have all developed on the steam engine in a relatively short historical time, the steam engine alone—however small or large it may have been and whatever type of machine it may have driven—remains the supreme technological emblem of the first industrial revolution in the history of modern civilisation. It is then not hard to imagine the psychological impact and then the continuing veneration of contemporary mankind with the steam engine, towards this machine which, from a technical point of view, could do what tens and even hundreds of men could have done, and which, from an economic point of view, changed the degree of civilisation of millions and millions of people. Thus, the steam engine is a landmark motif for the second half of the eighteenth century, which is established as the symbolic date for the beginning of the first great industrial revolution, and James Watt—who perfected the steam engine to the point of economic impact—is enshrined as the leading father of the terrible machine. Similar powerful psychological changes and mental mutations also occurred when electricity and electronics (culminating in digital applications) appeared in civilisation. The telegraph, telephone, radio, television, and later the computer, mobile telephony, and the internet, signify the second and third industrial revolutions respectively (Duignan 2021). In terms of psycho-moral perception, the most impactful inventions based mostly on electronics were robotics, automation—generally of many technological processes in large-scale production, cosmic flight, the personal computer and the internet (for current data and information search engines, communication and social networking, and online commerce).

In the context of the industrial revolutions, people's incomes have risen and, as a result, their quality of life has improved in many parts of the world. The cultivation of industrial revolutions as a model of socio-economic development derives from the Enlightenment democratic philosophy of modern historical times, which established the principle that society can only progress if all people are better off (Schwab 2016). By and large, the industrial revolutions can now be considered to have served their purpose, with today's world—at least in theory—having a chance of living a life incomparably better than that of its forebears throughout human history. In practice, however, things have not quite worked out as planned. One of the most significant expressions of this can be seen in the package of 17 major sustainable development goals developed and promoted by the UN (2015), behind which are at least 17 fundamental social, economic, and ecological problems and challenges of the contemporary world. Many of these problems—such as hunger, poor health, limited access to livelihood and productive (re)sources, lack of education, poverty in general, gender inequality, and lack of personal and community physical security—emerged in the destiny of humanity many centuries ago, but the industrial revolutions have failed, at least so far, to solve them for too much of the Earth's population.

From a political perspective, digitisation should not be approached as an ultimate goal in itself, but as an adjunct to Agenda 2030, i.e., aligned with the 17 major goals for sustainable development set by the UN. The achievement of these goals is the world's supreme motivation for this historical stage (e.g. Bundesregierung 2017). The economy, through all its fields, industries, actors, and actions, including entrepreneurship (of whatever kind), is already focusing its specific efforts to serve the great cause. Faced with the integration of sustainability principles in the form of new strategic levers, many entrepreneurs have already adapted, while many others have implemented digital technology in the most diverse forms of hardware and software in their organisations on the fly.

The particular bill of the digital revolution, the first of the industrial revolutions that is not alone the energy factor, is motivating mankind's hopes for the eradication of all its problems. The most eloquent proof of the better mentality is also to be found in the sustainable development goals—promoted by the UN under the "2030 Agenda". In particular, high hopes are placed in the revolutionary capacity of digitisation and even for example artificial intelligence to serve a digital entrepreneurship that can reinvigorate the global economy and reorient society towards a noble sustainable development.

2 Literature Review

On the taxonomy of industrial revolutions, economic history Alessandro Nuvolari believes that the traditional classification is rooted in an overly rigid historical chronology that assumes too close a link between technological change and economic outcomes. In order to provide a more accurate and useful historical description of innovation and sustainability policies, the author proposes a more flexible interpretative framework (Nuvolari 2018).

In the sense of this flexibility, the classification of technological revolutions may also imply a more nuanced qualitative or value approach. Andrew Atkeson and Patrick J. Kehoe, who once studied the transition from the second to the third industrial revolution, observed that after 1860–1900 (corresponding to the landmark "invention of electricity" motif), it took several decades before productivity really began to rise, and that this delay, considered paradoxical by economic historians, would be due to the reluctance of producers to give up the expertise accumulated with old technologies (Atkeson and Kehoe 2001).

In this context we ask, "to what extent can a radical change in established business models and, correspondingly, in strategic typologies, imposed by the adoption of digital technologies, now become useful for entrepreneurship?". In a study on entrepreneurial opportunities in the context of digital transformation, Reinhard Ematinger points out that the digitisation of the industry, beyond opening up new business opportunities, may also bring new risks—such as the risk of "losing touch" with traditional customers. Therefore, the only chance for survival that the author sees remains the development of new business models that generate new sales—both to old and new customers (Ematinger 2017).

Digitalization as a current megatrend is reflected in developments such as the digital transformation of industrial production, online commerce, sharing platforms, the Internet of Things (IoT), autonomous vehicles, Big Data, artificial intelligence, and blockchain applications such as cryptocurrencies. Digitalisation is fundamentally changing the way we live, learn, work and communicate with each other, how we produce and consume, and how we organise ourselves as a society. It presents us with new political, economic, social, environmental, cultural and ethical challenges, which are widely discussed in society. It thus becomes very important for civil society that the social debate on digitization is not limited to technological or economic aspects, but also includes comprehensive ecological and social effects such as the growing threat to privacy (Schneider 2019).

Concerned with how digital technology is integrated by digital entrepreneurship, the authors of this study now want to clarify the exact nature, from a strictly economic point of view, of the fourth industrial revolution and, correspondingly, its symbolic moment of debut on the historical scene.

Asking, in a recent study on the main objectives of the fourth industrial revolution, "whether this industrial revolution is a continuation of previous revolutions or can be perceived as a new revolution?", author Lucretia Dogaru believes that, due to the fact that the current revolution is ongoing (while the other three revolutions have taken incomparably longer), it is inappropriate to answer the question for the time being. (Dogaru 2020). From the content of the above-mentioned study (on the basis of which, in part, Table 1 was also drawn up), another important idea emerges: namely that the transitions between the first industrial revolutions were radical, based on a single moment-motivator, as in the best tradition of the political-social revolutions

Table 1 Technical and economic characteristics of the great industrial revolutions and their cultural-psychological consequences

The great industrial revolutions	Technical characteristics and economic aspects	Cultural-psychological meanings. Consequences
The first industrial revolution – began in 1775 in Britain and spread rapidly around the world	– goods production and maritime and rail transport become highly mechanised, at the expense of burning coal in steam engines; – the metallurgical and textile industries develop remarkably	– is the basis of modern Western civilisation; – thanks to the invention of trains and steamships, the development of freight transport and the multiplication of journeys are facilitated; – a new mentality about the use of energy sources is born
The second industrial revolution – began at the end of the nineteenth century (1870)	– electricity is introduced, both in industrial production and in domestic services (lighting, transport, etc.); – based on the burning of coal and natural gas, electro-energy requires the development of extractive industries (mining); – the motor car appears and its astonishing spread requires the development of the oil extraction industry and road and bridge-building; – the cinema, radio and television are invented; – the aeroplane is invented and a manufacturing industry is rapidly developing; – the iron and steel industry, which underpins all other industries, is booming; – new methods and means of communication are invented and developed (telegraph and telephone)	– Thanks to steamships, people are increasingly travelling the world's seas and oceans; – the increase in the number of cars gives people more freedom and opportunity to move around; – the advent of civilian air travel makes business travel and tourism in particular easier; – the invention of the motion picture gives the modern man great aesthetic satisfaction; the same is true for the radio and television, where the opportunity for news and live broadcasts prevails; – imposing skyscraper blocks are built; – world wars, despite all the misery they cause, accelerate the development of new technologies; – people start flying in the cosmos; – many people equip their homes with fridges, washing machines, vacuum cleaners, electric irons, making life easier

(continued)

Table 1 (continued)

The great industrial revolutions	Technical characteristics and economic aspects	Cultural-psychological meanings. Consequences
The third industrial revolution, also called the "Technological Revolution"; From the second half of the twentieth century (1969);	– nuclear power develops and renewable energy sources emerge; – in manufacturing and production industries, automation is increasingly adopted, with its technological cutting edge—robotics; – electronics and information technology are taking on unprecedented proportions in industrial production, telecommunications and domestic services; – digitisation is becoming increasingly important	– More and more people are benefiting from rapid technical and scientific progress; – mass production of consumer goods is leading to a futile consumerism; non-recyclable packaging and single-use products are spreading; – travel is booming, thanks to the development of transport; tourism is benefiting; – electronic means of learning are being introduced in education; – the world is beginning to feel the boomerang effect of the unreasonable exploitation of natural resources and pollution; – computers are entering many people's lives; – thanks to the development of electronics, the volume of communications increases exponentially; – thanks to the Internet, more and more people have easy access to information
The fourth industrial revolution (often referred to as the "Digital Revolution") – Internet / 2000 ? – Its establishment is symbolically marked by the 2016 Davos Conference?	– supports digital technologies, including artificial intelligence and nanotechnology; – involves the fusion of digital technologies with physical technologies and biological processes; – involves an energy revolution (with 'zero' harmful emissions and a global grid); – Google (as an internet search engine), Apple (as a provider of hardware, software and online services), Facebook (as a social network operator) and Amazon (as an online retail operator)	– The fourth technical revolution seems to be continuing the third; – the transition is seen as a pivotal moment in the evolution of humanity, as it is the first industrial revolution rooted not in a new type of energy but digitisation; – the world attributes to digitisation and robotisation the role of saviour for the current impasse; – all branches of the economy are beginning to rely on digitisation in one way or another; – digital means of learning and applying acquired theory are being introduced into education

Source Authors
Note The literature sources used to compile the table are: Griffin (2018), Atkeson and Kehoe (2007), Rifkin (2011), Vaclav (2005), Dogaru (2020)

of their time, while the transition to the fourth industrial revolution is not known exactly when it began, and with what fact.

On the other hand, the industrial revolution is defined as a progressive, highly complex technical process with a strong social, technological, and economic impact. At the same time, an industrial revolution has a major impact on business development, governance, and on improving people's lives. As a global phenomenon, the progress generated by industrial revolutions can radically change society, the economy, and politics and can alter social structures, investment, and people's mindsets (Dogaru 2020).

Therefore, going through the analytical logic of the present study, the authors consider that at this point of the approach, there is a need for a synthetic representation, implicitly more expressive, of the cultural-psychological meanings of the industrial revolutions, correlated with their technical characteristics and economic aspects. This is why Table 1 was drawn up.

With regard to the fourth industrial revolution included in the table, one particular aspect should be mentioned: there is no well-defined, symbolic moment for it. In the non-scientific or mainstream literature, it is widely believed that the advent of the Internet in 2000 was the turning point. After that year people started talking more and more about Industry 4.0, but the concept was probably for the first time officially recognised at the 2016 Davos meeting (Schwab 2016).

3 Methodological Analysis

The transition between two industrial revolutions, however long or short it lasts, is usually concentrated in a symbolic moment and/or a striking reason (such as, for example, the massive economic adoption of an invention).

The exact moment of inflection between the third industrial revolution and the fourth can also be assessed by comparing the qualitative or value assessments that humanity has of the most important applications of science and technology.

According to traditional phasing, the first industrial revolution began with the introduction of the steam engine into industrial production and transport. The second revolution was generated by the introduction of electricity into manufacturing, transport, and the domestic environment. The third revolution began with the adoption of applied electronics (industrial robotics, information technology, digitisation) in the economy and throughout civilisation. On the basis of this principle, the authors of this study now introduce the combined notion of 'moment marking motive' ('m-m-m'). The "m-m-m" complex would thus be characterised by three distinct coordinates: its chronological moment, its techno-economic nature and its psycho-moral value impact.

One can make an association of the notion of "m-m-m" with the factors of the new core innovations or "levels" that Leo Nefiodow tried to identify when arguing for the "sixth Kondratieff wave": technological, economic, social and temporal (Nefiodow 2017; Lungu 2020). Thus 'temporal' would correspond to 'timing', 'technological and economic' would correspond to 'reason', and 'social' would correspond to 'value impact'.

Once established by an appropriate scientific method, the exact chronological timing and economic dimensions of the Fourth Revolution could then be verified/validated by the "waves of economic evolution", first imagined by Kondratieff (see Popovici 2018) and later theoretically refined by Josef Schumpeter (Schumpeter 1939). However, when it has not been possible to establish the "moment-motive" that would become a symbol for the beginning of the fourth industrial revolution, the reverse procedure can be applied: one deduces from the Kondratieffian cycle scheme, which is the moment, after which one looks for data of all kinds to support the hypothesis. The authors of the present study tried this way, by developing the combined graph in Fig. 1. The graph juxtaposes the princely Kondratieff long-wave plot, processed after Nefiodow and Nefiodow (2014), with three curves signifying the first three industrial revolutions, inspired by a graph from "Digital Technology and Social Change: The Digital Transformation of Society from a Historical Perspective" (Hilbert 2020).

The "Kondratieff waves" represent evolutionary business cycles or, rather, evolutionary economic cycles. The economist's theory of long waves says that, in principle, at certain intervals, business rises and falls, reaching at certain times a maximum

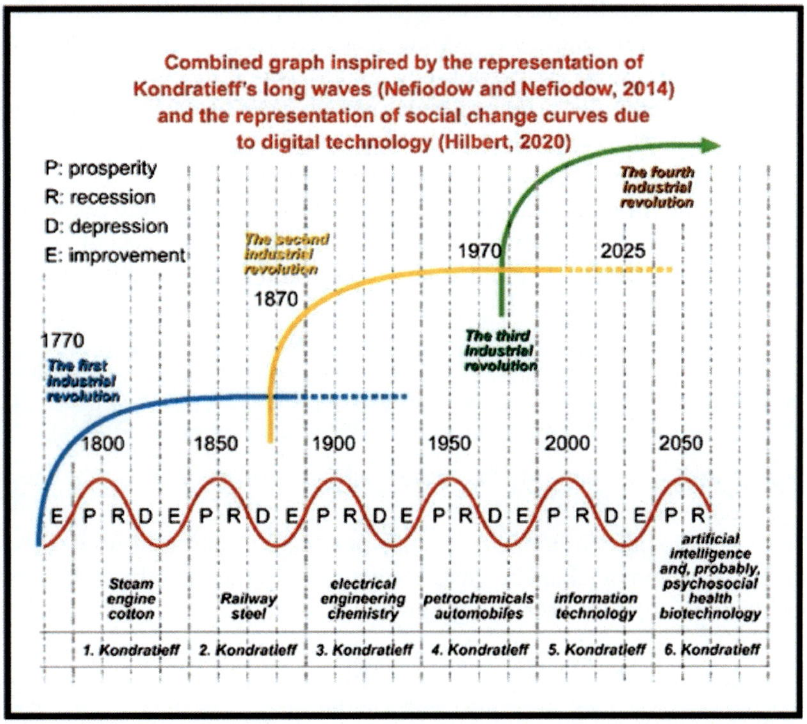

Fig. 1 A graph that combines the princely allure of Kondratieff's long waves with curves suggesting industrial revolutions. *Source* Authors

and a minimum. Each wave is characterised by an early phase of growth—which usually corresponds to historical periods of new business development, a period of growth slowdown—at the end of which development reaches a maximum, a phase of decline and a 'crash'. "Kondratieff's" long "Cycles" or "Waves", being regular, have a cadence of 40 to 60 years. However, if one shifts attention to the curves of the first three revolutions, one finds that there is neither regularity nor correlation with the Kondratieffian waves. This empirical method of detecting the Industry 4.0 momentum is therefore not yet feasible.

In another possible approach to the problem of determining the moment of transition between the third industrial revolution and the fourth, one might consider, for example, that it is not simply an official declaration—such as the one made in Davos (2016) —that can mark the beginning of such a complex and important phenomenon in the phasing of history, but much rather, perhaps, the emergence of a remarkable difference between a quiet digital generalisation (as data capture and processing through various applications and for various applications), and a consistent invasion of the human environment by artificial intelligence-based robotics.

Continuing to address other factors or issues circumscribing the Industry 4.0 industrial revolution, the question of using artificial intelligence in the context of digital entrepreneurship now arises.

AI (artificial intelligence) is known to be able to adapt automatically, i.e. differently to different conditions, in order to perform a premeditated action. Basically, it is an autonomous, and human behaviour. The prospects of artificial intelligence are fascinating to almost everyone, but they are also scary, to some people. According to a recent opinion poll conducted under the auspices of the European Parliament, 61% of Europeans have a favourable view of AI and robots, but 88% say these technologies require careful management (European Parliament 2020).

It is therefore difficult to assess, as yet, whether artificial intelligence can be seen as a peaceful spin-off category of digitisation, continuing the concept of automation, or is an early category of a field that might take hold at another historical stage.

4 Conclusions

Entrepreneurship is one of the driving forces of economic change and the entrepreneur is its essential element.

Since traditional entrepreneurship has practically embraced digital technology, digital entrepreneurship has become an effective formula for both good business practice and sustainable development. Digital technology has already started to change the way of life of mankind, and digital entrepreneurship seems to be the best initiative to integrate new technologies. However, there is not enough in-depth consideration of the taxonomy of the fourth industrial revolution.

In the view of the authors of this study, a firm answer to the question "whether new technologies should be appropriated or integrated by digital entrepreneurship, as a genuinely revolutionary set of techniques, or as a continuation of an electronic process serving automation?" will only emerge when man becomes dominated by artificial intelligence. But until then, increasingly surrounded and replaced by artificial intelligence, man will oscillate between enthusiasm and indignation. Very important in the equation for the success of peaceful coexistence between man and machine will be that contextual factor even for digital entrepreneurship namely democracy (Audretsch and Moog 2020).

In the new digital technology landscape, characterised by the predicted developments of artificial intelligence, the internet of things, autonomous vehicles, 3D printing systems, augmented reality, virtual reality, wearables, and nanotechnology, the relationship between man and machine will inevitably and radically change. And this change will also be reflected in the status of entrepreneurship, which, in order to be vital and vibrant, will have to integrate its 'digital' condition to the maximum, but with discernment and responsibility.

That being the case, the real defining moment that will impose digital technology as a revolution of its own could come when the world negotiates with artificial intelligence a reasonable balance between man and machine, and correspondingly, their entry together into another historical order.

References

Allen, J.P.: The Future of Small Business: Supporting Entrepreneurs in the Post-Crisis Era, Digital Entrepreneurship White Paper, learndigitalentrepreneurship.com (2020). https://www.learndigitalentrepreneurship.com/wp-content/uploads/2020/04/The-Future-of-Small-Business-v2.pdf

Atkeson, A., Kehoe, P.J.: The transition to a new economy after the Second Industrial Revolution; Working Papers 606, Federal Reserve Bank of Minneapolis (2001). https://ideas.repec.org/p/fip/fedmwp/606.html

Atkeson, A., Kehoe, P.: Modeling the transition to a new economy: lessons from two technological revolutions. Am. Econ. Rev. **97**(1), 64–88 (2007)

Audretsch, D.B., Moog, P.: Democracy and Entrepreneurship, Research Article (2020). https://doi.org/10.1177/1042258720943307

Baker, T., Welter, F.: Contextual Entrepreneurship: An Interdisciplinary Perspective (2018). https://www.nowpublishers.com/article/Details/ENT-078

Bundesregierung: Deutschland kommt voran. Jahresbericht der Bundesregierung 2016/17, Presse- und Informationsamt der Bundesregierung (2017). https://www.bundesregierung.de/resource/blob/975292/735564/b86c6fa8ecdf97109c4ae467ab9b3994/jahresbericht-der-bundesregierung-2016-2017-download-data.pdf

Dogaru, L.: The Main Goals of the Fourth Industrial Revolution. Renewable Energy Perspectives, Published by Elsevier B.V.; Procedia Manufacturing 46, pp. 397–401 (2020). www.sciencedirect.com; 2351–9789 © 2020 The Authors; https://pdf.sciencedirectassets.com/306234/

Duignan, B.: Inventors and Inventions of the Industrial Revolution, Encyclopædia Britannica, Inc. (2021). https://www.britannica.com/list/inventors-and-inventions-of-the-industrial-revolution

Ematinger, R.: Von der Industrie 4.0 zum Geschaftsmodell 4.0. Springer Gabler (2017). ISSN 2197–6708. https://doi.org/10.1007/978-3-658-19474-1

European Parliament: What is artificial intelligence and how is it used? (2020). https://www.europarl.europa.eu/news/ro/headlines/society/20200827STO85804/ce-este-inteligenta-artificiala-si-cum-este-utilizata

Griffin, E.: A Short History of the British Industrial Revolution, 2nd ed., Red Globe Press (2018). https://www.macmillanihe.com/page/detail/A-Short-History-of-the-British-Industrial-Revolution/?K=9781352003109

Hilbert, M.: Digital technology and social change: the digital transformation of society from a historical perspective Digital technology and social change: the digital transformation of society from a historical perspective. Dialogues Clin. Neurosci. **22**(2), 189–194 (2020). https://doi.org/10.31887/DCNS.2020.22.2/mhilbert; PMCID: PMC7366943; PMID: 32699519; https://www.ncbi.nlm.nih.gov/pmc/articles/PMC7366943/

Lungu, M.: Factors determining company performance in the IT industry. Manag. Market. Chall. Knowl. Soc. **15**(1), 59–77 (2020). https://doi.org/10.2478/mmcks-2020-0004

Milićević, S., Petrović, J., Đorđević, N.: ICT as a factor of destination competitiveness: the case of the republics of former Yugoslavia. Manag. Market. Chall. Knowl. Soc. **15**(3), 381–392 (2020). https://doi.org/10.2478/mmcks-2020-0022

Nefiodow, L.: The Sixth Kondratieff–The new Long Wave of the Global Economy, Almanac: Kondratieff waves: Cycles, Crises, and Forecasts (2014). https://www.sociostudies.org/almanac/articles/the_sixth_kondratieff_-_the_new_long_wave_of_the_global_economy/

Nefiodow, L.: The Sixth Kondratieff: A New Long Wave in the Global Economy (2017). ISBN-10: 1545485143; ISBN-13: 978-1545485149. https://www.amazon.com/Sixth-Kondratieff-Long-Global-Economy/dp/1545485143

Nuvolari, A.: Understanding successive industrial revolutions: a development block approach. Environ. Innov. Soc. Transit. **32**, 33–44 (2018). https://doi.org/10.1016/j.eist.2018.11.002

Popovici, A.A.: Ciclurile Kondratiev, Referat la seminarul nr. 16 din 22.V.2018 [Kondratiev Cycles, Report on seminar no. 16 of 22.V.2018], https://youtu.be/D93iDP1EccM; https://www.academia.edu/38569512/A_A_Popovici_Ciclurile_Kondratiev_%C5%9Fi_economia_global%C4%83_22_V_2018

Rifkin, J.: The Third Industrial Revolution; How Lateral Power is transforming Energy, the Economy, and the World. St. Martin's Press (2011)

Schumpeter, J.A.: Business Cycles: A Theoretical, Historical, and Statistical Analysis of the Capitalist Process, 1st ed. McGraw-Hill Book Company, Inc., New York and London (1939). https://www.mises.at/static/literatur/Buch/schumpeter-business-cycles-a-theoretical-historical-and-statistical-analysis-of-the-capitalist-process.pdf

Schneider, C.: Digitalisierung nachhaltig gestalten. Ein Impulspapier des Umweltbundesamtes (2019). https://www.researchgate.net/publication/340789954_Digitalisierung_nachhaltig_gestalten_Ein_Impulspapier_des_Umweltbundesamtes

Schwab, K.: The Fourth Industrial Revolution: what it means, how to respond, World Economic Forum (2016). https://www.weforum.org/agenda/2016/01/the-fourth-industrial-revolution-what-it-means-and-how-to-respond/

Vaclav, S.: Creating the Twentieth Century: Technical Innovations of 1867–1914 and Their Lasting Impact, 1st ed. Oxford University Press (2005)

Vrânceanu, D., Țuclea, C., Țigu, G.: Price search behaviour in digital markets–a perspective from Romania. Manag. Market. Chall. Knowl. Soc. **15**(2), 219–235 (2020). https://doi.org/10.2478/mmcks-2020-0014

The Impact of Covid-19 on Food Prices in Romania

Drăcea Lăcrămioara Alina, Mărăcine Daniela, Oprea Iulia, Girip Maria, and Suvorov Nicolae

Abstract During the pandemic caused by the SARS-COV-2 virus, the agri-food sector in Romania and Europe suffered due to the consumer market and the restrictions imposed to reduce the spread of the virus. Consumer prices in Romania in 2019 were optimal in terms of consumer price index and so was the aggregate consumer price index. Given the current situation and the obligation to adapt to the new conditions for a good development of the supply and purchase of food products for the population, the questions to be answered are "How has COVID-19 impacted the food market in Romania?" and "How have the prices of agro-food products evolved in Romania?". These aspects will be the subject of the analysis of this article, which will also discuss other relevant aspects that identify the impact of the pandemic on the Romanian market and the repercussions that followed to combat a food crisis at a national level and a financial crisis among the civilian population.

Keywords Covid-19 · Price · Consumption · Market · Evolution

1 Introduction

At the end of 2019, when SARS-COV-2 appeared in China, it seemed to be just a new virus among the multitude of already existing viruses, but it proved to be a real threat to the entire population of the globe and daily activities. The skepticism with which the contagion and spreading power of this virus were initially viewed quickly turned into an outbreak and then became a full-blown pandemic.

On the territory of Romania, the first confirmed cases were observed approximately 3 months after the appearance of COVID-19 on the Asian continent, namely on February 26, 2020, and it took no more than 3 weeks for the country to enter into total quarantine (Romanian Ministry of Health 2020).

D. L. Alina (✉) · M. Daniela · O. Iulia · G. Maria · S. Nicolae
Bucharest University of Economic Studies, Bucharest, Romania

A. M. Dima and M. Kelemen (eds.), *Digitalization and Big Data for Resilience and Economic Intelligence*, Springer Proceedings in Business and Economics, https://doi.org/10.1007/978-3-030-93286-2_9

For a year, Romania has gone through several measures taken by the authorities to combat and limit the spread of the SARS-COV-2 virus, from more restrictive ones, such as total quarantine and the closure of several economic agents in the field of hospitality, to some milder one, or even their relaxation or elimination.

The socio-economic effects of COVID-19 are devastating and unprecedented both globally and nationally. Due to the measures adopted, several sectors have been affected, and economic agents have suffered substantial losses, an example of this is those in the HORECA field who during 2020 had to keep their locations mostly closed, give up some of the staff or even give up business (Toderiță and Popescu 2020).

In 2018, Romania experienced the largest economic development in the last 10 years, according to GDP, but starting with December 2019, when the global spread of COVID-19 turned into a pandemic, restrictive measures were taken to control the disease. The measures imposed in Romania compared to other EU Member States were very drastic and necessary to reduce the cases of disease, but also deaths (Iancu et al. 2021).

Because of the country's Lockdown due to the SARS-COV-2 pandemic, the distribution of domestic and international products occurred with delivery delays, the Romanian agri-food markets were closed, and the agricultural sellers incurred great financial losses due to perishable products, as well as the lack of food storage places. In addition, the restrictions caused a series of unpleasant events such as the closure of schools, but the continuation of classes in online format, and the significant increase in the number of unemployed people whose jobs could not be done in the online environment (Aday and Aday 2020).

The aggressive restrictions that were imposed at the beginning of 2020 led to the formation of two separate modes of consumption, the first is aimed at purchasing food products online or by phone and preparing them in homes, and the second is the purchase of already prepared food products (from restaurants). These changes forced overnight the development of new acquisition concepts for the reduction of HORECA losses, as well as for the alimentary satisfaction of the population (Leddy et al. 2020).

The fear of getting or spreading the virus has aroused concern among the population and with the restriction of social life and its move to the online environment, depression and anxiety have developed, having a strong emotional impact on the inhabitants (Teufel et al. 2020).

The central objective of this research is to identify the impact of the pandemic on the Romanian food market and the reverberations of the economic changes generated by it at a national level but also to determine the relationship between the consumer price index and gross domestic product. This research is based on the literature in the field and aims to analyze the price dynamics of the main basic products of the Romanian population.

2 Literature Review

SARS-COV-2 has had a considerable economic impact globally, due to the restrictions imposed to reduce the number of cases, which led to an economic bottleneck, affecting most sectors that represented a pole of economic growth.

The pandemic has greatly affected all economic areas of the world, especially the HORECA field, with additional activities such as restaurants, grocery stores, agriculture being severely affected, and the prices of products in a fluctuating state. These containment measures, along with the high degree of uncertainty and deteriorating labor market conditions, are expected to continue to affect supply and demand.

In the European Union, the Commission has proposed a number of measures to support financially and economically all Member States affected by the coronavirus crisis. At the European level, it is trying to support the economic recovery of tourism by providing liquidity for companies in the field. The Commission, through the European Investment Fund, has provided EUR 8 billion for around 100,000 small enterprises affected by the crisis (European Commission 2020).

The European Commission offers to those companies whose economic activity is severely affected by the COVID-19 crisis a non-reimbursable financial support for the recovery of working capital, the maximum number of beneficiaries of this scheme being 100,500.

The non-reimbursable financial support has a value between 2000 euros and 150,000 euros, and the allocated money is granted in the form of a percentage of the turnover that the company registers at the last financial year ended 31.12.2019.

The enterprises eligible for the financing program are obliged to fulfill several conditions simultaneously (the turnover must be at least 5,000 euros at the date of the last financial year ended, they have obtained an emergency certificate issued by the Government, hold at least 15% of the financial aid received).

The value of the non-reimbursable financial support granted for the company differs depending on their turnover. In the enterprises where the turnover registered a value between 5,000 and 13,500 euros, the non-reimbursable aid will be 2,000 euros, and in the enterprises where the turnover exceeds 13,500 euros, they will be granted a non-reimbursable financial aid of 15% of the turnover, but without exceeding 150,000 euros.

The areas eligible for financing with non-reimbursable funds necessary for the establishment of capital are restaurants, cafes, hotels, travel agencies, and other fields of activity.

The eligible expenses that the grant can cover are coverage of due or current debts, purchase of stocks of SME materials, payment of rent, purchase of medical protective equipment, purchase of equipment, and payment of debts to the state budget.

Undertakings benefiting from non-reimbursable funds are obliged to assume a series of obligations, according to the financing contract they sign, such as to submit a progress report on the expenses within 180 days of the date when the funds were allocated, to maintain or to supplement the number of employees compared to the moment of submitting the application and mandatorily to keep all the documents related to this financing scheme for at least 10 years (Dumitrache 2020).

The loss of jobs has led to a decrease in economic activity, as well as an increase in unemployment. The EU and the Member States have adopted policy measures that will help mitigate the pandemic on labor markets in 2021–2022. According to ec.europa.eu, the unemployment rate has expected to rise in 2021 to 8.6%, compared to 7.7% in 2020, with a latent decrease in 2022 to 8.0%. The increase in unemployment in 2021 in the Member States is due to the efforts to phase out the emergency support measures granted in 2020, but also to the entry into the labor market of other people (European Commission 2020).

Although the European Commission and the World Trade Organization have tried to reduce the impact of SARS-COV-2 on the agri-food sector by adopting measures to condense customs procedures and break up trade barriers, there have been countries that have temporarily adopted export restrictions.

These prohibitions bring negative effects on the supply chain, affect the availability of food, and can build bottlenecks along the agri-food chain from the factors of production to distribution, encouraging the increase in prices and their volatility (WTO 2020).

Experts at the European Central Bank believe that inflation will experience large volatility in future quarters, and the constraints of fundamental factors influencing prices will remain moderate due to declining demand and will have gradual intensifications, depending on the economic recovery.

Thus, HICP inflation is expected to progress sharply from 0.3% in 2020 to 1.5% in 2021, reaching 2.0% in the fourth quarter of 2021, falling to 1.2% in 2022, and then rising to 1.4% in 2023.

This increase is due to a sharp acceleration in the inflation of the HICP on energy and food products, the change in values within the HICP, which has modified consumption behavior in the context of the pandemic.

According to the European Central Bank projections, HICP inflation for food and energy will rise from 0.7% in 2020 to 1.3% in 2023 and will develop intense quarterly volatility in 2021 and 2022.

The economic situation of a country can be determined by the analysis of indicators, such as inflation rate, gross domestic product (GDP), consumer price index (CPI), unemployment rate, but also the harmonized index of consumer prices (HICP) (European Central Bank 2021).

Inflation can be defined as a large-scale increase in the prices of goods and services; rising inflation leads to a decrease in purchasing power and affects the general expenditure of the population, but also to a slowdown in the economy.

The average monthly rate of inflation is the percentage by which prices have risen or decreased over a given period. This index is calculated as a geometric average of one month to another of the consumer price index having as a basis of calculation the value of the current month from which the value of the comparison base of the previous month is subtracted (which is equal to 100).

Average annual inflation rate—the growth of consumer prices in a year compared to the precedent year. This rate shall be calculated as a ratio, expressed as a percentage, between the average price index in a year and that of the anterior year, from which 100 shall be deducted. In turn, the average price indices are calculated as simple arithmetic averages of the monthly indices for every year, determined against the same basis (National Institute of Statistics 2021).

The Consumer Price Index (CPI) quantifies the overall progress of the prices of goods bought on the market and the tariffs of services utilized by the population in a certain period compared to the previous period (reference period). This indicator is a sensitive barometer that aims to synthesize and reflect the evolution of prices and tariffs of the diversity of products and services that go into the consumption of the population, and the calculation instrument is adapted to the objectives pursued, the concrete conditions, and the requirements to ensure domestic and international comparability (Mali 2010).

Currently, the knowledge stage in the field identifies and manages to take into account the correlation between the consumer price index and the volume of the GDP index determined at the national level between February 2020 and January 2021.

Following the analysis of the literature, it was been considered relevant and as a novelty element to carry out an analysis of the topical statistical data in the present paper in the context of the pandemic as a determining factor for the evolution of the consumer price index.

3 Methodology

This paper addresses a topical theme and aims to analyze, at the national level, the evolution of prices and sales of basic foodstuffs, as well as the impact of COVID-19 on the food market in Romania.

The analysis is oriented toward clarifying the concepts: inflation, the index of consumer prices, and GDP with their peculiarities, as well as influencing factors. Aspects about the SARS-COV-2 virus, as well as the correlation between GDP and the consumer price index, are also been presented.

The statistical data collected from the National Statistical Institute (NIS) based on both qualitative and quantitative statistics will be analyzed, and we will use the Pearson correlation coefficient and the Durbin Watson test to determine the relationship between the consumer price index and gross domestic product.

The analysis of statistical data is used to correctly and effectively assess the current situation in Romania with regard to the food market, highlighting the need for measures to recover the economy, both at the national and European level. It is important to focus on adapting to constant market changes and price fluctuations.

The Consumer Price Index (CPI) is calculated as a Laspeyres fixed-base index. From January 2021, the calculation of monthly fixed-base indices is made using the average price and the weights for 2019 (year 2019 = 100), which are determined based on the average expenditure in the Family Budget Survey.

The standard formula for calculating the Laspeyres index is

$$Ll_0 = \sum_{n=1}^{\infty} I_{l0}\left(\frac{P_0 Q_0}{\sum P_0 Q_0}\right), \tag{1}$$

Ll_0 = the aggregate index for the present month (l) from 2021 correlated with the reference year 2019;

Il_0 = current month's index compared to the 2019 average per aggregation step;

$\frac{P_0 Q_0}{\sum P_0 Q_0}$ = weights for aggregation steps (relative importance of average monthly expenditure per household for 2019).

Determination of price indices according to the variety:

$$I_{vi} = P_l^{vi} / \overline{\boldsymbol{P}}_0^{vi} \times 100 \tag{2}$$

$\boldsymbol{P}_l^{vi}$ = the price of the variety registered in the present month (l);

$\overline{\boldsymbol{P}}_0^{vi}$ = the annual average of the prices of the variety i in 2019.

The price of variety i registered in the present month ($Pl\ vi$) is calculated as a simple arithmetic mean from the three decadal records, as follows:

$$P_l^{vi} = P_{l1}^{vi} + P_{l2}^{vi} + P_{l3}^{vi} / 3 \text{ or } P_l^{vi} = P_{l2}^{vi} \tag{3}$$

where $\boldsymbol{P}^{vi}{}_{l1\ldots l3}$ = the nominal prices observed for 30 years in the current month, for the variety v_i.

The second formula applies to most assortments of non-food goods and services for which the collection is made only during the period 10–17 of the reference month.

The determination of price indices at assortment level, as a geometric average of the indices of varieties, is according to the formula:

$$I_{l/19}^{Si} = \sqrt[n]{\prod\nolimits_{i=1}^{n} ivi} \ldots, n \le 68 \tag{4}$$

n = number of price/tariff collection centers.

Estimation of indices at the stage of groups of food, non-food commodities and services as a weighted arithmetic average of the indices at the level of expenditure items included in the group, as follows:

$$I_{l/19}^{Ci} = \Sigma I_{l/19}^{Pi}\left(W_0^{Pi} / \Sigma W_0^{Pi}\right) \tag{5}$$

$I^{Ci}{}_{l/19}$ = group price index in the current month (l) compared to the average of 2019;

$\sum I^{Pi}{}_{l/19}$ = post level price index in the current month (l) compared to the average of 2019;

${W_0}^{Pi}$ = the weight of the station P_i;

$\sum {W_0}^{Pi}$ = the share of the group of goods and services.

The Harmonized Index of Consumer Prices (HICP) is a set of EU consumer price indices, determined in accordance with a harmonized technique and a unique set of definitions. The HICP is primarily designed to assess price stability in the euro area and the convergence of price development in the EU, but also for comparison of inflation at the European level. As of January 2016, the HICP series has been published with the reference year 2015 = 100.

The national nomenclature of goods and services used in determining the CPI is made up of 54 categories of food products, 50 categories of services, and 112 categories of non-food goods relevant to the consumption of the population.

For the determination of HICP at the European level, the ordering of expenditures according to the consumption destination (ECOICOP—Classification of Individual Consumption by Destination) is applied, which reorganizes the posts in the national system. This classification guarantees the similarity of the indices at the European level and is configured in accordance with the EU regulation 792/2016, on 12 detailed sections, 47 groups, classes, sub-classes.

The CPI applied the "national" criterion of consumption, analyzing the consumption expenditures of the inhabitants, without taking into account whether they are made inside or outside the country.

The weights applied in determining the CPI are acquired from the Family Budget Survey (ABF) and come from the structure of the average monthly expenditures made by a household for the payment of goods and services useful for satisfying the living needs. The updating of the population's expenditure structure is carried out annually. Therefore, from the beginning of 2021, to calculate the CPI, the weights obtained from the scheme of average expenses made by a household during 2019 are used.

Implementation of EC Regulation (EC) No 1114/2010 on the minimum standards for the quality of HICP weights was adopted in 2012. For year *t*, it represents the use of data on the value of household monetary expenditures on final consumption from national accounts for year *t*-2 and of expenditures from the Survey of Family Budgets *t*-2 to obtain the shares of harmonized indices. The weights thus determined are then updated to the prices of December *t*-1.

The HICP measures changes in the evolution of prices and tariffs for goods and services that have occurred in Romania. Thus, the "domestic" principle is used for the construction of the HICP, taking into account the consumption of all households in the territory of the country, regardless of nationality, residential or social status, except foreign embassies located on the territory of Romania (National Institute of Statistics 2021).

The Pearson correlation coefficient is determined as a fraction between the sum of the multiplied deviations and the multiplied standard deviations and evaluates the intensity of the network of the two variables. The sign of the coefficient indicates the direction, i.e., the way in which variables are reported, and the amount of the coefficient shows the intensity, a higher intensity implying a value much closer to one.

The Pearson correlation coefficient is calculated using the formula.

$$r_{xy} = \frac{\text{cov}(x, y)}{s_x s_y} = \frac{s_{xy}}{s_x \cdot s_y} \frac{\sum_{i=1}^{n} (x_i - \overline{x})(y_i - \overline{y})}{\sqrt{\left[\sum_{i=1}^{n} (x_i - \overline{x})^2\right]\left[\sum_{i=1}^{n} (y_i - \overline{y})^2\right]}} \quad (6)$$

where r_{xy} = The coefficient of Pearson correlation, x_i = single values of the variable, $\overline{x}$ = the average of single values of x, y_i = single values of y, and $\overline{y}$ = the average of the single values of y.

The Durbin-Watson test detects the correlation between the residual values and the variables of the model. This test is based on the calculation of the DW value and through the comparison between the tabular value DW and the test, and it can be observed that the existence of autocorrelation is as follows:

$$\text{DW} = \frac{\sum_{i=1}^{n} \left(\widehat{\varepsilon}_i - \widehat{\varepsilon}_{i-1}\right)^2}{\sum_{i=1}^{n} \widehat{\varepsilon}_i^2}, \quad (7)$$

where DW = Durbin-Watson test value, $\widehat{\varepsilon}$ = residual values.

This value is compared with the values d1 and d2 in the Durbin Watson test table according to the level of significance, and the decision can be determined according to the following rules.

4 Analysis/Results Interpretation

This paper brings a new highlight to the changes that the COVID-19 pandemic brought to the goods market. After this pandemic, the exchanges of goods will never be the same, considering the pace and the mobility of the assets. Even in the food industry, major changes arose and switched the consumption price index—prices began to grow for subsistence goods like cereals, oil, flour, and other related products.

But seeing this only at a smaller scale does not highlight the trend, therefore a much sizable analysis must be done, by the evidence brought by comparing GDP and prices. Having the information analyzed and combined in a single research is a necessary step for further studies that regard market changes during the pandemic.

The effects of the crisis caused by SARS-COV-2 are having repercussions, such as rising prices of agri-food products and even services. In order to provide food to the population, Romania decided to reduce exports of agro-food products in order to remain at a relatively normal price, but also to avoid the purchase of imported food products that come at much higher prices.

From the situation shown in Fig. 1, we can see a 3.2% increase in the consumer price in February 2021, compared to the same month of the previous year.

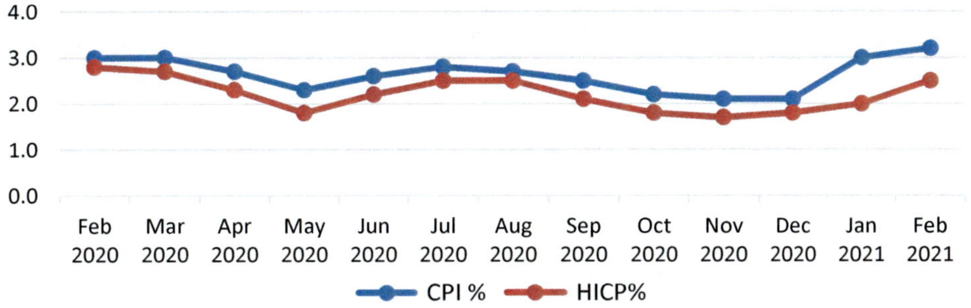

Fig. 1 Annual evolution of consumer prices (%). *Source* National Institute of Statistics

During 2020, the consumer price index registered a sharp decrease, reaching a percentage of 2.3 in May, which was reiterated by the first impact of COVID-19 on the food market.

During the period considered, we can see a permanent fluctuation in both the consumer price, with rates between 2% (minimum reached) in November and December 2020 and 3.2% (maximum achieved) in February 2021, as well as the harmonized index of consumer price, having rates between 1.6% (minimum reached) in November 2020 and 2.5% (maximum reached) in February 2021.

From March 2020 to February 2021, the average rate of consumer prices compared to the previous year (March 2019 to February 2020), determined according to the CPI, is 2.6%, while the average rate outlined on the basis of the HICP is 2.1%.

Following the data presented, of the total food products analyzed in Table 1, we see a significant decrease, amounting to 2.75% of the consumer price index in the period January 2021, i.e., 100.46%, compared to the period February 2020, i.e., 102.7% (National Institute of Statistics 2021) (see Table 2).

The main reasons why the consumer index registers significant decreases during the 2020 period are due to the increase in food prices, based on restrictive measures taken following the development of the epidemiological context regarding the SARS-COV-2 virus, which has imposed worldwide blocking of the running of goods for a specified period.

During the period under review, it was determined that products with low perishability recorded the highest values, following that in 2021 to experience a slight decrease, the main reason being to adapt and support farmers with European funds for keeping food prices relatively constant (Ministry of Agriculture and Rural Development 2020).

Table 1 Rules for determining the decision of the Durbin Watson test

$0 < DW < d1$	$d1 \leq DW \leq d2$	$D2 \leq DW \leq 4\text{-}d2$	$4\text{-}d2 \leq DW \leq 4\text{-}d1$	$4\text{-}d1 < DW < 4$
Positive autocorrelation	Indecision ←	Independence	Indecision →	Negative autocorrelation

Source Own processing using Ms Excel's data analysis

Table 2 Consumer price index and average monthly inflation rate

	February-21			Average monthly inflation rate	
	Compared to			Period 1 I–28 II	
	January-21	December-20	February-20	Year 2021	Year 2020
Food goods	100.46	101.09	102.70	0.5	0.8
Non-food goods	100.47	102.72	103.80	1.4	0.0
Services	100.20	100.45	102.32	0.2	0.4
Total	100.41	101.75	103.16	0.9	0.3

Source National Institute of Statistics

From the data presented in Fig. 2, where the value of the consumer price index of GDP in the period 2010–2019 is analyzed, we can see a constant decrease between the first and last year analyzed by 21.16%, while the volume index of GDP increased by 62.1% over the same period (Anghelache and Iacob 2020).

The financial crisis in Romania led to a short period of increase in the sales value of all products. As a Member State of the EU, it received financial support for the economic recovery of disadvantaged areas where GDP was less than 70% (especially in rural areas), the unemployment rate was reduced by supporting and developing qualification courses for integration into the labor market, but also by providing subsidies for the most affected economic sectors (Ministry of Agriculture and Rural Development 2020) (see Fig. 3).

From the data presented, we notice that there is a slight increase in the average price of most food products analyzed between 2019 and 2021. Especially for basic products, the visible impact is during 2020, when prices increased throughout the period, so we can see that cereals such as oats and sunflowers had increases of up to 0.16 Ron/kg, and 0.44 Ron/kg, respectively, beef 0.07 Ron/kg, eggs 0.03 Ron/piece,

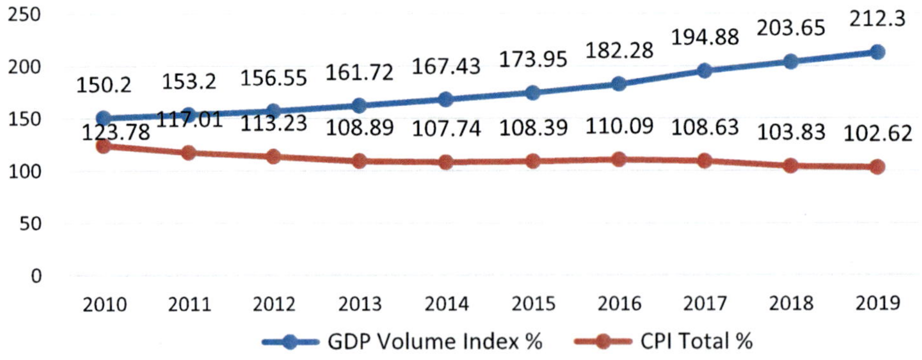

Fig. 2 Evolution of the consumer price index, GDP between 2010 and 2019 (%). *Source* National Institute of Statistics

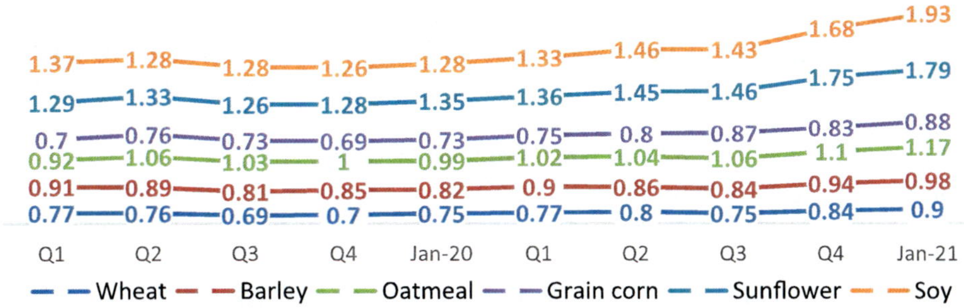

Fig. 3 Cereals price. *Source* National Institute of Statistics

cow milk 0.16 Ron/L. These increases are the result of the COVID-19 impact on the food market at both national and international levels due to the restriction of imports for a period.

There are also food products whose average prices have recorded decreases during the same time, by 2.06 Ron/kg for pork and by 0.7 Ron/kg in the case of potatoes. The reason for the price reduction is determined by the attention given to local producers.

During the analyzed period, demand increased too, just as the price of fruit and nuts; prices increased by 0.53 Ron/kg in the case of apples, by 0.14 Ron/kg for pears and 0.09 Ron/kg for walnuts.

It can be observed that the price in the category of live animal meat registers slightly ascending levels except for sheep meat, where the price had aggressive fluctuations from 4.20 Ron/kg to 10.22 Ron/kg, with an increase of 58.9% in a short period, returning, at an equally pronounced pace, to 5.00 Ron/kg at the end of 2020. These sudden price fluctuations are the result of limiting the export of live sheep meat.

We find that the average price of eggs during the analyzed period has experienced slight fluctuations, the highest price being recorded at the end of 2019, the beginning of 2020, and the beginning of 2021. The lowest recorded price, 0.51 Ron/piece, was observed in mid-2019.

The price per liter of cow's milk registered a steady increase, reaching at the beginning of 2021 the highest price of the analyzed period; as for the price of cow and sheep cheese, and that of honey, we can notice a slow increase (Toderiță and Popescu 2021).

4.1 Correlation Between Consumer Price Index and GDP Index Volume

To verify the influence of the consumer price index on GDP, an analysis based on the Pearson correlation coefficient is indicated. This analysis displays the level of connection of two variables and the intensity between them. The correlation coefficients (Consumer Price Index and GDP index volume) were calculated based on the available data with the Data Analysis program from MS Excel. They are shown in Table 3.

It can be observed the fact that there is a correlation coefficient of –0.81, which suggests a negative direct link.

Furthermore, we will establish the connections between Consumer Price Index (%) and GDP.

The function of analysis model is expressed based on the dependent and independent variables, which can be either unifactorial or multifactorial. The form is detailed as follows:

$$Y = a + b * X + \in, \tag{8}$$

where Y = the dependent variable, x = the independent variable, a = intercept, b = slope, and $\in$ = residual error (Katara 2021).

This model is identified using variables, and it can be used for verification and performing forecasts. The first autocorrelation order should be tested using the Durbin-Watson test.

For measuring the connection between Consumer Price Index (%) and GDP index volume (%), the below linear simple regression model can be considered (see Tables 4, 5 and 6).

It was identified a Multiple R (correlation coefficient) value of 0.813. This result means a close interdependence, i.e., when Consumer Price Index (%) increases, the GDP index volume (%) increases as well.

Table 3 Correlation variables

Indicators	GDP index volume (%)	Consumer price index (%)
GDP index volume (%)	1	–
Consumer price index (%)	−0.813348764	1

Source Own processing using Ms Excel's data analysis

Table 4 Linear model of simple regression between the consumer price index and GDP

Regression statistics	
Multiple R	0.813348764
R square	0.661536212
Adjusted R square	0.619228239
Standard error	13.52235833
Observations	10

Source Own processing using Ms Excel's data analysis

Table 5 Indicators of Anova

ANOVA	*df*	*SS*	*MS*	*F*	Significance *F*
Regression	1	2859.146	2859.146	15.63621	0.004210757
Residual	8	1462.833	182.8542	–	–
Total	9	4321.979	–	–	–

Source Own processing using Ms Excel's data analysis

Table 6 Values of regression coefficients

	Coefficients	Standard error	*t* stat	P-value	Lower 95%	Upper 95%	Lower 95%	Upper 95%
Intercept	490.74	79.80	6.14	0.00027	306.70	674.78	306.7	674.78
X variable 1	−2.85	0.72	−3.95	0.00421	−4.51	−1.18	−4.51	−1.18

Source Own processing using Ms Excel's data analysis

The determination coefficient (R Square) result was 0.661, which points out that GDP index volume is explained by the Consumer Price Index at a 66.1% rate.

In the above table it can be observed, the following validity indicators of the model. The *F* parameter value is compared with the critical F and may confirm or not the null hypothesis (the model's validity).

Therefore, the *F* value is 15.63 and the critical *F* is 0.004.

Considering this, it is observed that the *F* value compared to the critical *F* is considerably higher, and in connection with the importance level recorded by *F* (Significance *F*) being lower than 0.05 it can be said that the model is valid.

To confirm the validity, the function coefficients must be different from 0, meaning that the null hypothesis must be rejected. By comparing t-State with the critical value *t* (−3.95) it has been noticed that the two coefficients have a value *t* higher than the critical value, the confidence intervals do not have the null value, the value *P* is below the threshold of 0.05 so the null hypothesis is rejected.

To eliminate the potential first-order correlation, the residual values will be tested using the Durbin-Watson test. A value of 0.509 was generated for DW, which indicates a positive autocorrelation scenario. Taking into account all these aspects, the regression function can be written as follows:

$$\text{GDP} = -2.85 * \text{CPI}(\%) + 490.74. \tag{9}$$

From this function, it can be seen that the coefficient *x* (consumer price index) is –2.85, i.e., when the consumer price index value expands by one unit, the value of GDP will be reduced by 2.85 units.

There are several factors that have a high impact on GDP values: on the one hand, the stimulation of consumption in Romania, and on the other hand, the low investment flow, generated by the financial crisis.

5 Conclusions

From the lack of labor to the 'overnight' change in consumption patterns, the recent crisis puts substantial pressure on the entire agri-food sector of the European Union and, in particular, on small farmers. What remains a universal constant is that people have to eat; agriculture, in this context, must stand and ensure food security.

The analysis of data in the period 2010–2019 on the volume index of GDP shows that it has registered an alert increase throughout the last years, going up by 62.1% from 2019 to 2010.

Cereals are an important source of food for both humans and animals since ancient times are considered among the first steps of agricultural activity due to resistance to storage conditions.

The largest increase in prices was found for sunflower products, which increased by 0.44% in 2021 compared to 2020, and the smallest price increase in this period (more precisely 0.8%) was recorded for barley. Vegetables are foods rich in nutrients such as protein, vegetable fats, vitamins, and minerals. In Romania, vegetable consumption has increased considerably in recent years, and vegetable prices have been rising sharply, especially in 2020.

In the analyzed period, the price of fruit and nuts has recorded a gradual increase as early as 2020, by 0.53 Ron/kg for apples, 0.14 Ron/kg for pears, and 0.09 Ron/kg for nuts. Prices of products have increased at the same time with the demand for such goods. Additionally, the periods when fruits and nuts have the highest prices are in cold seasons when production is declining.

From the data referring to the average price of cow and sheep cheese, respectively, as well as the price of honey, we can see a slow increase, the highest price being recorded in the last month analyzed.

The correlation coefficient (Multiple R) with the value 0.813 reflects a close interdependence between the Consumer Price Index (%) and the volume of the GDP index (%) and shows that while one variable increases, the other one also increases.

The determination coefficient (R Square) result was 0.661, which points out that GDP index volume is explained by the Consumer Price Index with a 66.1% rate.

While using a model's case, the F value is 15.63 and the F critical value F is 0.004; it is considered that the F critical versus F value is substantially higher, and it can be stated that the model is valid.

After comparing t-State with the critical value t (-3.95) it has been noticed that the two coefficients have a value t higher than the critical value, the confidence intervals do not have the null value, the value P is below the threshold of 0.05, so the null hypothesis was rejected.

The harsh health and economic crisis generated by the SARS-COV-2 virus is uncertain now, and the most negative estimates show that it will end in 5 years. Forecasts show that the pandemic will deepen its manifestation by generating new periods of social distance, economic decline, and traffic restrictions.

HICP inflation is expected to progress sharply from 0.3% in 2020 to 1.5% in 2021, reaching 2.0% in the fourth quarter of 2021, falling to 1.2% in 2022, and then rising to 1.4% in 2023.

It is inferred that in 2021, the “food” component of HICP inflation will suffer a significant decrease because of the COVID pandemic and then increase by mid-2022, reaching 1.9% in 2023.

Between January 2020 and January 2021, from the analyses carried out, we found that all products are in the trend of growth compared to the same period of last year. The growth is determined by several factors such as drought, decrease in agricultural activities as well as the COVID-19 crisis, which caused countries to keep a good part of their grain, and importing and export decreased during this period of reference.

Several aspects mark the increase in vegetable prices, such as the fact that many foods are imported due to the climate of the country, which does not allow their production during the winter, and demand and supply represent important criteria for calculating the price. The food that is produced in the country has a high price because in recent times the world has been making the transition from physical to intellectual work and there are fewer and fewer farmers willing to work on the market. Lastly, the COVID-19 crisis seriously affected agriculture in 2020, and for its recovery, the European Commission has proposed a number of measures aimed at financially supporting farmers in the economic gap.

The high prices of fruit and nuts are driven by increased population awareness of the benefits of eating fruit and nuts, the increased level of consumers who prefer healthy food, habits in ("fashion") borrowed from the West, from more developed countries, who consume such products in much larger quantities.

In the future, an analysis of market changes should be considered regarding prices with a 10-year scale before the last economic crisis, with the tendencies and domains that suffered changes and GDP and 10 years after pandemic. The numbers could also be represented as a sinusoidal curve so the trends will be observed better. Nonetheless, the pandemic came with changes that can be seen at this moment, but the real changes can be observed in a 10-year period, by comparing the conclusion and results brought by this paper—this article is just a snapshot and in 10-years’ time after a thorough analysis, the whole picture could be observed.

References

Aday, S., Aday, M.: Impact of COVID-19 on the food supply chain. Food Qual. Saf. **4**(4), 167–180 (2020)

Anghelache, C., Iacob Ș. V.: Analysis of the evolution of consumer prices in Romania in 2019. Rom. Stat. Rev. (Suppl. 5), 3–17 (2020)

Dumitrache, M.: European Funds 2020: Covid-19 Affected Firms will be able to obtain Capital Working Grants. Academia de Finanțare (2020). https://academiadefinantare.ro/fonduri-europene-2020-firmele-afectate-de-covid-19-vor-putea-obtine-granturi-pentru-capital-de-lucru/. Accessed 2021/04/22

European Central Bank: ECB Staff Macroeconomic Projections for the Euro Area, pp. 2–13. European Central Bank, Frankfurt (2021)

European Commission: Directorate General for Economic and Financial Affairs. European economic forecast: Autumn 2020, Publications Office (2020). https://doi.org/10.2765/878338

Iancu, I., Darab, C., Cirstea, S.: The effect of the COVID-19 pandemic on the electricity consumption in Romania. Energies **14**(11), 3146 (2021). https://doi.org/10.3390/en14113146

Katara, H.: Regression Formula. WallStreetMojo (2021). https://www.wallstreetmojo.com/regression-formula/. Accessed 20 August 2021

Leddy, A., Weiser, S., Palar, K., Seligman, H.: A conceptual model for understanding the rapid COVID-19–related increase in food insecurity and its impact on health and healthcare. Am. J. Clin. Nutr. **112**(5), 1162–1163 (2020). https://doi.org/10.1093/ajcn/nqaa226

Mali, C.: Perfection and harmonization of the methodology for calculating the Consumer Price Index in Romania. [Symposium presentation]. In: The Symposium Consumer basket and inflation dynamics. Methodological aspects and problems of interpretation. National Bank of Romania, Bucharest (2010, January 26). https://www.bnro.ro/Cosul-de-consum-si-dinamica-inflatiei.-Aspecte-metodologice-si-probleme-de-interpretare-5151.aspx

Ministry of Agriculture and Rural Development: [Measure 21 fiche-Specific measure for exceptional temporary support under the EAFRD in response to the COVID outbreak] (2020). https://www.madr.ro/docs/minister/fisa-tehnica-m-21-update-24.09.2020.pdf. Accessed 2021/04/22

National Institute of Statistics of Romania: Evolution of consumption price in February 2021 (2021). https://insse.ro/cms/sites/default/files/com_presa/com_pdf/ipc02r21.pdf. Accessed 2021/04/22

National Institute of Statistics: [Consumer price index (CPI)], Annex Methodological specifications (2021). https://insse.ro/cms/ro/content/indicele-pre%C8%9Burilor-de-consum-ipc-70 . Accessed 25 April 2021

Romanian Ministry of Health: [Quarantine information] (2020). http://www.ms.ro/2020/02/26/29277/. Accessed 25 April 2021

Teufel, M., Schweda, A., Dörrie, N., Musche, V., Hetkamp, M., Weismüller, B., et al.: Not all world leaders use Twitter in response to the COVID-19 pandemic: impact of the way of Angela Merkel on psychological distress, behaviour and risk perception. J. Public Health **42**(3), 644–646 (2020). https://doi.org/10.1093/pubmed/fdaa060

Toderiță, A., Popescu, R.: How do we ensure Romania's food security during the pandemic. The role of small and medium-sized farms. CRPE Policy Brief nr. 44, pp. 4–8, Romanian Center for European Policies (2020). https://www.crpe.ro/wp-content/uploads/2020/04/CRPE_Policy-Brief-44.pdf. Accessed 24 April 2021

World Trade Organization: Responding to the covid-19 pandemic with open and predictable trade in agricultural and food products, WT/GC/208; G/AG/30 (2020). https://docs.wto.org/dol2fe/Pages/FE_Search/FE_S_S006.aspx?DataSource=Cat&query=%40Sybol%3d%22G%2fAG%2f30%22+OR+%40Symbol%3d%22G%2fAG%2f30%2f*%22&Language=English&Context=ScriptedSearches&languageUIChanged=true

Fiscal Consolidation in Romania in the Wake of the COVID-19 Pandemic: How Much and How Fast?

Bogdan Andrei Dumitrescu and Cătălina Adriana Hândoreanu

Abstract The economic shock generated by the COVID-19 pandemic and prior procyclical fiscal policies has left Romania with a severely deteriorated budgetary balance in 2020 and a rapidly rising public debt. Policymakers are confronted with difficult choices amid the need to balance restoring fiscal sustainability with an adequate response to the economic shock generated by the pandemic. By resorting to public debt equations, this paper projects the public debt evolution in Romania during 2021–2030 in light of the announced fiscal consolidation plans for 2021–2024 and afterward by proposing a continuation in the reduction of the budgetary deficit, albeit at a slower pace. In order to account for possible variations in the determinants of public debt, a sensitivity analysis is performed, considering both optimistic and pessimistic scenarios. The paper concludes that fiscal consolidation under the current plan for 2021–2024 and going further until 2030 at the proposed pace is essential for keeping public debt near prudent levels. Moreover, under a pessimistic scenario, even with a successful fiscal consolidation, considered to be represented by an exit from the Excessive Deficit Procedure in 2025 and a reduction in the budgetary deficit to around 1% of GDP in 2030, public debt in Romania could be at the end of the interval considered in the vicinity of the 60% threshold set by the Maastricht Treaty.

Keywords Public debt sustainability · Fiscal consolidation · Public debt equations

1 Introduction

The outbreak of the COVID-19 pandemic in 2020 has had a severe impact on economies and fiscal positions around the world. The majority of countries have witnessed severe drops in the economic growth rate, and in many instances, it turned negative. Also, budgetary balances were affected, on the one hand by the decrease of revenues as a result of a less intense economic activity and on the other hand by

B. A. Dumitrescu (✉) · C. A. Hândoreanu
Bucharest University of Economic Studies, Bucharest, Romania
e-mail: bogdan.dumitrescu@fin.ase.ro

A. M. Dima and M. Kelemen (eds.), *Digitalization and Big Data for Resilience and Economic Intelligence*, Springer Proceedings in Business and Economics, https://doi.org/10.1007/978-3-030-93286-2_10

expenditure increases needed to cope with the public health situation and with the economic and social costs of the pandemic.

According to the data from the National Institute of Statistics and the Ministry of Finance, in 2020 Romania experienced a real GDP contraction of 3.9%, while the budgetary balance reached a very high deficit, i.e., 9.1% of GDP. To the budgetary imbalance contributed: prior procyclical fiscal policies, leading to an increase in the budgetary deficit during 2015–2019 from 0.6 to 4.4% of GDP (ESA2010 methodology, data from the Ministry of Finance), despite economic growth averaging above 4% per year (based on data from the National Institute of Statistics); the measures taken in light of the COVID-19 pandemic in 2020 with a net budgetary impact estimated by the Romanian Fiscal Council (2021) at around 1.2% of GDP; the economic shock generated by the health crisis, which decreased budgetary revenues. Given the breach of the 3% threshold for the budgetary deficit in 2019, the European Commission launched the Excessive Deficit Procedure against Romania in 2020. Considering these very high levels of the budgetary deficit, a fiscal consolidation in Romania is inevitable in the coming years in order to stabilize public debt and gradually reduce it to more prudent levels.

Thus, given past policies, the fiscal space of Romanian authorities to stimulate the economy in face of the COVID-19 pandemic was very limited. The budgetary situation in 2020 was similar to the one faced by Romania in the previous recession from 2009 to 2010, although back then public debt was below 25% of GDP. At that moment, as shown by Dumitrescu (2015a), Romania was forced to undertake a very fast fiscal consolidation mainly as the result of the financing constraints, Romania initially losing market access. The economic and social costs of the fast consolidation process, as the budgetary deficit was reduced by more than 8 pp during 2010–2015, were substantial. In the current crisis, financing needs are being met more smoothly, which will allow fiscal policymakers to undertake a more gradual fiscal consolidation, despite public debt being above 45% of GDP.

We believe that the size and pace of the fiscal consolidation in Romania will be driven in the coming years by two elements. First, the Excessive Deficit Procedure will exert significant pressures to reduce the budgetary deficit below 3% of GDP. Under the current plans of the Government, the trajectory involves a small adjustment of the budgetary deficit to 8.2% in 2022, followed by a more alert one to 3% of GDP until 2024. Given the relatively large size of the needed adjustment and the fact that in 2024, Romania will hold local, presidential, and general elections we believe that deficits of around 3% of GDP will be possible only in 2025. Moreover, the fiscal consolidation will have economic and social costs, although they can be partially alleviated by the significant funds allocated to Romania from the Next Generation EU instrument. Second, the fiscal consolidation after 2025 should be driven by the need to bring public debt to more prudent levels. In an analysis conducted by the National Bank of Romania (2015), it was identified a sustainability threshold for the public debt in Romania at around 45%, above which the probability of a recession increases by 50%. This limit could be considered a relatively safe level for the public debt and policymakers should implement measures to reach it. However, given that this level is already outrun and public debt is difficult to reduce, we will consider that fiscal consolidation will be driven by the target to bring public debt to a level of 50% of GDP in 2030.

Against this background, using the deterministic approach, the present paper assesses the trajectory of the public debt in Romania during 2021–2030 under the necessary fiscal consolidation, driven by the two elements mentioned above. Also, it determines the pace of fiscal consolidation that is necessary and feasible after the 2025–2030 interval. An important question is if a successful fiscal consolidation will manage to keep public debt in the vicinity of a prudent level. Another question is related to the influence of variations in the macroeconomic framework on the public debt trajectory, which can be highlighted with a sensitivity analysis.

The remainder of this paper is organized as follows: Sect. 2 provides an overview of the scientific literature, Sect. 3 presents the methodology, Sect. 4 reveals the interpretation of the results, while Sect. 5 draws the conclusions and implications for policymakers.

2 Literature Review

Identifying a prudent public debt level for an economy is not straightforward, although the dedicated literature provides us with some insights in this regard. First, several authors highlight the differences between developed and emerging countries. For example, Cecchetti et al. (2011) point to a threshold regarding the public debt for developed economies, above which economic growth is affected negatively and in a nonlinear way, with a more severe impact as the level of debt increases. Moreover, given future challenges such as population aging or providing some buffers for this level not to be overrun even in the occurrence of shocks suggest that an eventual target for the public debt should be much lower. Also, delayed measures designed to decrease public debt enlarge the costs of fiscal adjustments. The same argument was made by Reinhart and Rogoff (2009) who identified the same negative and nonlinear effect of public debt on economic growth for advanced economies. However, their identified threshold is 100% of GDP. Moreover, they find that the probability of occurrence of financial crises and also of their severity is higher when public debt exceeds the threshold.

Debt tolerance for emerging economies might be much lower than for advanced economies, as argued by Reinhart et al. (2003), because of the limited ability of the former to access capital markets. Among the factors influencing debt, intolerance are found to be past credit events, inflation, quality of public institutions, structure, and term of the debt.

Cantore et al. (2017) point out that the initial governmental debt to GDP ratio is important for the policymakers' decision regarding the fiscal consolidation speed. The higher the initial level of the public debt, the faster the equilibrium point will be reached. The authors point out that the Governments that are able to issue long-term bonds will reach more slowly the optimal debt consolidation plan than the ones which are only able to issue short-term bonds. Despite the optimistic conclusions for high-debt countries, the research must be particularized for each analyzed country. To this point, in the case of Romania, the degree of financial intermediation is the lowest in the EU (around 27% of GDP in 2020) and banks already have in their balance sheets a large share of Government securities (above 20% in 2020), and the additional space for further lending to the Government seems to be limited.

The topic of budgetary deficits in relationship with economic growth, especially for developing countries and emergent markets, is a vast one, being in the focus of both economists and international financial institutions. Despite the existing literature, there is no consensus between the researchers about the "correct" level or impact of the fiscal multipliers on the consolidation process. Analyzing fourteen countries from Latin America and the Caribbean, Carriere-Swallow et al. (2018) demonstrate that fiscal consolidation is contractionary for a short-term horizon in Latin America and the Caribbean Countries. Blanchard and Leigh (2013) switch the fiscal consolidation analysis from identifying the fiscal multipliers to a proposal of the right moment of performing the consolidation. Their analysis underlines that the decision must be tailored for each economy and each moment. The authors conclude that not only the assessment of short-term multipliers must be made, but also other factors like private demand must be taken into consideration. Also, for CEE countries, the literature on fiscal multipliers is quite poor. Mirdala (2009) studies the effects of a fiscal shock on the output of six CEE countries, including Romania, but he identified a positive lasting effect of seven years of budgetary expenditure on the output only in the case of Romania. The conclusion, which is contrary to the economic theory, is explained by the increase in collection efficiency, not necessarily by an increase in charged taxes.

An argument can be made that fiscal consolidations are preferable to be performed in good economic times. Thus, a large new body of literature, such as Spilimbergo et al. (2009) and Auerbach and Gorodnichenko (2012) document that fiscal multipliers are larger in bad economic times and thus output losses determined by fiscal consolidations are higher during recessions. Such an evolution can be attributable to the central bank behavior, in the sense that a fiscal stimulus is not accompanied by interest rate hikes, especially during downturns. Moreover, in bad times the share of credit-constrained economic agents is higher and, as a result, the impact of fiscal policy on production is more potent. Dumitrescu (2015b) analyzed the fiscal policy impact on real GDP growth and estimated the impact of the Romanian fiscal consolidation program initiated in 2010. Multipliers determined using a VAR approach have small values, in line with the theory of open economy, with variation for the boom (lower) and recession periods (higher). Thus, relatively low values for the fiscal multipliers in Romania would point to a frontloaded fiscal consolidation, but considering also their somewhat higher values during downturns, a more gradual fiscal adjustment, as the one proposed by the Romanian authorities seems reasonable.

3 Methodology

This paper aims to assess the public debt trajectory in Romania during 2021–2030 on the background of the fiscal consolidation program, which will be undertaken in the next period, in order to assess if the fiscal adjustment in Romania is compatible with keeping public debt at a reasonable level. Thus, the paper emphasizes the public debt evolution in Romania in the context of the Government‘s intention and obligation to bring the budgetary deficit under the 3% threshold set by the Stability and Growth Pact and relates this process to debt stabilization. Moreover, the paper calculates the required fiscal adjustment, after the 3% level of the budgetary deficit is reached, presumably in 2025, to bring public debt to a more prudent level in 2030. Also, a sensitivity analysis of the trajectory of public debt under the considered fiscal consolidation plan is performed, using scenarios for various macroeconomic variables affecting this trajectory.

The methodology used in this paper is based on the public debt equations. Although several versions are proposed in the literature, such as Escolano (2010), we choose to rely on the one proposed by Cafiso (2012a). According to the latter, the trajectory of public debt as a percent of GDP is given by:

$$b_t = -w_t + \frac{1+i_t}{(1+\pi_t)*(1+\eta_t)} b_{t-1} - sfa_t \tag{1}$$

where t is the year, b designates public debt, w stands for the primary balance, i is the nominal interest rate paid on public debt, π is the inflation rate as measured by the GDP deflator, η is the real GDP growth rate, while sfa stands for stock-flow adjustment.

In essence, the previous equation says that the evolution of public debt depends on the primary balance, the nominal GDP growth rate, and the interest rate paid for the debt, to which is added a stock-flow component (the latter explaining why in practice actual debt differs from the one determined by the previous factors of influence). Starting from Eq. (1) it is useful to determine a relationship for the change in public debt:

$$\Delta b_t = -w_t + \left(\frac{1+i_t}{(1+\pi_t)*(1+\eta_t)} - 1\right) * b_{t-1} - sfa_t \tag{2}$$

The term multiplied with the public debt in the previous year is called effective rate on the outstanding debt (CR) and reflects the difference between the real GDP growth rate and the real interest raid paid on public debt, a very important determinant of the trajectory of public debt. The product between this effective rate and the previous year’s debt is called the snowball effect, as it points to the tendency of public debt, without accounting for the primary balance. Thus, if the real GDP growth rate exceeds the real interest rate, the public debt as a percent of GDP will decline even when the primary balance is equal to 0, while in the opposite situation, primary surpluses are needed in order to stabilize the public debt.

Equation (2) can be transformed, following some algebraic manipulations, as shown by Cottarelli et al. (2010), into a relationship depicting the contributions to the public debt trajectory of the main determinants, i.e., nominal interest rate, inflation, economic growth, and stock-flow adjustment:

$$\Delta b_t = -w_t + \left(\frac{i_t}{(1+\pi_t) * (1+\eta_t)} - \frac{\pi_t}{(1+\pi_t) * (1+\eta_t)} \right) * b_{t-1} - \frac{\eta_t}{(1+\eta_t)} - sfa_t \tag{3}$$

Equations (1)–(3) can be used to determine the public debt trajectory or each factor's contribution to the public debt dynamics both for the past and for the future, considering projections for the main determinants of public debt.

Relevant for the objectives of the paper is also to compute a trajectory for the primary balance and consequently for the budgetary balance leading to a target debt level. For that purpose, we will also rely on the equation determined by Cafiso (2012b) based on the public debt equations:

$$\overrightarrow{w} = \frac{CR}{1-(1+CR)^{-m}} * (b_0 - (1+CR)^{-m} * b_m^*) \tag{4}$$

where $\overrightarrow{w}$ is the average primary balance during the adjustment period, CR is the effective rate on outstanding debt, m is the number of years of adjustment, b_0 is the initial level of public debt, b_m^* is the target level for the public debt.

The historical data for public debt and its determinants are taken from Eurostat, the Romanian Ministry of Finance, and the most recent Convergence Program for Romania. For the period 2021–2024, we used forecasts of the European Commission, but also national projections from the Report concerning the macroeconomic situation for 2021 and its projection for the 2022–2024 period, which was published by the Romanian Ministry of Finance alongside the budget draft for 2021. For the period 2025–2030, we used similar macroeconomic projections as for 2022–2024, given that the economic growth projected of 4% for 2021–2024 is close to potential growth estimated by several stakeholders, and that the projections for inflation are in the vicinity of the central bank target. In addition, we make the assumption that interest expenses remain at the level of 2021, which is consistent with a small decrease in funding costs alongside a moderate increase in the debt stock. The last assumption is also in line with the declared intention of the European Central Bank to keep interest rates at a low level for an important period of time, a decision which is likely to influence also the interest-rate policy of the National Bank of Romania.

We assume that for 2021 the budgetary deficit will turn out to be at the level of the 8.2% of GDP target set by the Ministry of Finance in the budget draft, while the correction to the 3% limit under the Excessive Deficit Procedure is projected to be achieved until 2025. We chose this period having in mind the gap toward the

3% threshold and also that in 2024 local, general, and presidential elections will take place. Thus, the annual average reduction in the budgetary deficit in the 2022–2025 period is considered to be around 1.3%. We think that the fiscal adjustment in this period will be driven by the constraints of the Excessive Deficit Procedure. Going forward, we consider that the period 2026–2030 should be characterized by a continuation of the adjustment needed to bring public debt to a more prudent level. Considering the peak of the public debt in the next years and the goal of gradually reducing it, we choose as a target for the public debt in 2030 a level of 50% of GDP and we calculate the fiscal adjustment path needed to reach this goal. Variations in the macroeconomic determinants of the public debt trajectory are depicted in the sensitivity analysis.

4 Results Interpretation

The public debt in Romania witnessed a sharp increase in 2020 of 12 pp of GDP to 47.3% after 9 years of evolution in a relatively narrow interval, i.e., 34–39% of GDP. The main causes were represented by the economic contraction induced by the COVID-19 pandemic of around 4%, but it is also the result of the high budgetary deficit from 2020, amounting to 9.1% of GDP. The latter is rather the result of previous expansionary and procyclical fiscal policies, which lead to a 4.4% budgetary deficit in 2019, although the economy was advancing a pace higher than 4%, In fact, during 2016–2019 the budgetary deficit was on average 3.1% of GDP, while the average economic growth was above 5% as a result of significant tax cuts and expenditure increases, especially with public wages. If we use Eqs. (2) and (3) from above in order to calculate the contributions to public debt increase in 2020, we find that 7.6 pp of GDP is attributable to the primary balance, 1.4 pp to the economic decline, and 2.7 pp of GDP to the stock-flow adjustment (as a result of meeting in advance future financing needs in order to consolidate a buffer at the level of the Treasury).

The public debt trajectory in the period 2022–2025 is computed based on Eq. (3). For the period 2026–2030, after the 3% level for the budgetary deficit is supposed to be reached in 2025, the adjustment is calculated based on Eq. (4), leading to an annual pace of deficit reduction of around 0.35 pp of GDP, and a value for the budgetary deficit in 2030 of approximately 1.2% of GDP. A sensitivity analysis is performed, using as scenarios higher/lower economic growth by 1 pp separately and in conjunction with lower/higher interest rate paid on public debt by 1 pp. Thus, we construct two optimistic and two pessimistic scenarios for the public debt trajectory during 2022–2030. The contributions of the main determinants to the actual or projected change in public debt and its trajectory under the baseline scenario and also under the scenarios considered for the sensitivity analysis are presented in Table 1.

Thus, in the context of high—although declining—budgetary deficits, public debt is expected to continue its increase in Romania during 2022–2024 peaking at a level of around 58.7% of GDP and reaching 57.9% of GDP in 2025, the estimated year in which the budgetary deficit will reach the 3% threshold. A continuation

Table 1 Contributions to public debt evolution during 2018–2030 (actual and projected)

Year	Change in public debt (% of GDP)	Primary balance contribution (% of GDP)	Nominal interest rate contribution (% of GDP)	Inflation contribution (% of GDP)	Economic growth contribution (% of GDP)	Stock flow adjustment contribution (% of GDP)
2018	−0.4	1.8	1.0	−2.0	−1.5	0.3
2019	0.6	3.2	1.1	−2.1	−1.4	−0.2
2020	12.0	7.6	1.5	−1.3	1.4	2.7
2021	5.1	6.6	1.5	−1.1	−2.0	0.0
2022	3.6	5.3	1.5	−1.2	−2.0	0.0
2023	2.0	4.0	1.5	−1.3	−2.2	0.0
2024	0.6	2.7	1.5	−1.4	−2.2	0.0
2025	−0.7	1.4	1.5	−1.4	−2.3	0.0
2026	−1.0	1.0	1.5	−1.4	−2.2	0.0
2027	−1.3	0.7	1.5	−1.3	−2.2	0.0
2028	−1.6	0.3	1.5	−1.3	−2.1	0.0
2029	−1.9	0.0	1.5	−1.3	−2.1	0.0
2030	−2.1	−0.4	1.5	−1.2	−2.0	0.0
Average contribution	1.1	2.6	1.4	−1.4	−1.7	0.2

Source Own calculations, Eurostat, Ameco, Ministry of Finance

of the reduction of the budgetary deficit at a pace of 0.35% per year until 2030 is consistent with reaching at that moment the target debt level of 50% of GDP. However, the baseline scenario relies on strong economic growth during 2022–2030 and reasonable interest rates. In a pessimistic scenario of lower economic growth by 1 pp public debt is expected to be at a level of 53.8% of GDP in 2030, while if interest rates also increase by 1 pp compared to the current level, there will be almost no reduction in public debt with an estimated level of 58.8%. Thus, in a pessimistic scenario, which still assumes economic growth of 3% per year and a sustained fiscal adjustment, public debt will be hovering around the 60% reference value. However, in more optimistic scenarios public debt could reach a level of 46.5% of GDP in 2030, provided that economic growth is higher by 1 pp, or even below 45% of GDP if interest rates further decline by 1 pp. Given the high amount of fiscal adjustment needed in Romania in the coming years and the already low level of interest rates, we think that the optimistic scenarios have a lower probability compared to the pessimistic ones. The public debt trajectories under the baseline scenario and the optimistic and pessimistic ones are presented in Table 2.

Table 2 Projections for the public debt trajectory in Romania during 2022–2030—baseline, optimistic, and pessimistic scenarios

Year	Public debt in the baseline scenario	Optimistic scenario 1: growth +1 pp	Optimistic scenario 2: growth +1 pp, interest −1 pp	Pessimistic scenario 1: growth −1 pp	Pessimistic scenario 2: growth −1 pp, interest +1 pp
2022	56.0	55.5	55.0	56.5	57.0
2023	58.0	57.1	56.2	59.0	60.2
2024	58.7	57.2	56.0	60.1	61.9
2025	57.9	56.1	54.5	59.9	62.4
2026	56.9	54.6	52.8	59.3	62.4
2027	55.6	52.9	50.8	58.4	62.1
2028	54.0	51.0	48.5	57.1	61.3
2029	52.1	48.9	46.1	55.6	60.3
2030	50.0	46.5	43.4	53.8	58.8

Source Own calculations, Ameco, Ministry of Finance

5 Conclusions

Procyclical fiscal policies in Romania during 2015–2019 leading to the launch of the Excessive Deficit Procedure by the European Commission in 2020, and the economic shock generated by the COVID-19 pandemic in 2020 left Romania with a 9.1% budgetary deficit at the end of 2020 and a rapidly rising public debt. This paper has shown that, even under the favorable hypothesis of a successful exit from the Excessive Deficit Procedure by 2025, public debt will peak at a level of 58.7% in 2024, slightly decreasing to 56.9% of GDP in 2025, even in the context of a 4% economic growth during 2022–2025. However, at this moment, the challenging measures underlying the more than 5 pp. needed reduction in the budgetary deficit during 2022–2025 are not presented.

Clearly, even after 2025, the need to bring public debt to a more prudent level will be present, although the reach of safe level in 2030, i.e., below 45% of GDP given previous estimates of the National Bank of Romania, is unlikely. This paper has calculated a yearly pace of fiscal adjustment amounting to 0.35% of GDP needed to bring the debt level at around 50% in GDP in 2030 and the budgetary deficit in the vicinity of the 1% level. This level will be presumably close to the medium-term objective. Such an evolution would be an achievement in our opinion, given the current trajectory of public debt. Moreover, in less optimistic scenarios, public debt will be closer to the projected level from the end of 2022 or even in the vicinity of the 60% threshold set by the Maastricht Treaty. Given these calculated trajectories for the public debt during 2022–2030, we appreciate that a successful fiscal adjustment, materialized in the exit of the Excessive Deficit Procedure at the end of 2025, and a further reduction of the budgetary deficit to around 1% of GDP, is essential for keeping public debt at a reasonable level.

The limits of this analysis are given by the fact that we have used a deterministic approach to the public debt evolution, without accounting for all the contemporaneous interconnections between the variables. Most likely, applying a stochastic framework for analyzing the public debt trajectory, a direction for future research, will point to additional risks, so the conclusions of the current paper urging for fiscal prudence are likely to be augmented.

References

Auerbach, A.J., Gorodnichenko, Y.: Measuring the output response to fiscal policy. Am. Econ. J. : Econ. Policy **4**(2), 1–27 (2012)
Blanchard, O., Leigh, D.: Fiscal consolidation: at what speed? VoxEU.org–CEPR's policy portal (2013)
Cafiso, G.: A guide to Public Debt equations. In: Social Sciences Research Network WP (2012a)
Cafiso, G.: Debt developments and fiscal adjustment in the EU. Interecon. Rev. Eur. Econ. Policy **47**(1), 61–72 (2012b)
Cantore, C., Levine, P., Melina, G., Pearlman, J.: Optimal fiscal and monetary policy, debt crisis and management. In: IMF Working Paper 17/78 (2017)
Carriere-Swallow, Y., David, A.C., Leigh, D.: The macroeconomic effects of fiscal consolidation in emerging economies: evidence from latin America. In: IMF Working Paper 18/142 (2018)
Cecchetti, S., Mohanty, M., Zampolli, F.: The real effects of debt. In: BIS WP no. 352 (2011)
Cottarelli, C., Forni, L., Gottschalk, J, Mauro, P.: Default in today's advanced economies: unnecessary, undesirable, and unlikely. : IMF Staff Position Note (2010)
Dumitrescu, B.A.: Arguments in the debate austerity versus growth in Romania. Rom. J. Fiscal Policy (RJFP) **6**(1), 54–62 (2015a)
Dumitrescu, B.A.: The fiscal consolidation consequences on economic growth in Romania. Rom. J. Econ. Forecast. **XVIII**(3), 136–151 (2015b)
Escolano, J.A: Practical guide to public debt dynamics, fiscal sustainability, and cyclical adjustment of budgetary aggregates. In: IMF Technical report (2010)
Mirdala, R..: Effects of fiscal policy shocks in the European transition economies. In: MPRA Paper no. 19481 (2009)
National Bank of Romania: Financial Stability Report (2015)
Reinhart, C.M., Rogoff, K., Savastano, M.A.: Debt intolerance. In: NBER WP no. 9908 (2003)
Reinhart, C.M., Rogoff, K.: This Time is Different. Eight Centuries of Financial Folly. Princeton University Press, Princeton (2009)
Romanian Fiscal Council–Fiscal Council's Opinion on the State Budget Law, the Social Security Budget Law for 2021 and the 2021–2023 Fiscal Strategy (2021)
Spilimbergo, A., Symansky, S., Schindler, M.: Fiscal Multipliers. In: IMF Staff Position Note SPN/09/11 (2009)

Solutions for Post-pandemic Economic Recovery: The Case of China

Erokhin Vasilii, Tianming Gao, and Ivolga Anna

Abstract The global economy is now under extremely severe pressure from a great variety of political, economic, social, environmental, and public health challenges. The COVID-19 outbreak has rapidly transformed from a medical phenomenon to a threat of disruption to global supply chains and economic recession in most countries of the world. Despite the similarity of problems, the impact of the pandemic on individual countries has appeared to be different in terms of the severity of both human and economic losses. China is the first country that experienced the outbreak in early 2020 and now it is one of the first to recover from it. A set of effective and efficient health security, economic, and social measures allowed China to restart economic activities in the domestic market and restore foreign trade with its counterparts. This paper presents an assessment of major macroeconomic parameters of China in 2020 compared to previous periods, discusses the efficacy of economic, fiscal, and investment solutions made by China's government during the pandemic, and assesses how these measures have affected China's recovery in terms of GDP, investment in fixed assets, exports and imports, money supply, and the price index.

Keywords China · GDP · Export · Import · Investment · Pandemic · Trade

1 Introduction

Continuing to this day, the COVID-19 pandemic has already had an extremely negative impact on the global economy, while its overall outcomes can hardly be predicted (Erokhin 2021). The countries that are more deeply integrated into global production and supply chains are most severely affected by the restrictions on cross-border trade, transport, and other forms of mobility and business. In recent years, one of

E. Vasilii (✉) · T. Gao
Harbin Engineering University, Nantong Str. 145, Harbin 150001, China
e-mail: basilic@list.ru

I. Anna
Stavropol State Agrarian University, Zootekhnichesky Str. 12, 355017 Stavropol, Russia

A. M. Dima and M. Kelemen (eds.), *Digitalization and Big Data for Resilience and Economic Intelligence*, Springer Proceedings in Business and Economics, https://doi.org/10.1007/978-3-030-93286-2_11

the undisputed leaders among such economies is China, whose contribution to the global GDP exceeds 12% (Trading Economics 2021), or even 18%, according to the purchasing power parity parameter (Statista 2021). The World Trade Organization (WTO) reports that China's share of global exports in 2019 was 13.2%, in global imports—10.8% (WTO 2020). The COVID-19 pandemic started in China and affected all areas of the country's economic activity, peoples' lives, consumer demand, investment, and many other spheres. However, strict measures to contain the spread of the disease within the country (Vasiev et al. 2020) allowed China to start recovering by mid-2020, while many other countries are still being exposed to new waves of the pandemic. This study aims to summarize economic, fiscal, and investment solutions made by China's government during the pandemic and assess how these measures have affected China's recovery in terms of major macroeconomic parameters.

2 Literature Review

The effects of the COVID-19 pandemic on the global economy have received tremendous attention in the literature since the beginning of 2020, when the first cases were found outside China. Many scholars have been attempting to assess the economic losses due to lockdowns, closure of businesses and entire sectors such as air travel, tourism, entertainment, disrupted supply chains, and many more negative effects associated with anti-pandemic measures. According to Toffolutti et al. (2020) and Blay-Palmer et al. (2020), the pandemic is not only impacting people's lives but is disrupting supply chains. As the virus spreads and public health protection measures tighten, there are many ways in which global markets have been strained (border closures, quarantines, supply chain disruptions, etc.). The pandemic is affecting countries directly by distorting supply and demand, and indirectly by degrading the purchasing power of the population. Shevchenko (2020), Grishin et al. (2020), and Rodríguez-Caballero and Vera-Valdés (2020) generalized the content and forms of economic consequences of the pandemic for the global market, while Kvashnin (2020) and Černikovaitė and Karazijienė (2021), among others, conducted comprehensive per-country studies.

The effects of the pandemic containment measures have also been addressed on a per-country basis, including by Bricco et al. (2020), Guerriero et al. (2020), Goolsbee and Syverson (2020), and Papava and Chkuaseli (2021). However, due to the uncertainty of the dynamics of the pandemic, the estimations remain rather rough. Most of the countries continue experiencing new waves of the COVID-19 outbreak, while governments extend or introduce new containment measures that affect the economic environment. Given the scarcity of knowledge, studying the experience of those few countries (China, in the case of this study) that have curbed the spread of the disease is particularly valuable, as amid the relevant stability of the situation, the economic consequences of particular decisions can be tracked and measured. In China, preliminary estimations of the pandemic's effects on the economy have been made by Chen et al. (2021), Vasiev et al. (2020), Liu et al. (2020), and Shalamov and Kudrov (2020). The majority of scholars, however, investigated particular sectors of the economy, while the complete picture has not been effectively generalized. Thus, it is worthwhile to say that the impacts of the COVID-19 containment measures on China's economy have remained insufficiently explored.

3 Methodology

The main economic impacts of the COVID-19 pandemic on economic development, which can be experienced by all countries, include difficulties in the operation of labor and trade markets, negative effects on monetary systems, currency exchange rates, and government reserves, disruptions in supply chains in high-tech industries, a significant reduction in cross-border movements of people, tourism, and services in general, changes in the socio-economic activity of people, as well as increased problems of poverty and food insecurity. The research question explored in this paper is how the pandemic containment policies could alleviate these adverse economic effects, what policies have demonstrated their efficacy in China which was the first among countries to face the COVID-19 crisis, and how China's experience could be utilized in other economies.

Major economic parameters of China are analyzed in terms of GDP, investment in fixed assets, exports and imports, money supply, and the price index. The effects of pandemic containment measures are estimated by comparing the values of the respected six variables in 2020 (quarterly) compared to 2018 and 2019. The generalized data table is provided in the Appendix (Table 1). The data for this study are derived from the National Bureau of Statistics of China, the World Trade Organization, and Statista and Trading Economics data aggregators.

4 Analysis/Results Interpretation

Although the number of newly reported COVID-19 cases in China began to decline in February 2020, and restrictive measures were significantly relaxed in March–April 2020, the losses in the first quarter of 2020 were extremely sensitive for the economy: a drop in GDP by 6.8%, a reduction in foreign trade and domestic consumption, and a rise in urban unemployment up to 6%. The situation has improved by applying economic, financial, and fiscal instruments and relying on stimulating domestic consumption (Shalamov and Kudrov 2020).

In February 2020, China's Ministry of Industry and Information Technology issued the Notification on Responding to the Epidemic Situation (Tzou 2020) and announced packages of financial and banking support for small and medium enterprises along with twenty directions. In particular, they included assistance in coordinating and solving problems such as the return of employees to work, supply of raw materials, transportation of goods and other cargo, purchase of masks and other materials for the prevention and control of the disease. Infrastructure services were advised to implement a phased deferral of payments for electricity, water, and gas, which were necessary for supporting the activities of small and medium enterprises. The People's Bank of China together with the Ministry of Finance issued CNY 184 billion ($28.9 billion) of special loans, while nine national banks and ten provincial and municipal banks allocated a total of CNY 182.1 billion ($28.6 billion) of concessional loans to 4,708 key enterprises at the national and provincial levels (on average, CNY 40 million ($6.3 million) per enterprise) (Tzou 2020; Liu et al. 2020). In March 2020, China's Ministry of Commerce together with the respective departments in various sectors proposed four packages of measures to support over 60 million small stores and other businesses:

- Taxation. The government has significantly relaxed the tax regime for businesses, including small and medium-sized enterprises, which were almost completely exempt from paying taxes until the end of 2020 (Lukonin and Zakliazminskaia 2020). For all small and medium taxpayers, the VAT rate was reduced from 3 to 1%, while the smallest businesses and those in the consumer services sector were exempt from VAT.
- Social insurance. From February to June 2020, enterprises were exempted from payments under three social insurance payments (old-age insurance, unemployment insurance, and occupational accident insurance). The volume of social insurance paid by large firms was halved and collected on a phased basis.
- Credit policy. Apart from the special loans mentioned above, support was provided in the form of subsidizing part of the interest rate. In addition, a deferral was provided for enterprises that were experiencing difficulties in repaying loans. Banks and other financial institutions received recommendations from the central government to expand loan programs at low-interest rates and provide targeted support to individual entrepreneurs.
- Support in reducing production costs. From February to June 2020, the total price of electricity for the industrial and trade sectors was reduced by 5%. In addition, there was implemented a reduction in the rent payments for the state-owned property. Businesses experiencing difficulties were allowed to apply for deferred payments to the housing savings fund.

Similar support measures were applied in most other countries in Asia, Europe, and North America: emergency social and economic support for people and businesses, allocation of funds to support small and medium enterprises, reduction of key interest rates, and liquidity injection. However, even with such massive support, global GDP in 2020 declined by 4.4%, the US economy—by 4.3%, Japan—by 5.3%, Germany—by 6%. China's policy was different in the way that at the earliest stages of the pandemic, a set of measures was taken to increase the supply of the population, forgive debts, exempt small and medium businesses from taxes, and reschedule interest payments on loans. Along with the introduction of a strict quarantine, the state immediately announced comprehensive centralized assistance to both businesses and people: public health care, food supplies, and financial support. This ensured a high level of trust in the government and helped to avoid public protests. Without such measures, the GDP dynamics would be negative (Fig. 1), whereas, in 2020, the GDP grew by 2.3% (Liu et al. 2020).

Another distinct difference in China's policy from those in other countries was the reliance on the world's largest domestic market, one of the main competitive advantages of China. Before the pandemic, about 58% of the country's GDP was provided by domestic consumption, while foreign trade occupied only 11% (National Bureau of Statistics of China 2021). A significant increase in funding for various social programs (by 11.5% in the first quarter of 2020 and then by almost 13% quarterly until the end of the year) helped to support domestic demand. After a sharp drop in consumption by 21.7% in March 2020, demand began to recover (−17.2% in April, −11.3% in May, −7.5% in June) (Fig. 2). Despite the recovery in consumption in the second half of 2020, the volume of retail sales in 2020 declined by 3.9% compared to 2019 (Cheng 2020).

The reliance of the national economic development on the domestic market was emphasized by China's government well before the pandemic and it proved to be extremely effective in an emergency situation. The main guidelines of this policy are formulated in six "stability factors" (employment, stability of the financial sector, development of foreign trade, foreign and national investment, and efficiency of economic planning) and six "guarantee factors" (unemployment control, poverty alleviation, business support, food, and energy security, maintenance and development of infrastructure, and strengthening supply chains). Much attention is paid to attracting investment from abroad and implementing domestic investment projects.

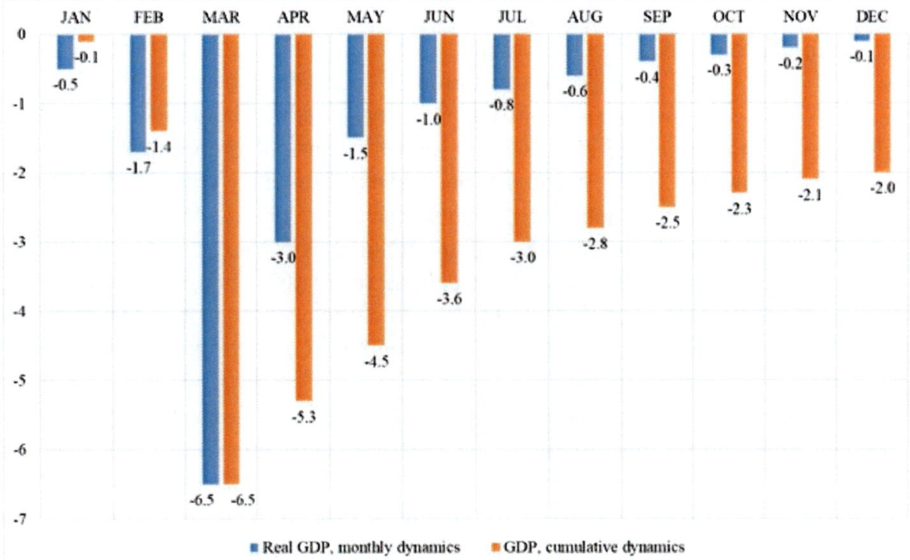

Fig. 1 Recovery of production in China in 2020. *Source* Authors' development based on the National Bureau of Statistics of China (2021)

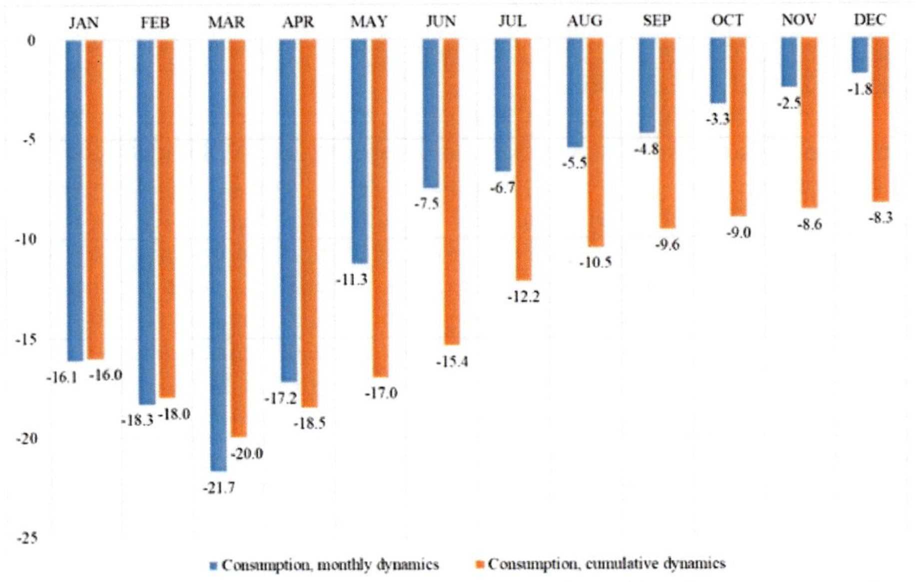

Fig. 2 Recovery of consumption in China in 2020. *Source* Authors' development based on the National Bureau of Statistics of China (2021)

Although in March 2020, the decline in fixed capital investment in China was 39.3%, since the second quarter of 2020, there has been a recovery (Fig. 3). Due to the implementation of state programs and a number of large infrastructure projects, investments in 2020 exceeded the pre-pandemic level of 2019.

Against the background of such relatively favorable forecasts, the business activity index (PMI) is also growing. Expectations of Chinese manufacturers and businessmen have improved significantly since March 2020. The indices in the manufacturing and non-manufacturing sectors showed a particularly remarkable recovery, remaining above 50%. The highest expectations of an early recovery in economic activity are registered in the construction sector.

However, even though China is likely to remain the only growing economy among all countries in the world by the end of 2020, there are also a number of serious problems, risks, and imbalances that need to be taken into account to ensure a sustainable pace of post-pandemic development. They can be combined into the following six blocks.

First, the main factor of uncertainty for the world is the volatility of the epidemiological situation. In most countries, vaccination campaigns are facing many challenges, and it is difficult to predict when positive economic effects occur. China continues to implement a strategy to prevent the spread of the virus from entering the country, which entails quite strict restrictions on the cross-border mobility of people and commercial cargo. The pace and nature of the economic recovery will

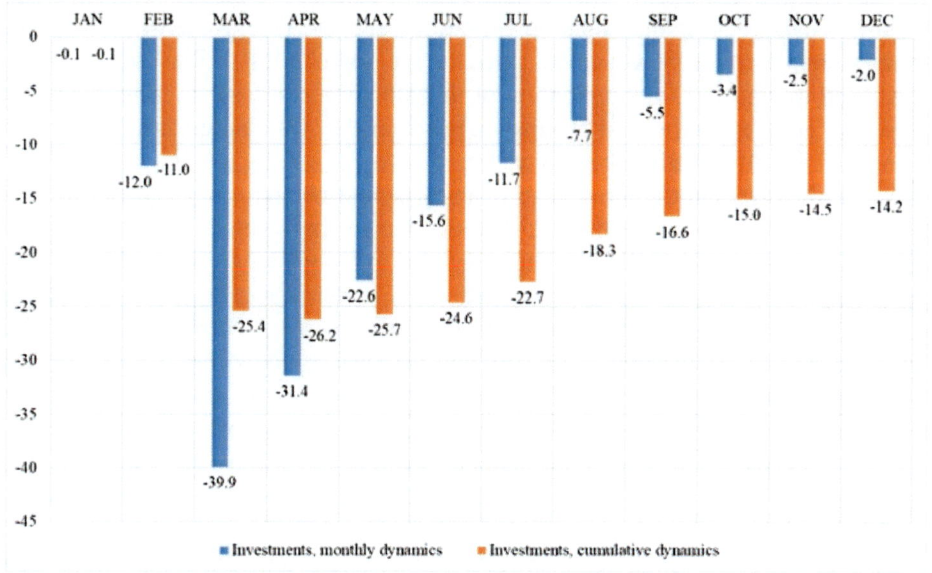

Fig. 3 Recovery of investments in China in 2020. *Source* Authors' development based on the National Bureau of Statistics of China (2021)

depend directly on how long and in what forms the restrictions will continue. Moreover, given the crucial role that China plays in global production, supply, and cargo logistics chains, restrictions within China directly affect the entire global market.

The second factor is the disparity in the rate of recovery of supply and demand, which has been observed since the second quarter of 2020. The GDP growth at the end of the year was 2.3%, while consumption declined by 3.9%. Some experts (Cheng 2020; Liu et al. 2020; Erokhin 2021) predict a decline in the share of domestic consumption in the GDP against the background of the pandemic to 54.3% compared to almost 58% in 2019. Against the background of state support, the vast majority of entrepreneurs managed to restart their businesses after the lockdown in the first quarter of 2020. But the workload in most enterprises is still below the level of 2019. Only 52% of companies in the market operate at a workload level of more than 90% compared to last year. Thus, along with supporting businesses, it is necessary to focus on stimulating demand.

Such structural imbalances in the recovery rates of various industries threaten the overall sustainability of the economy. In the first quarter of 2020, the decline in the primary, secondary, and tertiary sectors in China was 3.2%, 9.6%, and 5.3%, respectively. Some industries were more exposed to the negative impact of the pandemic. In industrial production and construction, the decline was 10.2% and 17.5%, respectively, while the service sector decreased by 35.5%, trade—by 17.8%, transportation and storage—by 14.0%. In contrast, the financial sector grew by 6.0%, while information and communication technologies grew by 13.2%. As a result of the uneven dynamics of the situation in various sectors, the problems of unemployment and poverty have worsened, since the sectors with less skilled labor have been affected the most. The continuation of this situation can lead to an increase in the income gap between social groups—a problem that China's government has long and successfully fought for many years.

Fourth, we cannot ignore the shifts in consumer behavior that directly affect the situation in the domestic market. The decline in the level of income of workers in underperforming industries and the threat of job losses due to the closure of enterprises have led to a significant reduction in demand. The general uncertainty of the future economic situation has reduced the investment activity. Many Chinese people tend to save money. The available reserves in many respects allowed most people to survive relatively easily in terms of their means of subsistence during the period of strict quarantine. However, the consumer "conservatism" that intensified against the background of the pandemic became a serious obstacle to the rapid recovery of the market. In 2017–2019, bank deposits of enterprises in the first quarter of the year averaged about 800 billion RMB. In January–March 2020, they rose to 2.9 trillion RMB. Such an increase in reserves means a significant reduction in current spending and investment, given that the profits of enterprises have also significantly decreased.

To prevent the accumulation of funds in banks and stimulate turnover, the government significantly reduced interest rates on the interbank market. More than 2 trillion RMB was distributed through special transfers to the grassroots level of the banking system. From January to May 2020, private investment declined by 9.6%, while in general, the monetary policy in recent years has been aimed at ensuring the growth of investment from various sources.

Finally, it should be noted that many of the previous factors of China's unprecedented economic growth in recent years are now losing their significance, and the global crisis due to the pandemic may accelerate this process. Compared to China's rapid integration into global production and supply chains in the 2000s, the impact of economic globalization as a driver of China's growth is now significantly reduced. This trend began long before the pandemic and it was clearly manifested in the trade tension between the USA and China in 2018–2019. The share of the trade surplus in China's GDP has been gradually declining for more than a decade—from 8.6% before the financial crisis in 2007 to 1.5% in 2019. At the same time, the deficit in trade in services is growing. The growth rate of exports and imports fell from an extremely high of 31.8% and 38.8% in 2010 to just 0.5% for exports in 2019, while the volume of imports in 2019 decreased by 2.7% compared to 2018. It is clear that the pandemic and restrictions on cross-border mobility and trade, as well as the general decline in the global economy, will further affect the slowdown in China's foreign trade.

5 Conclusions

China experienced the most negative impact of the pandemic on its economy in the first quarter of 2020. Since April 2020, the pressure has been weakening. Our study shows that such a result could be attributed to the set of measures implemented by the government in February–March 2020. The support measures were primarily aimed at saving the most vulnerable sectors of the economy, small and medium enterprises, rather than stimulating growth in general. The COVID-19 economic problems are mainly related to shrinking consumption in all sectors. Unlike many Western countries, China has focused on fiscal measures, rather than monetary ones. The support was provided in the forms of simplification of the tax regime and tax exemption, deferred payments under social insurance programs, subsidizing interest rates on business loans, as well as supporting enterprises in reducing production costs. China focused on maintaining demand in the domestic market while ensuring high liquidity in the economy. The short-term effects of economic measures can now be evidenced in China's GDP growth of 2.3% in 2020. However, it is necessary to study the long-term consequences for both the national economy and the global market as a whole. A critical problem in these future studies is the uncertainty of the pandemic situation in the world, which forces governments to seek a balance between the needs to prevent new outbreaks and to relaunch economic activities to avoid recession, social unrest, and the wave of bankruptcies.

Appendix

See Table 1.

Table 1 Major macroeconomic parameters of China before and amid the pandemic

Parameters	2018	2019	2020				Year, total
			Q1	Q2	Q3	Q4	
GDP change, %	+6.7	+6.1	−6.8	+3.2	+5.0	+6.5	+2.3
Investments in fixed assets, $ trillion	9.241	7.892	1.186	3.978	6.776	8.566	8.566
Sales of consumer goods, $ trillion	5.539	5.891	1.108	2.434	4.156	6.244	6.244
Exports, $ trillion	2.487	2.499	0.478	1.099	1.811	2.449	2.449
Imports, $ trillion	2.136	2.078	0.465	0.931	1.485	2.026	2.026
Trade balance, $ trillion	0.351	0.421	0.013	0.168	0.326	0.423	0.423
M2 money supply change, %	+8.1	+8.7	+10.1	+11.1	+11.5	+12.0	+12.0
M1 money supply change, %	+1.5	+4.4	+5.0	+6.5	+7.0	+7.0	+7.0
Social support change, %	+10.3	+10.7	+11.5	+12.8	+12.7	+12.8	+12.8
Consumer Price Index change	+2.1	+2.9	+4.9	+3.8	+3.2	+3.0	+3.0
Producer Price Index change	+3.5	−0.3	−0.6	−1.9	−2.7	−3.0	−3.0

References

Blay-Palmer, A., Carey, R., Valette, E., Sanderson, M.: Post COVID 19 and food pathways to sustainable transformation. Agric. Human Values, 1–3 (2020)

Bricco, J., Misch, F., Solovyeva, A.: What Are the Economic Effects of Pandemic Containment Policies? Evidence from Sweden. International Monetary Fund, Washington, DC (2020)

Černikovaitė, M., Karazijienė, Z.: Social-economic effects of the COVID-19 pandemic in lithuania. In: SHS Web of Conferences, vol. 92, p. 01006 (2021)

Chen, Q., He, Z., Hsieh, C.-T., Song, Z.: Economic effects of lockdown in china. In: Agarwal, S., He, Z., Yeung, B. (eds.) Impact of COVID-19 on Asian Economies and Policy Responses, pp. 3–10. World Scientific Publishing, Singapore (2021)

Cheng, E.: China Says Its Economy Grew 2.3% in 2020, but Consumer Spending Fell (2021). https://www.cnbc.com/2021/01/18/china-economy-release-of-fourth-quarter-full-year-2020-gdp.html

Erokhin, V.: Impact of the COVID-19 pandemic on China's economy: preliminary estimate and recovery outlook. Market. Logist. **33**(1), 5–16 (2021)

Goolsbee, A., Syverson, C.: Fear, lockdown, and diversion: comparing drivers of pandemic economic decline 2020. J. Public Econ. **193**(30), 104311 (2021)

Grishin, V., Domashchenko, D., Konstantinova, L., Koshkin, A., Ustyuzhanina, E., Shtykhno, D., Shubenkova, E.: Life after the pandemic: economic and social consequences. Vestnik Plekhanov Rus. Univ. Econ. **3**, 5–18 (2020)

Guerriero, C., Haines, A., Pagano, M.: Health and sustainability in post-pandemic economic policies. Nat. Sustain. **3**, 494–496 (2020)

Kvashnin, Y.: Greece amid coronavirus pandemic: economic aspects. Sci. Anal. Her. IE RAS **16**(4), 64–70 (2020)

Liu, X., Liu, Y., Yan, Y.: China macroeconomic report 2020: China's macroeconomy is on the rebound under the impact of COVID-19. Econ. Polit. Stud. **8**(4), 395–435 (2020)

Lukonin, S., Zakliazminskaia, E.: Transformation of the socioeconomic model of China in the context of a pandemic. Outl. Glob Trans. Polit. Econ. Law **13**(6), 198–216 (2020)

National Bureau of Statistics of China: National Data (2021). https://data.stats.gov.cn/english/index.htm

Papava, V., Chkuaseli, M.: Economic consequences of the COVID-19 pandemic and the economic ability of a government as a factor of production. Int. Bus. Econ. Stud. **3**(2), 67–71 (2021)

Rodríguez-Caballero, C.V., Vera-Valdés, J.E.: Long-Lasting economic effects of pandemics: evidence on growth and unemployment. Econometrics **8**(3), 37 (2020)

Shalamov, G., Kudrov, A.: Features of china's development in the conditions of the coronavirus pandemic. Financ. Econ. **7**, 194–196 (2020)

Shevchenko, V.: Economic shocks of the pandemic impact: the european case. Three Seas Econ. J. **1**(2), 53–59 (2020)

Statista: China's Share of Global Gross Domestic Product (GDP) Adjusted for Purchasing-Power-Parity (PPP) from 2009 to 2019 with Forecasts until 2025 (2021). https://www.statista.com/statistics/270439/chinas-share-of-global-gross-domestic-product-gdp/

Toffolutti, V., Stuckler, D., McKee, M.: Is the COVID-19 pandemic turning into a european food crisis? Eur. J. Pub. Health **30**(4), 626–627 (2020)

Trading Economics: China GDP (2021). https://tradingeconomics.com/china/gdp

Tzou, S.: Impact of the coronavirus epidemic on the china's economy and the government and regional countermeasures. Power Adm. East Rus. **91**(2), 37–44 (2020)

Vasiev, M., Bi, K., Denisov, A., Bocharnikov, V.: How COVID-19 pandemics influences Chinese economic sustainability. Foresight STI Gov. **14**(2), 7–22 (2020)

World Trade Organization: China (2020). https://www.wto.org/english/res_e/statis_e/daily_update_e/trade_profiles/CN_e.pdf

Individual Work Valuation in a Digital World—The Case of Personal Token's Pricing

Litwiński Michał, Marchewka-Bartkowiak Kamilla, and Nowak Karolina

Abstract Personal tokens (specifically, utility tokens) can serve as a measure of work valuation. Valuing one's work is usually based on three sources: comparing competition prices, determining the costs incurred, identifying the value offered to the investor/client. The aim of the paper is to identify the types of individual work that is valued by means of personal tokens and offered in the virtual world. We would also like to recognise the motives and incentives of different individual service providers who valuate their services (performed both online and in the real world) using personal tokens. The theoretical basis for this analysis is the theory of the basic individual values and work values implemented firstly by S. H. Schwartz. Conclusions will be drawn on the basis of case studies. The authors will analyse the data and information available on the personal tokens platform (personaltokens.io) in order to specify the measures for assessing the motives of work valuation based on personal tokens. One of the results of the study is the identification of a new motive for virtual work, which is the network theme.

Keywords Individual work · Labour value · Personal tokens

1 Introduction

The research problem addressed in the article concerns personal tokens as a new measure of valuing individual work offered by their owners. The authors focus therefore on a specific kind of digital tokens, namely utility tokens. The starting point for

---

Litwiński M. · Marchewka-Bartkowiak K. (✉) · Nowak K.
Poznan University of Economics and Business, Al. Niepodległości 10, 61-875 Poznań, Poland
e-mail: Kamilla.Marchewka-Bartkowiak@ue.poznan.pl

Litwiński M.
e-mail: Michal.Litwinski@ue.poznan.pl

Nowak K.
e-mail: Karolina.Nowak@ue.poznan.pl

A. M. Dima and M. Kelemen (eds.), *Digitalization and Big Data for Resilience and Economic Intelligence*, Springer Proceedings in Business and Economics, https://doi.org/10.1007/978-3-030-93286-2_12

the evaluation of the application of the abovementioned new crypto-asset technologies will be the identification of the types of services/products offered by the owners of personal tokens and the potential motives behind their decision to tokenise their work.

Our study is embedded in the broad context of research on contemporary labour market transitions related to the spread of a new model of work within economy 4.0 (Hackl et al. 2017; Ruiner 2021). We address the important question of how work is valued in this context (Schofield 2019). Indeed, existing ways of valuing work, based on the traditional model of full-time, horizontal work, do not cover the new ways of valuing work associated with the technological breakthroughs that have encompassed the contemporary labour market. The changes occur not only in the expansion and transformation of the catalogue of services offered, but also in the modification of the motives of people performing work, which affects the way in which the work provided is valued (Huws 2014). Individuals taking up employment with the use of new technologies are usually characterised by a value system that allows them to realise the main idea of the Flexible Labour Market.

The study of contemporary forms of valuing work with the use of new technologies is therefore crucial for recognising and understanding contemporary changes in the labour market. In particular, it seems important to identify those types of services that can be provided thanks to the emergence of new technologies and to begin to identify the motivations of participants in the new system (thanks to the analysis of changes in values, respected by the labour market participants; Gallie 2019). These two factors influence the valuation of the services provided.

Having regard to the above considerations, we posed the following research questions: (1) what type of work is subject to tokenisation; (2) what motives, in terms of axiological background, do token issuers have; (3) on what principles do they value their work while applying personal tokens? We also hypothesise that the main types of work offered by the issuers of personal tokens will be professions characterised by a specific value system, realising the main idea of the Flexible Labour Market.

The aim of the paper is to identify the types of individual work that is valued by means of personal tokens and offered in the virtual world. We would also like to recognise the motives and incentives of different individual service providers who valuate their services (performed both online and in the real world) using personal tokens.

Such an analysis is a significant contribution to the discourse regarding work valuation in the world that is being transformed by new technologies. Previous research on tokens is conducted in technological (Adhami et al. 2018), legislative (Dierksmeier and Seele 2016), and financial (Castrén et al. 2020) dimensions. It is worth noting that the research on the issue of labour valuation through personal tokens that we undertake is actually not currently conducted due to the novelty of the tokenisation process itself and the "taking root" in the labour market of new labour models based on digitalisation and the use of new technologies. The novelty of our research is not only that we take up a new topic, concerning new phenomena occurring in the labour market, but also that we study it in an interdisciplinary way, taking into account the financial and axiological dimension (we use Schwartz's theory of the basic individual values and work values).

The main results of our research are: (1) identification of the main characteristics of personal tokens, under which work is offered, in comparison with other types of tokens; (2) identification of the types of services, offered by PT issuers; (3) recognition of the axiological motivation of PT issuers, i.e. identification of the values PT issuers referred to in their description of the service offer and to what extent the values declared by PT issuers "realised" the main ideas of the Flexible Labour Market.

2 Literature Review

The issue of self-work valuation is related to the increasingly intense discussions about changes in the Flexible Labour Market (Benner 2002; Schittekatte and Meeus 2020). In particular, it refers to the emergence of new business models and new work models based on the idea of Wikinomics, a behaviour that combines openness, partnership, sharing, and global action (Tapscott and Williams 2006). These new models of work are characterised both (1) from the objective side (the market, the service recipient) by: projectivity, timeliness (deadline), value estimation, reputation, horizontal labour market, and (2) from the subjective side (the employee, the contractor) by: independence, creativity, ingenuity, innovation, time and space mobility (Florida 2019). This model is based on the interpenetration of professional and private spheres.

An example of this type of work is that undertaken by gig workers. These are workers who perform and complete short-term on-demand (i.e. gig) work for a variety of employers (Torpey and Hogan 2016; Best 2017), using technological tools in their work (Colbert et al. 2016).

One of the main problems that arise in connection with the latter is to define what is work and what is not (Ross 2013; Autor and Dorn 2013), and consequently, to consider the important question of how to value such work. Existing valuation models, based on a full-time, vertical view of work, do not take into account the ongoing changes of the contemporary labour market of Economy 4.0 (gig workers and gig economy; De Groen et al. 2017). Valuing one's own work is typically based on three sources: comparing competitor prices, identifying costs incurred (Heneman and LeBlanc 2003), and identifying the value offered to the investor/client (Prainsack and Buyx 2018). An interesting answer to the question of how work is valued in the digital world is personal tokens.

3 Methodology

Empirical data for the study were obtained from the personal tokenisation platform www.personaltokens.io in the period December 2020–April 2021. The research is therefore a case study. The indicated platform is not only a newly explored source of data (to the knowledge of the authors of the study, no research has yet been conducted using it), but also a valuable collection of information dedicated strictly to the subject matter.

The analysis of types of services offered by digital token issuers and their motives has been embedded in the classification proposed by the authors of the paper. The development of this type of typology is associated with certain problems: (1) the nature of the services is ambiguous (sometimes it is not possible to assign them to a single profession); (2) many services have appeared on the market relatively recently and, in addition, they are performed fully remotely, thus eluding the work typologies recognised in the research community; (3) there is a lack of considerations in the literature dedicated to the need to classify the work offered by digital token issuers. Referring to the latter, it is worth noting that the strand most similar to the area studied by the authors of this paper is the valuation of work within the gig economy. A classification of the services offered within the latter has been proposed, among others, by Kässi and Lehdonvirta (2018). Nevertheless, the motivations of issuers of digital utility tokens are of a peculiar nature, so that their activities in the market of offered services cannot be fully identified with the gig economy.

Therefore, the authors of the study, also bearing in mind the purpose of the research presented here, proposed a classification of the services offered, based on the motivation for digital token issuers to join the platform on which they can offer their services. These motivations include an interest in new technologies, an interest in financial (or more broadly, economic) issues, and a preference to be a part of a network. Within the framework of the study, the service description of each of the 155 digital token issuers (personal token issuers who offered services by means of those tokens) was analysed and then classified into a specific group based on the typology characterised in Table 1.

The theoretical basis for determining the axiological motivation of token issuers valuing their services is the theory of the basic individual values and work values implemented firstly by Shalom H. Schwartz (Ros et al. 1999). According to this theory, there are 10 main axiological areas, to which people refer in their valuation of work (see Fig. 1). The study assumes that each of these areas is a reference point for the evaluation and valuation of their work by the issuers of personal tokens.

In the next part of the article, based on the criterion of valuation of 1 work hour, 12 cases of personal tokens were selected on the basis of which the issuer's axiological relation to work was estimated in a five-point Likert scale with the use of content analysis of communication artefacts (information contained in personal profiles of issuers on the examined platform) (justification for the choice of the scale—see Höhne et al. 2021): 1-not necessary, 2-not desirable, 3-objectionable, 4-desirable,

Table 1 Classification of services provided by digital token issuers

Class of services	Examples of provided services
Financial/Economic—E/F	Accounting
	Consulting (financial, investment, real estate, business, tax advisory)
	Currency exchange
	Human resources
Social (community services)—S	Trainings (incl. online courses)
	Platform CEO/founder
	Advertising/Promotion of ideas
	Language courses
	Consulting (e.g. photography, architecture, social media)
	Creative writing
	Travelling
	Celebrity (actor, musician, athlete)
	Community development (YouTuber, blogger)
	Mentoring, coaching
	Fundraising
Technology—T	Web development
	Game development
	Software development
	New technology development
	Software testing
	IT consulting
	Computer graphics
	Video production

Source Own elaboration

5-necessary. In the last part of the research, an analysis of the relationship between the valuation of 1 labour/service hour using personal tokens by both token owners (labour supply) and the customer network (labour demand) was conducted. The study used, among other things, financial data relating to the market valuation on a given date (5 April 2021) in the ratio personal token:ethereum:dollars.

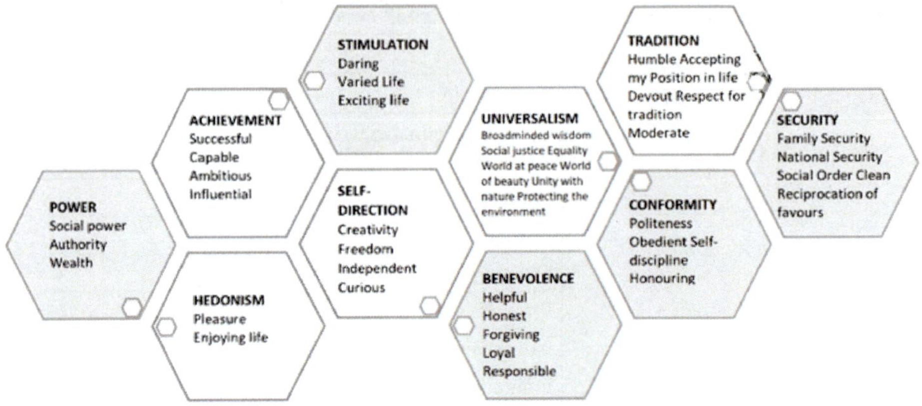

Fig. 1 Types of axiological areas (values) taken into account when evaluating work. *Source* Own elaboration based on Ros et al. (1999), p. 52

4 Analysis/Results Interpretation

4.1 Nature and Characteristics of Personal Tokens

Personal tokens are a kind of digital tokens based on blockchain technology, more widely referred to as distributed ledger technology (DLT). The issue of digital tokens is now widely considered both in the context of cryptocurrencies (narrow approach) and crypto-assets (broad approach). Taking into account the new blockchain technology regulations proposed at the European Union level in 2020, digital tokens can become the basis for developing technological instruments within the framework of open and decentralised finance.

This article adopts, as a basis for determining the characteristics of personal tokens, the definition proposed by the European Commission in 2020 as part of the drafts of the new regulations that comprise the Digital Finance Strategy, in particular in the Markets in Crypto-Assets Regulation—MiCA. According to this definition, "crypto-asset means a digital representation of value or rights which may be transferred and stored electronically, using distributed ledger technology or similar technology" (COM 2020, 593). Thus, taking into account the general nature of crypto-assets, it can be pointed out that personal tokens (PT) are a type of token otherwise known as digital tokens, which are characterised primarily by the individual ownership of their issuers (both in the celebrity and common person categories) and are mostly intended to provide digital access to a good or service, available on DLT, that are only accepted by the issuers of that token. More detailed characteristics of personal tokens are presented in Table 2.

Digital personal tokens can therefore serve as digital tools for the financial valuation of services and products offered in both the virtual and real worlds as part of the professional work of their issuers.

Table 2 Personal token (PT) features

Criteria	Tokens features
Type of the creating (issuing) entity	Issued by an individual entity (individual, non-institutional tokens)
The value or rights represented	Utility type—the most popular Exchange type (payment tokens) Investment type (security tokens)
Method of technological link	Non-native
Price/value stability standard	Non-stable
Digital contract	Non-fungible
Issuer branding	Celebrity personal tokens (PT) Common personal tokens (PT)

Source Own elaboration

Table 3 Classification by type of service

Class of services	Number of cases	Percentage
Financial/Economic	33	21.29
Social (community services)	90	58.06
Technology	32	20.65

Source Own elaboration

4.2 Classification of Services Offered by PT Issuers

The research conducted on a group of PT issuers shows that the most frequent type of service is community service (Table 3). More than 50% of the analysed 155 issuers of personal tokens provide this type of work, while the financial and technology classes each account for about 20% of the remaining owners of utility tokens.

The 12 tokens, which are further analysed in detail, have a similar structure in terms of the nature of the services offered (Table 4). The largest proportion of issuers of personal tokens provides work having the character of services to the community, while the financial and technological classes account for 1 and 3 cases, respectively.

4.3 Axiological Valuation of Work by 12 Token Issuers

An examination of the axiological basis of work valuation by issuers (Fig. 2) of personal tokens, based on the 10 axiological areas distinguished by Schwartz, shows that the leading values to which all issuers, referred as a study group, were: power, achievement, hedonism, stimulation, self-direction, while the other values did not constitute a strong axiological support for token valuation by issuers.

Table 4 Type of services provided by analysed 12 token issuers

Token name	Class of services
RAF	Financial/Economic F/E
BEN	*Social (community services)—S*
ARTCOIN	*Social (community services)—S*
ZIBICOIN	*Social (community services)—S*
LSZ	*Social (community services)—S*
PAGEMAN	*Social (community services)—S*
PP	*Social (community services)—S*
POKATO	*Social (community services)—S*
DDT	*Social (community services)—S*
JKCOIN	Technology—T
DEX	Technology—T
FULOFMO	Technology—T

Source Own elaboration

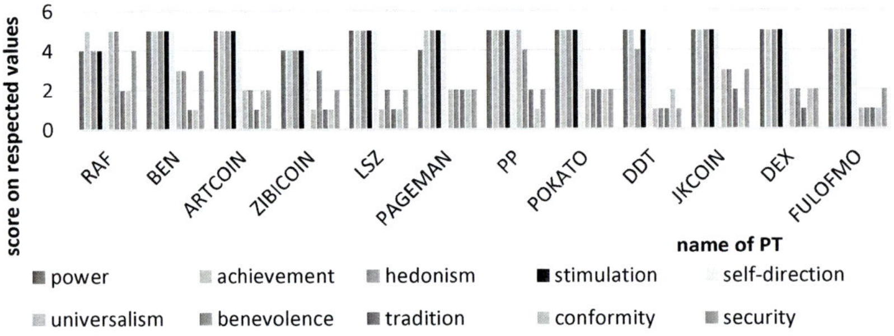

Fig. 2 Axiological view of work by analysing 12 PT issuers. *Source* Own elaboration

Considering the split of tokens by the services offered, it can be seen that the groups of issuers providing social and technological services are very similar in terms of the values considered (Table 5).

For personal tokens under which financial services are offered, there is a significant difference (compared to the two remaining classes) when it comes to axiological areas such as universalism, benevolence, and security. This is a rather surprising observation, since stereotypically in the previous labour market model (before the emergence of new online or gig economy work models) services of a financial nature were axiologically close to those of a social nature (Autor and Dorn 2013). It would also seem that issuers who offered technological services within their tokens—i.e. services from the new labour market model based on the ideas of Wikinomics, flexibility, or sharing—would be axiologically differently motivated in relation to the evaluation/valuation of their own work than before.

Table 5 Median axiological "saturation" of the tokens under study, taking into account the types of services offered

Axiological field	All type services	Financial/economics services	Social/community services	Technology services
Power	5.0	4.0	5.0	5.0
Achievement	5.0	5.0	5.0	5.0
Hedonism	5.0	4.0	5.0	5.0
Stimulation	5.0	4.0	5.0	5.0
Self-direction	5.0	4.0	5.0	5.0
Universalism	2.0	5.0	2.0	2.0
Benevolence	2.0	5.0	2.0	2.0
Tradition	1.0	2.0	1.0	1.0
Conformity	1.5	2.0	1.5	1.0
Security	2.0	4.0	2.0	2.0

Source Own calculations based on data from the PT platform

4.4 Personal Tokens Valuation

The above statements were finally verified by means of financial valuation of the services offered by the owners of personal tokens, based on the example of valuation of 1 working hour. As can be seen in Fig. 3, owners of 12 different tokens were quite diversified when it comes to the valuation of their work time (from 100 to 5 000 tokens). The most popular groups of work hour pricing values were 100, 1000, and 2 000 tokens.

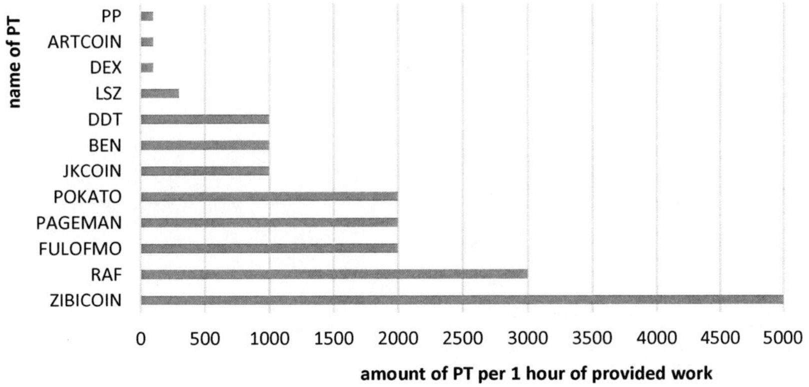

Fig. 3 Amount of PT per 1 h of individual work of their owners. *Source* Own calculations based on data from the PT platform

As further analysis shows, the highest prices of 1 h for a labour service offered by using personal tokens were not directly related to high customer interest as assessed by the number of transactions carried out involving a respective token (Table 6).

Therefore, as follows from the analysis of market valuation by network clients (Table 5 and Fig. 4) and the study of the type of services offered (Tables 3 and 4) at the current, initial stage of development of the personal tokens market, the motivation of the owner and the class of service offered may be a secondary criterion for token valuation. It is observed that, in addition to the motives for issuing tokens identified above (see the analysis of the axiological background of the decision to use tokens

Table 6 Valuation of services and PT transactions on the platform

Token	1 h of work	Class of services	Number of transactions[a]	PT in $*
ZIBICOIN	5,000	F/E	1	0.000062
RAF	3,000	S	1	0.004179
FULOFMO	2,000	T	2	0.000166
PAGEMAN	2,000	S	3	0.031207
POKATO	2,000	S	1	0.041582
JKCOIN	1,000	T	116	0.024949
BEN	1,000	S	1451	0.025276
DDT	1,000	S	8	0.031207
LSZ	300	S	18	0.009876
DEX	100	T	26	0.009876
ARTCOIN	100	S	5	0.000020
PP	100	S	17	0.031207

[a]Number of transactions and valuation as of 5 April 2021
Source Own calculations based on data from the PT platform

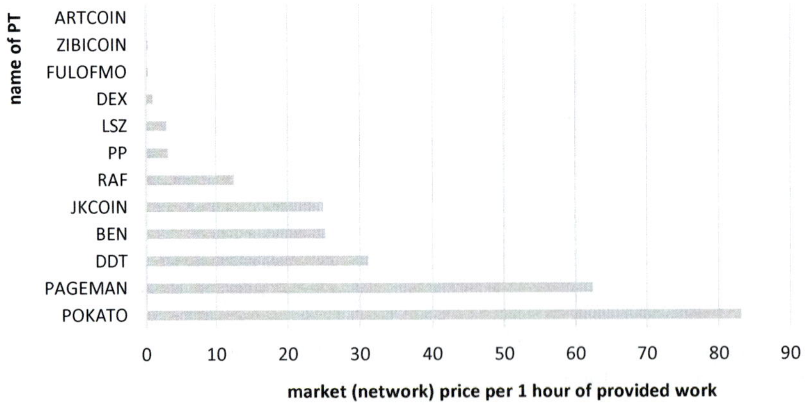

Fig. 4 Market (network) price per 1 h of individual work of PT owners. *Source* Own calculations based on data from the PT platform

in labour valuation), token owners are driven by the additional motive of obtaining a network effect. This would mean that the main purpose of the token issue is not necessarily to sell services or goods, but to increase the number of users of a given personal token, which may in the long term translate into increased utility of the virtual job offer.

5 Conclusions

Based on the research conducted, the following conclusions were drawn. Personal tokens, within the framework of which services were offered, showed characteristic features of personal tokens, i.e. they were non-negotiable, non-stable, and non-convertible, most often of utility nature, and their issuers were individual persons.

The study allowed for answering the first of the research questions—three main types of work were distinguished, offered as part of tokenisation—technological, social, and financial.

The most important group of services offered by token owners is that of a social nature. As we supposed, this is related to the motivations (analysed in relation to the value system) of people providing services using personal tokens, which was related to the analysis conducted within the second research question.

In this context, it should be pointed out that the main motivations of issuers were, on the one hand, to "appear" on the web and, on the other, to be able to express themselves (themselves and their skills, their work). When it comes to the axiological dimension of the ways issuers value their services, the dominant values represented axiological areas related to the sphere of individual cognitive activity and emotional experience (power, achievement, hedonism, stimulation, self-direction). This conclusion confirms our hypothesis that the main types of work offered by the issuers of personal tokens are professions, characterised by a specific value system, realising the ideas of the Flexible Labour Market. These are the ideas of value/flexibility and efficiency/success.

The results of the analysis carried out within the third research question showed that the valuation was neither based on a kind of provided services, nor related to the level of customer interest. It seems that at the current stage of development of the personal tokens market, the main motive for the valuation of the offered work may be a new factor—the appearance in the virtual world and the development of a network of contacts (customers), which will enable to achieve a network effect in the long term.

The main limitation of our study was the availability of data. Difficulties in interpreting the data involved the need to use methods of linguistic analysis of communication artefacts (descriptions of tokens and the services offered within them, made by issuers on the platform), which involve the risk of incomplete intersubjectivity of interpretation. In order to mitigate this, we used a specific communicative perspective—a cultural approach—thanks to which the artefacts were inter-pretended as expressions of a specific valuing attitude, allowing us to determine the respect of certain types of values by the issuers (according to the adopted 10 axiological areas).

Further research on personal tokens as a measure for labour valuation can be developed in the following directions. Firstly, it would be worthwhile to examine the personalisation process itself in the context of changes in the service buyer–seller relationship. Secondly, formulating a proposal for the valuation of networked labour (e.g. by examining how PT issuers build trust) is equally worth achieving. Thirdly, we suggest building a model enabling quantitative presentation of the impact of individual variables on the price of the personal token under which the work is offered and its fluctuation over specific time periods.

Acknowledgements The article was prepared through the project financed within the Regional Excellence Initiative programme of the Minister of Science and Higher Education of Poland, covering the years 2019–2022, grant no. 004/RID/2018/19, financing of 3,000,000 PLN.

References

Adhami, S., Giudici, G., Martinazzi, S.: Why do businesses go crypto? An empirical analysis of initial coin offerings. J. Econ. Bus. **100**, 64–75 (2018)

Autor, D.H., Dorn, D.: The growth of low-skill service jobs and the polarization of the US labor market. Am. Econ. Rev. **103**(5), 1553–1597 (2013)

Benner, C.: Work in the New Economy Flexible Labor Markets in Silicon Valley. Blackwell Publishing, Oxford (2002)

Best, S.: The U.S. Gig economy: economic imposition or economic choice? Bus. Manag. Rev. **8**(4), 60–67 (2017)

Castrén, O., Kavonius, I.K., Rancan, M.: Digital currencies in financial networks. EBA Staff Paper Series **8**, 3–48 (2020)

Colbert, A., Yee, N., George, G.: The digital workforce and the work place of the future. Acad. Manag. J. **59**(3), 731–739 (2016)

De Groen, W.P., Lenaerts, K., Bosc, R., Paquier, F.: Impact of digitalisation and the on-demand economy on labour markets and the consequences for employment and industrial relations. Final Study. CEPS Special Report, August 2017. http://aei.pitt.edu/88531/1/EESC_Digitalisation.pdf (2017). Accessed 12 Mar 2021

Dierksmeier, C., Seele, P.: Cryptocurrencies and business ethics. J. Bus. Ethics **152**, 1–14 (2016)

Florida, R.: The Rise of the Creative Class. Basic Books, New York (2019)

Gallie, D.: Research on work values in changing economic and social context. Ann. Am. Acad. Pol. Soc. Sci. **481**(1), 26–42 (2019)

Hackl, B., Wagner, M., Attmer, L., Baumann, D.: New Work: Auf dem Weg zur neuen Arbeitswelt. Springer Gabler, Wiesbaden (2017)

Heneman, R.L., LeBlanc, P.V.: Work valuation addresses shortcomings of both job evaluation and market pricing. Compens. Benefits Rev. **35**(1), 7–11 (2003)

Höhne, K., Krebs, D., Kühnel, S.M.: Measurement properties of completely and end labeled unipolar and bipolar scales in Likert-type questions on income (in)equality. Soc. Sci. Res. 102544 (2021)

Huws, U.: Labor in The Global Digital Economy the Cybertariat Comes of Age. Monthly Review Press, New York (2014)

Kässi, O., Lehdonvirta, V.: Online labour index: measuring the online gig economy for policy and research. Technol. Forecast. Soc. Chang. **137**, 241–248 (2018)

Prainsack, B., Buyx, A.: The value of work: addressing the future of work through the lens of solidarity. Bioethics **32**, 585–592 (2018)

Proposal for a regulation of the european parliament and of the council on Markets in Crypto-assets, and amending Directive (EU) 2019/1937 COM (2020) 593

Ros, M., Schwartz, S.H., Surkiss, S.: Basic individual values, work values, and the meaning of work. Appl. Psychol. Int. Rev. **48**(I), 49–71 (1999)

Ross, A.: In search of the Lost Paycheck. In: T. Scholz (ed.) Digital Labor. The Internet as playground and factory. Taylor & Francis, New York (2013)

Ruiner, C., Debbing, C.E.: Digital supply chains and new work—friends or foes? In: M. Klumpp, C. Ruiner (eds.) Digital Supply Chains and the Human Factor. Lecture Notes in Logistics. Springer, Cham (2021)

Schittekatte, T., Meeus, L.: Flexibility markets: Q&A with project pioneers. Utilities Policy **63**, 1–11 (2020)

Schofield, A.: Personalized pricing in the digital era. Competition Law J. **18**(1), 35–44 (2019)

Tapscott, D., Wiliams, A.: Wikinomics. How Mass Collaboration Changes Everything. Port-folio. Penguin Group, London (2006)

Torpey, E., Hogan, A.: Working in a gig economy. BLS.gov (2016)

Factors Affecting Consumers' Attitude and Intentions Toward Online Events During the COVID-19 Pandemic

Otilia-Elena Platon, David-Florin Ciocodeică, Margareta-Stela Florescu, Ştefan Claudiu Căescu, and Olguţa-Anca Orzan

Abstract For the events industry, the measures imposed in order to prevent the spread of Coronavirus have generated indefinite postponement or cancellation of many types of events, and event organizers started to relocate their activities online. It is necessary to measure and evaluate the impact of the COVID-19 pandemic on the events industry from the consumers' perspective. An online survey on a sample of 423 respondents was conducted in this regard. The research aimed to validate a structural model created in order to identify the influence of the COVID-19 pandemic and other factors of influence on the consumers' attitudes and intentions toward online events. The proposed conceptual model was tested and validated using the specific methodology of structural equation modeling (SEM). The research results could be used by event organizers to meet consumer needs, to overcome the obstacles, and to improve the format and the deployment of online events.

Keywords COVID-19 · Online events · Event marketing

1 Introduction

So far, the COVID-19 pandemic has generated over 226 million infections and over 4.6 million deaths globally (WHO 2021). It has also provoked fears of imminent

O.-E. Platon (✉) · D.-F. Ciocodeică · M.-S. Florescu · Ş. C. Căescu
Bucharest University of Economic Studies, Bucharest, Romania
e-mail: otilia.platon@mk.ase.ro

D.-F. Ciocodeică
e-mail: david.ciocodeica@stud.ase.ro

M.-S. Florescu
e-mail: margareta.florescu@ari.ase.ro

Ş. C. Căescu
e-mail: stefan.caescu@mk.ase.ro

O.-A. Orzan
University of Medicine and Pharmacy "Carol Davila", Bucharest, Romania

A. M. Dima and M. Kelemen (eds.), *Digitalization and Big Data for Resilience and Economic Intelligence*, Springer Proceedings in Business and Economics, https://doi.org/10.1007/978-3-030-93286-2_13

economic and social crises (Nicola et al. 2020) and a lot of uncertainty. Social distancing, self-isolation, and travel restrictions have led to changes in all economic sectors. This pandemic has affected communities, businesses, and organizations worldwide, as well as financial markets and the global economy.

Prior to 2020, the events industry made a significant contribution to the economy (Ozili and Arun 2020). In 2018 business events hosted over 1.5 billion participants across over 180 countries (Ozili and Arun 2020). The events industry generated over \$1.07 trillion of direct expenses, representing expenses for business event planning, the production of business events, travel-related aspects, and exhibitors' direct expenses. The industry also created 10.3 million direct jobs globally and generated \$621.4 billion of direct GDP worldwide (Ozili and Arun 2020).

During the Coronavirus outbreak, a large number of cancellations financially affected the events industry. Events such as trade fairs, exhibitions, conferences, corporate events, product launches, live concerts, music performances, cultural events, weddings, parties, and many more were either cancelled or postponed to a later date.

Event marketing is used as an inclusive term, encompassing a diverse range of organizational events, from large congress or trade shows to small workshops and seminars (Crowther 2011). Event marketing is defined as the promotion and management of an event, such as conferences, seminars, exhibitions, fairs, art performances, company anniversaries, and other similar events (Kotler and Keller 2009). At the same time, event management represents the design and coordination of an event and, without a doubt, the success of an event depends both on the efficiency of the event marketing and on its management (Moise et al. 2012). The most important criteria taken into account when carrying out an event is: the type of event, the location where the event takes place, the period in which the event takes place, the participation fee, and the way it is managed (Moise et al. 2012).

Many changes occurred with the emergence of the COVID-19 pandemic in the field of event management. Since the events with a large number of people were cancelled or postponed, the event organizers had to rethink their actions and adapt to this situation. Some companies relocated most of their activities online. Virtual conferencing began to be the new and widely used means of communication. Therefore, events are changing and are integrating these new ways of communication. In the context of online marketing, social media has become one of the fastest means of communication. Social networks offer a great opportunity to interact with event organizers, marketers, and participants (Harb et al. 2019). In the online environment, the communication barriers are less restrictive, bringing a high degree of flexibility in the exchange of information, content, knowledge, ideas, and opinions. An important factor during any event is the interactive communication of those who conduct the event with the potential customers, sponsors, and the public (Moise 2014).

The lack of events due to the COVID-19 pandemic has affected both brands and the social life of consumers (TrendHunter 2020). Event organizers had to resort to other methods to carry out their activity so, as to withstand the pandemic period, the most accessible option was to relocate the events in the online environment. Therefore, as an alternative, some brands decided to invest more in online events so that consumers can interact with products and can have social experiences, by connecting virtually with other consumers (TrendHunter 2020).

The behavior of event consumers changed during the pandemic, after the appearance of self-isolation and social distancing measures and the prohibition of many events. During this period, marked by uncertainty and anxiety, consumers are looking for ways to escape and relax, to distract themselves from the unusual reality they are currently facing (TrendHunter 2020). These consumers turn to new hobbies, new relaxation activities, or decide to attend various types of virtual experiences (TrendHunter 2020), as a means to connect with other persons, to interact with them, or to gain knowledge from different fields.

Due to the growth of online activities, the consumer experience in the online environment has gained relevance in the literature, becoming more important than the concept of "services quality" (Klaus and Maklan 2011) including in areas such as online events. The consumer experience is a vital element in order to increase the success of online events and, as a result, it is necessary to understand how this experience can be shaped, managed, and influenced.

Organizing an event in the online environment is not an insurmountable challenge because the main elements of any event—the organizers, participants, and speakers—are already there (Roerdink et al. 2008). Moreover, this alternative format of online events and the real-time experience is almost as captivating as offline events. In addition to "live" interaction, online experiences are a key point of connection between the event organizer and consumers (McGillivray 2014). Online events are set in a dynamic and information-rich context (Morgan-Thomas and Veloutsou 2013) and event organizers are often promoting interactivity and real-time experiences to engage consumers with the event itself, but also with other consumers (Filo et al. 2015).

The COVID-19 pandemic will have a long-term impact and will most probably determine significant changes in consumers' beliefs, attitudes, and behavioral intentions toward online events. Therefore, it is necessary to measure and evaluate the impact of this pandemic from the consumers' perspective. Currently, there are no studies to evaluate influencing factors, such as the COVID-19 pandemic and the specific features of virtual events, in relation to consumers' attitudes and intentions toward online events. Therefore, this paper aims to study and test the relationship between these variables. The main objectives of this paper are to answer the following questions:

(1) what are the main internal and external factors that influence the decisions of event consumers during the pandemic,
(2) how do the features and deployment of online events influence the attitude of event consumers during the pandemic, and
(3) what are the behavioral intentions of event consumers in the current pandemic situation?

Since the field of online events is expanding during this period, this study is important because it can lay the groundwork and be a starting point for future research. Event organizers could also use this evaluation to meet consumer needs, to adjust plans, to determine future actions, to improve the format and the deployment of online events, or to stimulate investment in online events.

For this article, we developed a quantitative research, conducted through an online survey, which aimed to validate a structural model. The model is based on eight hypotheses and is designed to identify the influence of the COVID-19 pandemic and other emotional and rational factors of influence on the consumers' attitudes and intentions toward online events.

2 Literature Review

Event organizers prefer the exclusively online version for conferences, workshops, or competitions due to some advantages: it is much easier to organize and control the event in terms of safety rules, the participants can connect from anywhere in the world and it is easier to promote the event and inform the public about it (Su et al. 2019). Event organizing companies can reduce costs and increase profitability through online events. Online events have many benefits even if they do not have the same impact on consumers. In the case of online events, the organizational costs decrease, so the tickets are much cheaper and affordable for consumers. Although it is quite effective to organize an online event and there are many advantages, it is also different and some important aspects of physically supported events are lacking (Zhang and Ghorbani 2020). There are also some barriers to accepting and attending online events. Some consumers are reluctant about this type of event, due to the lack of direct social interaction and to the impossibility of recreating the atmosphere of conventional events. Some consumers also consider that events no longer have the same impact and no longer generate the same satisfaction offered by attending a conventional event. Although attending online events does not compare with the affiliation felt by participants in offline events, this new form of deploying an event is a suitable alternative for the moment that generates enough advantages. Event organizers need to consider the growing number of consumers who are willing to attend online events and understand the factors that make up their virtual experience (Su et al. 2020).

Taking into consideration all the information presented above, we identified five key variables that can affect the attitude and intentions of online event consumers, namely: the features of online events, the consumers' motivations, the external influences, the COVID-19 influence, and the barriers to accepting or attending online events.

Attitude is defined as "a person's favorable or unfavorable evaluation of an object" (Fishbein and Ajzen 1975). A person's attitude generally determines a predisposition to behave in a certain way rather than the behavior itself (Fishbein and Ajzen 1975). In the case of online events, it is more likely that the consumers who have positive attitudes toward online events to attend them than consumers who have a neutral or negative attitude.

Behavioral intention refers to "a person's intentions to perform various behaviors" (Fishbein and Ajzen 1975). Behavioral intention is considered to be a conative component of attitude and it is determined by attitude and subjective norm (Davis 1989). Therefore, the strength of an intention is explained by "the person's subjective probability that he will perform the behavior in question" (Fishbein and Ajzen 1975).

The subjective norm is defined as "a person's perception that most people who are important to him think he should or should not perform the behavior in question" and it has a direct effect on the person's intention to act (Fishbein and Ajzen 1975). In this research, the subjective norm was replaced with a series of internal and external factors that can influence the consumers' intentions, namely: the features of online events, the consumers' motivations, and the external influences.

The main objectives of this research are to identify the most important features of online events for consumers, what motivates consumers to attend online events during the pandemic, what types of barriers can negatively influence consumers' attitude toward online events, what are the main external factors that motivate and influence the decisions of event consumers during the pandemic, how do the features and deployment of online events influence the motivation of event consumers to attend online events during the pandemic, and what are the behavioral intentions of event consumers in the current pandemic situation.

Based on the research objectives, a set of eight research hypotheses were formulated, as shown in Fig. 1, namely:

H1: The influence of the COVID-19 pandemic has a direct and positive effect on the consumers' attitude toward online events.

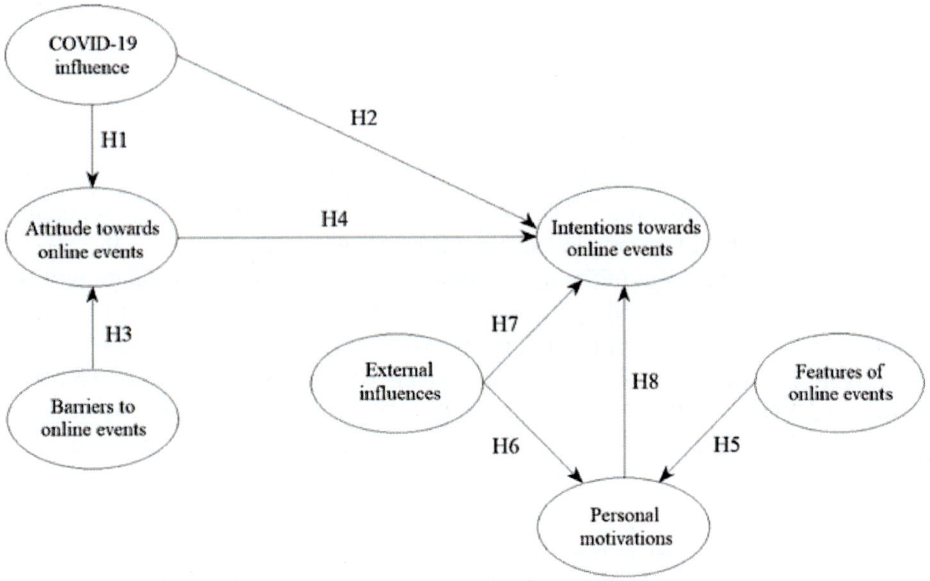

Fig. 1 Proposed structural model. *Source* The authors' contribution

H2: The influence of the COVID-19 pandemic has a direct and positive effect on the consumers' intentions toward online events.
H3: The barriers to online events have a direct and negative effect on the consumers' attitude toward online events.
H4: The consumers' attitude toward online events has a direct and positive effect on their intentions toward online events.
H5: The features of online events have a direct and positive effect on the consumers' motivation to attend online events.
H6: The external influences have a direct and positive effect on the consumers' motivation to attend online events.
H7: The external influences have a direct and positive effect on the consumers' intentions toward online events.
H8: The consumers' personal motivations have a direct and positive effect on their intentions toward online events.

3 Methodology

The research aimed to identify the factors affecting consumer attitude and intention toward online events during the COVID-19 pandemic. The data was collected through an online survey, based on a structured questionnaire with 19 closed-ended questions. All latent variables included in the model were measured with 5 or 6 items, using 5-steps semantic differentials. The data was collected during November 2020 and IBM SPSS Statistics 21 and WarpPLS 7.0 were used for data analysis.

The main objectives of the research were related to the validation of the conceptual model regarding the consumers' motivations, attitudes, and intentions toward online events. The research also aimed to identify the types of online events that consumers attend, the frequency of attending online events, the platforms used for attending online events, and the sources used to inform about online events.

The proposed conceptual model was tested and validated using the specific methodology of structural equation modeling (SEM). The study was conducted on a sample of 423 respondents, but 65 respondents declared that they had not attended an online event in the last 6 months, thus for the model validation only the answers provided by the other 358 respondents were taken into consideration. Of this total sample, 36.3% were men and 63.7% were women. The distribution of respondents by age was as follows: 86.3% between 18 and 23 years old, 6.7% between 24 and 29 years old, 3.6% between 30 and 35 years old, and 3.4% over 36 years old. In terms of graduate studies, 78.2% have high school studies, 16.2% university studies, and 5% postgraduate studies. In terms of the statute on the labor market, the distribution of the sample was as follows: 79.6% students, 15.3% employees, 4.5% entrepreneurs/freelancers, and 0.6% unemployed. In terms of income, 19.8% have no personal income, 18.2% earn below 1000 RON, 26% between 1000 and 2000 RON, 13.4% between 2001 and 3000 RON, 4.2% between 3001 and 4000 RON, 4.7% between 4001 and 5000 RON, 8.4% over 5000 RON, and 5.3% did not want to answer. The distribution of respondents by the environment of residence was as follows: 75.8% were from the urban area and 24.2% were from the rural area.

4 Analysis/Results Interpretation

The proposed conceptual model was tested and validated using the specific methodology of structural equation modeling (SEM). The data used in this research do not have a normal distribution since the skewness values for the overall sample items ranged from −1.411 to +0.019 and the kurtosis values ranged from −0.652 to + 2.612. However, these values do not pose problems regarding their use in factor analysis.

The accuracy of the measurements was tested based on the values of the Cronbach's Alpha and the composite reliability coefficients. The values of the Cronbach's Alpha (ranging from 0.724 to 0.886) and the composite reliability coefficients (ranging from 0.820 to 0.916), presented in Table 1, demonstrate that all latent variables have very good values, generally over 0.80. These values indicate a very good accuracy of the measurements performed in the research and also indicate that the constructs are internally consistent.

According to the data in Table 1, the principle of convergent validity is fulfilled since almost all AVE values are greater than the recommended threshold of 0.50 but lower than the values of composite reliability coefficients, ranging from 0.478 to 0.687.

The latent variable Barriers to online events has a lower Average variance extracted (AVE) value than the threshold of 0.50, but the values of Cronbach's Alpha and composite reliability fall within the good–very good range. By removing items from the measurement of this scale, the values of Cronbach's Alpha and the composite reliability did not improve, therefore even though the AVE was slightly below 0.50

Table 1 Latent variables coefficients

Variable	Cronbach's alpha	Composite reliability	Average variances extracted (AVE)
Features of online events	0.860	0.896	0.592
Personal motivations	0.810	0.868	0.570
COVID-19 influence	0.779	0.851	0.538
External influences	0.818	0.873	0.579
Barriers to online events	0.724	0.820	0.478
Attitude toward online events	0.886	0.916	0.687
Intentions toward online events	0.859	0.899	0.641

Source The authors contribution

it might be considered acceptable given the fact that the scale was used for the first time for this research.

The discriminant validity was fulfilled since the correlations among latent variables with square roots of AVEs have values between 0.692 and 0.829 on the main diagonal of the correlation table, while the rest of the corresponding cells were registered lower values. The p-values for all of the correlations are lower than the threshold $p < 0.05$, with only one exception: the correlation between the variables Barriers to online events and Attitude toward online events has a p-value of 0.055.

The research hypotheses were tested by calculating the standardized path coefficients, corresponding to the causal relationships in the model. The hypotheses were validated under the conditions of $\beta > 0.10$, at a significance threshold $p < 0.05$. Therefore, according to the results presented in Fig. 2, seven proposed hypotheses were validated and one proposed hypothesis was rejected.

The three most important conditions that must be met in order to validate the model are related to the probability values associated with the APC and ARS indicators, which must be less than 0.05, and to the AVIF indicator value, which must be less than 5, or ideally less than 3.3. Thus, the calculated values of the Average path coefficient (APC) = 0.283, $p < 0.001$, Average R-squared (ARS) = 0.416, $p < 0.001$, and Average block VIF (AVIF) = 1.432, show that the model can be validated.

The R^2 coefficients of determination, calculated by the WarpPLS 7.0 program using ordinary least-squares regression, indicate the explanatory power of the predictor variables on the three dependent variables within the model, as shown in Fig. 2. According to the results, the values of all R^2 coefficients of determination are higher than 0.10, ranging from 0.375 to 0.469, showing that most of the predictive

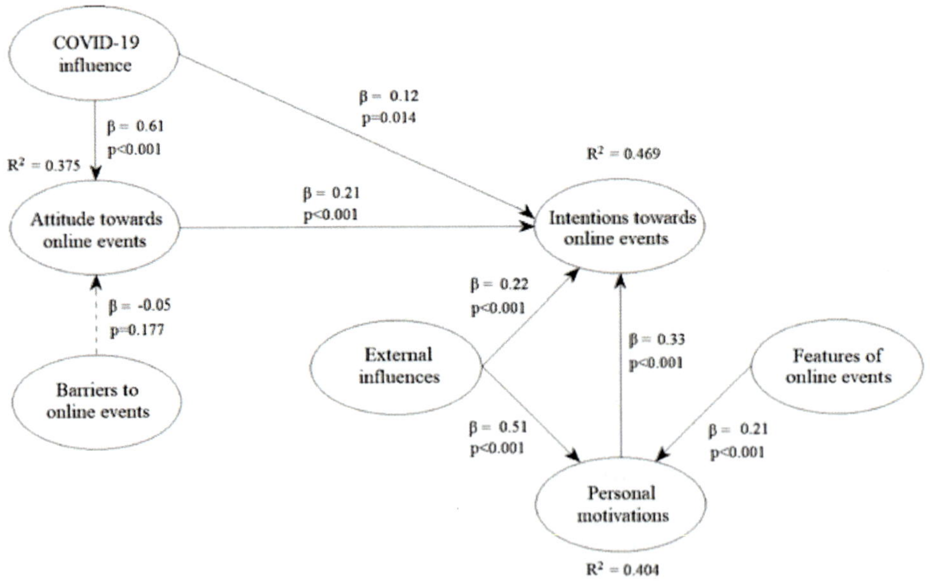

Fig. 2 Final structural model with the hypotheses supported. *Source* The authors' contribution

variables have a moderate explanatory power. The model has moderate R^2 values because there is an inherently great amount of unexplainable variation associated with consumer behavior.

According to the research results, the influence of the COVID-19 pandemic has a direct and positive effect on the consumers' attitude toward online events. In the context of the COVID-19 pandemic, compared to offline events, consumers consider online events to be a safer alternative in terms of preventing the spread of the SARS-COV-2 virus, a more efficient alternative in terms of organizing time and activities, a more enjoyable alternative in terms of social interaction with other participants, a simpler alternative in terms of how to register and participate and a more comfortable alternative in terms of overall effort to participate. All these factors directly influence the consumers' attitude toward online events in a favorable manner. Therefore the consumers enjoy more participating in online events, consider it is a better option to attend online events, consider they can have a useful experience participating in online events, and feel more confident and relaxed when they attend online events.

As the research results showed, the barriers to online events do not have a direct and negative effect on the consumers' attitude toward online events. Barriers such as the obligation to pay the attendance (ticket/participation fee), the distrust in the way the event takes place, the lack of direct interaction with event participants/organizers, the limited experience in using online equipment/technologies/platforms, and the lack of time to attend the online event do not have a negative influence on the consumers' attitude toward online events.

The influence of the COVID-19 pandemic also has a direct and positive effect on the consumers' intentions toward online events. Given the fact that in the context of the COVID-19 pandemic consumers consider online events to be a better alternative to offline events, they are more willing to attend or to interact with online events. In addition, this willingness is supported by the fact that the consumers' attitude toward online events has a direct and positive effect on their intentions toward online events.

The consumers' intentions toward online events are supported to a larger extent by their personal motivations and are influenced by external factors. According to the research results, the consumers' personal motivations have a direct and positive effect on their intentions toward online events. Consumers consider that by attending online events they gain knowledge, they get to meet other people who have the same interests as them, they get to discuss important topics with other people and they get up to date with news from different fields. Attending online events is also a good choice for leisure.

The consumers' motivation is influenced by the features of online events. As the results showed, features of online events, such as the theme of the event, the usefulness of the event, the attractiveness of the event, the date/period of the event, the event's agenda, the event guests/speakers, have a direct and positive effect on the consumers' motivation to attend online events. Also, the external influences have a direct and positive effect on the consumers' motivation to attend online events.

If the event was organized by recognized companies/individuals, if it had important moderators/guests/speakers, if the event was recommended by trustworthy people, if it was promoted offline and/or online (websites, social media, etc.), and if the event attracted the attention of many other people interested in participating, then the consumer may feel more motivated to participate in an online event.

Also, the external influences have a direct and positive effect on the consumers' intentions toward online events. Therefore, all the factors mentioned above can influence the consumers' intentions toward online events, such as: the intention to continue to inform themselves about the online events that interest them, the intention to continue to participate in similar online events as often or more often than at present, the intention to give positive feedback/reviews to online events that they enjoyed participating in, the intention to recommend the online events to their friends and acquaintances and the intention to participate in online events with various topics.

5 Conclusions

The research showed that there are certain elements of importance to consumers regarding the features of online events. The most important elements are represented by the theme of the event and its utility and attractiveness. Therefore, in order to succeed with an online event, the organizers need to concentrate mainly on these attributes. In order to be useful, an online event must match the interests of the participants and must bring added value for them. It is also important that the event is presented in an interesting and appealing manner so as to attract as many participants as possible, but also to live up to the expectations created. It is also important that the theme is well-chosen, depending on the occasion of the event and also on the target audience. The agenda of the event, the guests of the event/speakers, as well as the date/period of the event represent other important elements for consumers. The agenda should reach points of interest for the participants and should be very well-structured, not very busy and it should not waste much time with moments of pause. It is recommended to invite known, experienced, and representative guests/speakers because they are key components of an event. Potential participants are enthusiastically encouraged to take part in online events largely when the event is organized by important and recognized companies or persons and when the moderators/guests/speakers are well-known persons. It is also necessary to organize events of medium duration, with short, but strategic breaks, in order to keep the participants present in the "story" of the event. The event should be scheduled on days and hours accessible to as many participants as possible.

From the research results, we concluded that elements such as the type of event (public/private), the event organizer, and the event platforms are not elements of interest to consumers and could not influence their intention to participate in a significant manner.

Regarding the consumers' motivation to participate in online events, the research revealed a series of important aspects. Consumers consider that participating in online events contributes to their personal development and enriches their knowledge. By interacting with other participants with similar interests and by engaging in online discussions, consumers can gain more knowledge, can analyze different perspectives, and can gain more ideas, increasing the rate of cognitive learning and critical thinking skills. Engaging in online events represents a way to socialize and create new friends, with a common interest. It also helps consumers to maintain a connection with important specialists from various fields and to remain up to date with relevant information. Some consumers consider that online events are a good choice for leisure.

Event organizers should explore topics of current interest to contribute to the improvement of the participants' knowledge. They should also take into consideration the importance of networking and create discussion groups meant to stimulate the discussions related to the events. This way participants can keep in touch with one another and can transfer and continue the discussions about the event in other environments.

Compared to offline events, consumers consider that online events are a safer alternative in terms of preventing the spread of the infectious SARS-CoV-2 virus.

They consider that online events are time efficient, accessible in terms of registration and participation, and also more compliant in terms of participants' effort. Event organizers must highlight all these advantages and must implement a very accessible system for registration and participation.

Even if consumers consider online events have many advantages, there are some barriers to acceptance or attendance such as: the distrust in the event, the lack of direct interaction with the participants/organizers, the obligation to pay a participation fee, the lack of experience in using technology and the lack of time needed to participate in the event. To satisfactorily address these grievances, event organizers should create a trustworthy and interesting experience in order to somehow equate the payment of the fee.

Participants in online events during this period consider this type of event to be a more effective and enjoyable option and are willing to continue participating in online events as often or even more often as now. Therefore, there are suitable premises for event organizers to continue to invest in online events and to create unique experiences for participants in order to not perceive major differences between online and offline events.

References

Crowther, P.: Marketing event outcomes: from tactical to strategic. Int J. Event Festiv. Manag. **2**(1), 68–82 (2011)

Davis, F.D.: Perceived usefulness, perceived ease of use and user acceptance of information technology. MIS Q. **13**(3), 319–340 (1989)

Filo, K., Lock, D., Karg, A.: Sport and social media research: a review. Sport Manag. Rev. **18**(2), 166–181 (2015)

Fishbein, M., Ajzen, I.: Belief, attitude, intention and behaviour: an introduction to theory and research. Reading, MA, Addison-Wesley (1975)

Harb, A.A., Fowler, D., Chang, H.J., Blum, S.C., Alakaleek, W.: Social media as a marketing tool for events. J. Hosp. Tour. Technol. **10**(1), 28–44 (2019)

Klaus, P., Maklan, S.: Bridging the gap for destination extreme sports: a model of sports tourism customer experience. J. Mark. Manag. **27**(13), 1341–1365 (2011)

Kotler, P., Keller, K.L.: Marketing Management, 13th edn., p. 46. Prentice-Hall, Englewood Cliffs, NJ (2009)

McGillivray, D.: Digital cultures, acceleration and mega sporting event narratives. Leis. Stud. **33**(1), 96–109 (2014)

Moise, D.: Marketingul si managementul evenimentelor [Events marketing and management], ASE, Bucharest (2014)

Moise, D., Georgescu, B.: Zgură, D: Strategies for interactive communication, with external and internal stakeholders, in events' marketing. Proc. Soc. Behav. Sci. **46**, 5361–5365 (2012)

Morgan-Thomas, A., Veloutsou, C.: Beyond technology acceptance: brand relationships and online brand experience. J. Bus. Res. **66**(1), 21–27 (2013)

Nicola, M., Alsafi, Z., Sohrabi, C., Kerwan, A., Al-Jabir, A., Iosifidis, C., Agha, M., Agha, R.: The socio-economic implications of the coronavirus pandemic (COVID-19): a review. Int. J. Surg. **78**, 185–193 (2020)

Ozili, P.K., Arun, T.: Spillover of COVID-19: impact on the global economy. In: SSRN, https://papers.ssrn.com/sol3/papers.cfm?abstract_id=3562570 (2020). Last Accessed 05 Nov 2020

Roerdink, M., Coolen, B.H., Clairbois, B., Lamoth, C.: Online gait event detection using a large force platform embedded in a treadmill. J. Biomech. **41**(12), 2628–2632 (2008)

Su, H., Zhang, H., Liang, Y., Mu, Y.: Online event-triggered adaptive critic design for non-zero-sum games of partially unknown networked systems. Neurocomputing **368**, 84–98 (2019)

Su, H., Zhang, H., Sun, S., Cai, Y.: Integral reinforcement learning-based online adaptive event-triggered control for non-zero-sum games of partially unknown nonlinear systems. Neurocomputing **377**, 243–255 (2020)

TrendHunter: https://www.trendhunter.com/protrends/virtual-events (2020). Last Accessed 01 Nov 2020

WHO Coronavirus: (COVID-19) Dashboard, https://covid19.who.int/ (2021). Last Accessed 17 Sept 2021

Zhang, X., Ghorbani, A.A.: An overview of online fake news: characterization, detection, and discussion. Inf. Process. Manage. **57**, 10–15 (2020)

Non-financial Performance of Energy Companies Listed on the Bucharest Stock Exchange and Relevance for Stakeholders

Puime Felix, Panait Mirela, Andrei Jean Vasile, and Gigauri Iza

Abstract Sustainable development is a complex process that requires the concerted effort of various categories of stakeholders. Companies have become aware of the role they can play in the transition to the green economy, which is why they are voluntarily involved in various CSR programs. In addition, economic agents try to provide the most complete information of their financial and non-financial performance so that stakeholders have a broader picture of the efforts of companies not only to maximize profit for shareholders, but also the value created for society in general. Starting from these considerations, the article proposes the analysis of the non-financial performances of the companies in the energy sector listed on the Bucharest Stock Exchange. These companies show a responsible attitude toward the environment and society, trying to mitigate the negative externalities generated by the production activity. Extensive information is presented in sustainability reports, with companies trying to carry out systematic consultation and sustained information of the stakeholders considering the character of public companies and the provisions of the European directive on the disclosure of non-financial information. Therefore, the social and environmental behavior of the companies in the energy sector has substantially improved under the pressure of different categories of stakeholders and under the influence of certain European regulations transposed in the Romanian legislation. However, the analysis revealed a differentiated behavior of these companies despite the fact that they belong to the same field of activity, they are listed companies and, in general, the state is the majority shareholder.

P. Felix (✉)
University of A Coruña, A Coruña, Spain
e-mail: felix.puime@udc.es

P. Mirela · A. J. Vasile
Petroleum-Gas University of Ploiești, Ploiești, Romania
e-mail: mirela.matei@upg-ploiesti.ro

P. Mirela
Institute of National Economy, Bucharest, Romania

G. Iza
St. Andrews Georgian University, Tbilisi, Georgia

A. M. Dima and M. Kelemen (eds.), *Digitalization and Big Data for Resilience and Economic Intelligence*, Springer Proceedings in Business and Economics, https://doi.org/10.1007/978-3-030-93286-2_14

Keywords Reporting · Disclosure · Non-financial performance · Energy

1 Introduction

Companies have become increasingly aware of their role in promoting the principles of sustainable development, and international institutions such as the United Nations are creating specific tools to guide companies in this complex process (Said et al. 2015; Ismail and Mahmood 2019; Latif et al. 2020; Mahmood and Uddin 2020, Nicolo et al. 2020; Siminica et al. 2020; Tarquinio et al. 2020; European Commission 2021; García-Sánchez et al. 2021). More and more, companies are involved in social responsibility programs, transnational companies being CSR promoters at national and international levels. Important is not only the concrete actions carried out by companies to maximize their contribution in the economies in which they act socially and environmentally, but also the way in which they report the results obtained.

Sustainability reporting is an essential component of corporate social responsibility (CSR) as companies need to publicly disclose information concerning the achieved results of their corporate responsibility programs, including the impact of their daily operations on the environment, society, and other stakeholders. The society is expecting companies in the energy sector to present non-financial reports describing their sustainable performance. Sustainability or CSR reporting is an effective tool for a company to communicate with stakeholders. Besides, it allows companies to evaluate their influence on the environment, society, and economy, to improve their performance by decreasing negative footprints and simultaneously reducing operational costs.

Increased demand for ethical and sustainable practices (Matei 2013; Raimi and Isiaka 2020; Petrescu et al. 2020; Tarquinio et al. 2020; Ates 2021; Gigauri and Djakeli 2021; Voica and Stancu 2021) and information about CSR performance force companies to engage in CSR reporting efforts, and publish their reports annually to communicate with all groups of stakeholders (Vartiak 2016). Moreover, the ongoing COVID-19 pandemic crisis dictates companies to protect their reputation through CSR practice (García-Sánchez and García-Sánchez 2020; Gigauri 2021), and take into account the remarkable role of sustainability reporting.

Furthermore, Sustainability Reporting has become mandatory for large European companies. The EU law requires non-financial reporting of large companies to disclose information regarding their operations and management of social and environmental issues. In general, the purpose of sustainability reports is to help shareholders, investors, consumers, and other stakeholders to evaluate the performance of companies not only in terms of their financial success, but also their responsible behavior and approach to business (European Commission 2021). In particular, 2014/95/EU Directive requires large companies to disclose information concerning environmental responsibility, social and employee matters, respect for human rights, anti-corruption activities, and diversity on company boards (European Commission 2021). The significance of Corporate Sustainability Reporting is increasing as the European Commission adopted a proposal in April 2021, which has amended the existing requirements and aims at extending the scope to all large companies, demanding the assurance audit of reported information, introducing detailed reporting requirements in accordance with the EU sustainability reporting standards, and asking companies to tag digitally the reporting information to fit into the European single access point (European Commission 2021).

Along with the mandatory financial information, public companies have disclosed their voluntary non-financial information (Rezaee and Tuo 2017). Interestingly, the research has proved that the high level of voluntary disclosure of non-financial information was linked with better sustainable performance (Rezaee and Tuo 2017). The analysis of CSR reports of Italian companies, published to fulfill legal requirements concerning mandatory social and environmental reports, demonstrated a high level of credibility and understandability, but a low level of exhaustivity, which is suggesting the significance of experience in voluntary non-financial reporting (Balluchi et al. 2021).

Likewise, energy companies are engaging in CSR and sustainability activities as a response to the growing demands from stakeholders to disclose information (Karaman et al. 2021), but also to improve their sustainability. They need to meet the expectations of the society as non-financial disclosures have become a standard of business practice and recent studies confirm the positive correlation between CSR performance and reporting of energy companies (Karaman et al. 2021). Additionally, good CSR performance is related to the disclosure of verifiable information, whereas poor CSR performance tends to disclose unverifiable information (Koseoglu et al. 2021). However, sustainable development implies focusing on environmental and social issues while generating economic gains (Koseoglu et al. 2021). Further, many companies mention Sustainable Development Goals (SDGs) in their non-financial reporting (Di Vaio and Varriale 2020).

Studies demonstrate that firm size plays a prominent role in the disclosure of non-financial performance, and particularly large companies tend to disclose their CSR efforts, while CSR report disclosure improves the financial performance of small companies (Ting 2021). Importantly, environmental disclosure is essential on financial markets as it is argued to be a tool for risk reduction (Tzouvanas et al. 2020), and therefore, provides needed information for decision-making to investors.

The present research explores the sustainability activities of Romanian companies from the energy sector. The data for the study was derived from the websites of the energy companies listed on the Bucharest Stock Exchange and was obtained additionally from the GRI Sustainability Disclosure Database for these companies.

This study is notable for focusing the analysis on the non-financial performance of energy companies given the negative externalities generated by their activity. For this reason, these companies are more careful with the information they present to stakeholders given the divestment process that is manifesting itself internationally, more and more portfolio investors giving up their shares in fossil fuel companies and targeting companies with low impact on the environment such as those that produce renewable energy.

The rest of the paper is organized as follows. The next section reviews the relevant literature for the theoretical background of the study and is followed by a description of the research methodology. The subsequent section reports the study results and discussion of the findings. The final section draws conclusions, acknowledges the limitations, and provides new avenues for future studies.

2 Literature Review

Given the complexity of the phenomenon of sustainable development, the promotion of specific principles can be done through different channels, and companies can be some of the promoters of this concept. Through various mechanisms, the principles of sustainable development shape business strategy (Curtó-Pagès et al. 2021). Taking into account the EU Directive 2014/95/EU on Non-Financial Reporting, this law could be considered a political commitment by including the SDGs as an important reporting framework.

More and more researchers are focusing on socially responsible investments as portfolio investors have become increasingly aware of the role they can play in the capital market by changing the behavior of listed companies. The managers of the companies listed on the stock exchange have become attentive to the published information considering the behavior of the different categories of stakeholders. In addition to the financial information that must be published periodically given the rigors of the capital market, listed companies provide more and more information on CSR programs. In the last ten years, researchers have also focused on analyzing the non-financial performance of companies and their impact on stakeholders.

The relationship between Non-financial Reporting, Environmental Strategies, and Financial Performance is analyzed by Pizzi (2018) taking into account the transposition of the European directive 95/2014 into Italian legislation, from 2017. The researchers select 118 companies listed at the Milan Stock Exchange, and the analysis is conducted for 2013–2015. The philosophy of this paper is based on the Ohlson assumption about company evaluation (Feltham and Ohlson 1995; Ohlson 1995). According to Ohlson, the company market value is based on and derives from financial business components and non-financial business components. The conclusions of the study reveal that the homogenization of the information presented to the stakeholders contributes to the improvement of the possibilities to make comparisons between companies. In this way, the investment process is favored by the harmonization of the presentation of non-financial data.

Caputo et al. (2020) focused on Non-Financial Reporting Harmonization in Europe taking into account the directive 95/2014. Even if the sample included 223 companies listed on the Milano Stock Exchange, which fell under the regulations of the European directive, only 147 companies had published their non-financial data for 2017 by the study date. The results of the study reveal the importance of the European directive in supporting the adoption of more sustainable business models at the level of Italian companies.

For the Spanish market, Curtó-Pagès et al. (2021) conducted a study on a sample of 58 listed companies to the Bolsas y Mercados Españoles (BME, Spanish Stock Exchanges and Markets). The researchers analyzed non-financial reports for the period 2016–2019. The results of the study reveal that the 2030 Agenda improves the commitment of Spanish listed companies to the SDGs. A greater inclination for non-financial reporting was observed in the case of companies using standards such as the GRI or that are signatories of the UN Global Compact. So, connecting to international initiatives improves the behavior of European companies that are increasingly concerned about their social and environmental performance.

Another study about the Spanish market was run by (Escamilla-Solano et al. 2019) on 103 companies listed on the Spanish continuous market. Spanish researchers have analyzed the link between the publication of non-financial information and the economic performance of listed companies, proving that the reputation and legitimacy of companies, and business profitability are significantly affected.

For the Romanian market, several studies are related to the impact of the transposition into the Romanian legislation of the European directive regarding non-financial information reporting. The study by (Beleneși et al. 2021) focuses on listed companies, for the period 2017–2019. The aim of the study was the set-up of a composite non-financial disclosure Index. The leaders in disclosure of relevant information regarding social and environmental impact are companies from the energy field OMV Petrom, Transgaz, and Electrica. The conclusions of the study reveal an intensification of the companies' concerns for non-financial reporting, but there are notable differences depending on the field of activity.

The study conducted by (Tiron-Tudor et al. 2019) on companies listed on the Bucharest Stock Exchange reveals the importance of transposing the European directive into the Romanian legislation. The reporting of non-financial performances is differentiated according to certain factors, the most important being the company's size, performance, and the sensitivity of the activity field. An important element in publishing non-financial information is also mimetic isomorphism and less normative isomorphism.

Prior to the European directive, companies in the energy sector were the subject of studies aimed at either their environmental performance in terms of information published in CSR sections or their involvement in greenwashing actions aimed only at creating a positive image among stakeholders (Vollero et al. 2011; Andrei et al. 2014; Vollero et al. 2016).

Therefore, the present study stands out by selecting the sample of companies, which belong to a sensitive field of activity, are more concerned with creating and consolidating a positive image among stakeholders. For this reason, the managers of these companies are interested in good communication with stakeholders and the widest possible information on their social and environmental performance.

3 Data and Methodology

The Bucharest Stock Exchange, founded only in 1995, is an emerging market, where shares and bonds issued by companies with private capital but also with majority state capital are mainly traded. The privatization process of state-owned companies contributed to the establishment of this stock exchange after the fall of communism. Subsequently, private companies and international institutions have chosen the Bucharest Stock Exchange to list the shares and bonds issued. Currently, 83 companies are listed on the regular market.

The Bucharest Stock Exchange (BSE) calculates and distributes in real-time eight stock indices—BET, BET-TR, BET-XT, BET-XT-TR, BET-BK, BET-FI, BET-NG, BET Plus—and an index developed with the Vienna Stock Exchange, the ROTX index.

The BET-NG, which was launched in 2008, is a sectorial index for energy companies (Fig. 1). This index reflects the evolution of the companies listed on the regulated market of the Bucharest Stock Exchange that have the main field of activity the production or distribution of energy and related utilities. The maximum share of a company in the index is 31% (Table 1). Currently, there are 10 companies in the index basket, some with majority state capital, and others with foreign capital. The evolution of BET-NG is similar to BET, with the energy companies being among the blue chips listed on the Romanian capital market (Fig. 2).

The analysis focuses on energy companies listed on the Bucharest Stock Exchange that are part of the official BET NG index basket. We opted for the selection of these energy companies for several reasons.

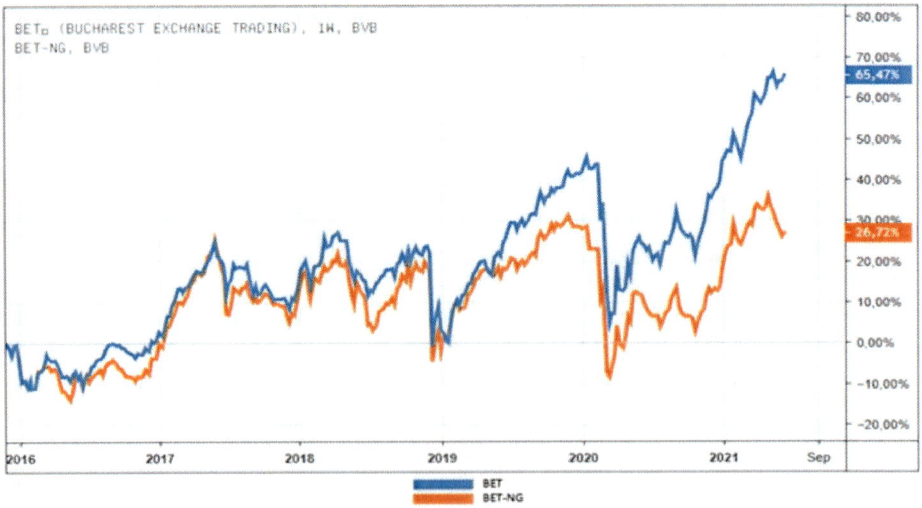

Fig. 1 Evolution of BET and BET NG. *Source* Authors based on www.bvb.ro

Table 1 The basket of BET NG Index

Symbol	Company	Share in BET NG (%)	Included in BET index	Share in BET (%)
SNP	OMV PETROM S.A	31.00	YES	15.37
SNG	S.N.G.N. ROMGAZ	24.77	YES	7.84
EL	SOCIETATEA ENERGETICA ELECTRICA	11.74	YES	3.72
TGN	S.N.T.G.N. TRANSGAZ	11.63	YES	3.68
SNN	S.N. NUCLEARELECTRICA	11.54	YES	3.65
TEL	C.N.T.E.E. TRANSELECTRICA	5.10	YES	1.61
COTE	CONPET	2.05	YES	0.65
RRC	ROMPETROL RAFINARE	1.58	NO	–
PTR	ROMPETROL WELL SERVICES	0.36	NO	–
OIL	OIL TERMINAL	0.23	NO	–
Total		100		36.52

Source Authors based on BSE data, www.bvb.ro

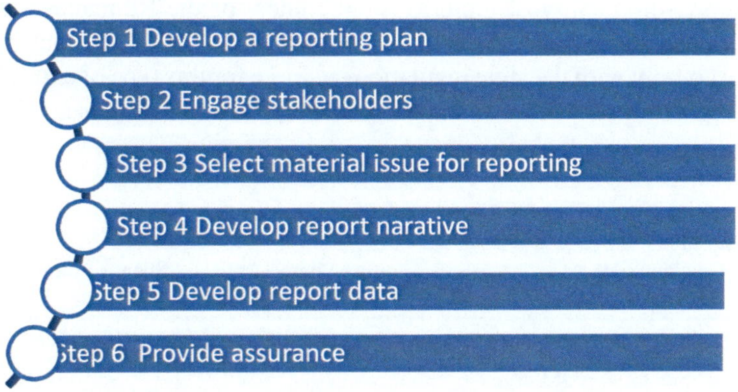

Fig. 2 Steps of preparation of the sustainability reports. *Source* Authors based on IPIECA, Sustainability reporting guidance for the oil and gas industry, p 17

- Energy is an intensely debated topic in the literature, researchers analyzing various aspects related to energy intensity, energy transition, energy production and consumption, and sustainable development (Hysa et al. 2020; Abbasi and Adedoyin 2021; Shahzad et al. 2021).
- Various categories of stakeholders are increasingly paying attention to the information published by energy companies given the negative externalities they generate but also the challenges generated by the energy transition (Andrei et al. 2014; Voica et al. 2019).
- The companies in the field of oil, gas, and utilities are important actors in the Romanian economy, considering the resources that Romania has and the tradition

in the field of extracting and processing these resources. Most of these companies were state-owned companies that were privatized, some of them with foreign capital. The importance of these companies for the Romanian economy is also proved by the selection of seven (out of ten) companies from the energy sector in the BET index basket, the first index of the Bucharest Stock Exchange, launched in 1997 that currently includes 17 companies registered in Romania. The share of these companies in the BET index basket is over 36%.

- The listing on the stock exchange implies numerous transparency requirements for the listed companies, and this is the reason why these companies publish a lot of information according to the legal regulations and those imposed by the stock exchange. For this reason, for these companies, the data on their economic activity is very extensive and updated periodically.

In order to identify a sectoral behavior for these companies, we searched the BSE website for information on their shareholding structure.

Most of these companies have as main shareholder the Romanian state, represented by the Ministry of Energy (Table 2). Only three companies in the BET NG index basket have the majority of foreign capital (OMV Petrom, ROMPETROL RAFINARE and ROMPETROL WELL SERVICES).

Therefore, the quality of majority shareholders of the Romanian state in these companies ensures a similar behavior on certain levels, in the sense that these companies must comply with the legal regulations in force for this type of entities. The most relevant regulations that have an impact on the reporting of non-financial information are:

Table 2 Shareholder structure for companies in the BET NG index basket

Symbol	Company	Share of state (%)	Share of foreign investors
SNP	OMV Petrom	20.6389%	51.0105%
SNG	S.N.G.N. ROMGAZ	70.0071%	–
EL	SOCIETATEA ENERGETICA ELECTRICA	48.7948%	–
TGN	S.N.T.G.N. TRANSGAZ	58.5097%	–
SNN	S.N. NUCLEARELECTRICA	82.4981%	–
TEL	C.N.T.E.E. TRANSELECTRICA	58.6882%	–
COTE	CONPET	58.7162%	–
RRC	ROMPETROL RAFINARE	44.6959%	48.1136%
PTR	ROMPETROL WELL SERVICES	–	10.6797% 73.0111%
OIL	OIL TERMINAL	59.6222%	–

Source Authors based on public data available on www.bvb.ro

- Government Emergency Ordinance no. 109/2011 on corporate governance of state-owned enterprises, with subsequent amendments and completions (approved by Law no. 111/2016);
- Government Decision no. 722/2016 regarding Methodological norms for establishing indicators on the financial and non-financial performance and the variable component of the remuneration of the members of the board of directors or, as the case may be, of the supervision of the state-owned enterprise, as well as of the directors, respectively of the members of the directorate.

The National Anticorruption Strategy is the reason why these companies publish the declaration of adherence to the National Anticorruption Strategy and the Integrity Plan.

For the evaluation of the non-financial performances of these companies, the information available on the websites of the respective issuers was analyzed. The main sections that have been identified as presenting relevant information are the sections.

- *About us section* (which presents important projects carried out by companies that consider the sustainable approach in production);
- *CSR section*;
- *Investors Relation section* where the annual reports on the financial situation and possibly the non-financial statements are;
- *Corporate Governance section*;
- *Public information section* where general data are presented regarding the activities of companies made in accordance with the provisions of Government Decision no. 878–2005.

The GRI database query provides additional information on CSR reports, sustainability report published by these entities, respectively (Table 3).

The query of the GRI database reveals a weak involvement of energy companies in non-financial reporting compared to similar entities in the same field (energy and energy utilities). At the European level, 341 organizations were found and they published 1880 reports.

4 Results and Discussions

Starting from the general information on the CSR programs carried out, the energy companies started to publish CSR reports and later sustainability reports according to GRI standards. This process of sustained involvement in the process of promoting the principles of sustainable development is due both to the trend registered internationally and to the specific European regulations that have been transposed into the Romanian legislation.

The listing on the Bucharest Stock Exchange did not impose on the companies any additional criteria regarding the reporting of information on the promotion of

Table 3 GRI Reports for listed companies

Symbol	Company	Report for year
SNP	OMV PETROM S.A	2020 GRI – G4, 2019 GRI – G4, 2017 GRI – G4, 2015 GRI – G4, 2014 Non GRI, 2013 GRI G3.1., 2012 Non GRI
SNG	S.N.G.N. ROMGAZ	2017 GRI Standards
EL	SOCIETATEA ENERGETICA ELECTRICA	2019, 2018, 2017 GRI Standards
TGN	S.N.T.G.N. TRANSGAZ	–
SNN	S.N. NUCLEARELECTRICA	–
TEL	C.N.T.E.E. TRANSELECTRICA	2018 GRI Standards 2017 GRI Standards
COTE	CONPET	–
RRC	ROMPETROL RAFINARE	KMG International Reports 2017 GRI – G4 2016 GRI – G4 2015 GRI – G4 2013–2014 GRI – G4
PTR	ROMPETROL WELL SERVICES	
OIL	OIL TERMINAL	–

Source Authors based on SDD—GRI Database (globalreporting.org)

sustainable development, which is the reason why we identified different variants of presenting this information, such as:

- Sustainability reports;
- CSR reports;
- Non-financial statement prepared in accordance with the European directive, which is presented separately or in the annual report of the administrators;
- Policy on quality, environment, health and safety at work;
- Policy on energy;
- Social and personnel policy;
- Ethics and integrity in business, fighting corruption policy;
- Environmental reports.

The top three companies in the BET NG index basket (OMV Petrom, Romgaz, and Electrica) stand out from the point of view of the efforts made to report the relevant information on non-financial performance. These companies have published sustainability reports that are prepared according to GRI standards, which proves not only a concern to promote the principles of sustainable development but also the involvement of stakeholders in this process by conducting regular consultations with it for the preparation of reports.

Most sustainability reports comply with GRI Standards—core option and GRI G4 Oil and Gas Sector supplement. In addition, some of them take into consideration other guidance or standards like IPIECA oil and gas industry guidance on voluntary sustainability reporting or Sustainability Accounting Standards Board—S.A.S.B.

The preparation of the sustainability report is a complex process that involves several stages (Fig. 2) and meetings of the representatives of the companies and the stakeholders, considering the social and environmental impact specific to these entities.

The reports are made based on the materiality analysis. Materiality has developed into an applicable framework to evaluate sustainability disclosure and business performance (León et al. 2016). It has become the main component for measuring sustainable performance (Carpejani et al. 2018), to make it relevant for stakeholders (Lubinger et al. 2019). This relatively new concept, which integrates materiality into sustainability reporting, associates with economic aspects as well as provides relevant information for investors to make decisions (Formisano et al. 2017; Slacik and Greiling 2019). Additionally, the principle of materiality is an important part of the Global Reporting Index (GRI) and has become a crucial aspect of sustainability assessment (Whitehead 2016). The materiality framework aims at evaluating the SDGs information that appears in a sustainability report of a company (Sardianou et al. 2021).

According to the materiality principles, a sustainability report should include information relevant to stakeholders in contrast to the irrelevant information that is not material to the stakeholder in the decision-making process (Slacik and Greiling 2019). While financial materiality emphasizes issues investors are interested in, sustainability materiality is concentrated on broader concerns to meet all stakeholders' needs for information (Whitehead 2016). Therefore, the analysis of materiality enriches non-financial reports of firms as it demonstrates social, environmental, and economic impacts of their business practice, and allows transparency in the communication with their stakeholders (Formisano et al. 2017).

The materiality matrix analyzes risks and opportunities of sustainability for organizations and enables them to identify relevant matters to align their strategies and sustainability goals (Formisano et al. 2017; Bellantuono et al. 2018). It is used to report on compliance in sustainability and demonstrates whether the interests of stakeholders are taken into account or a company is pursuing goals not relevant to stakeholders as well as how a company, in general, addresses all stakeholders with the sustainability report (Beske et al. 2020). The model of materiality analysis identifies priorities in sustainability reporting and informs investors and stakeholders about the business capacity for creating and sustaining value (Hsu et al. 2013). The selected prioritized issues should also be of importance to companies, and facilitate them to achieve a greater level of accountability (Calabrese et al. 2016).

Furthermore, materiality analysis is an advised method to assess sustainability reports, especially when they concern social and environmental disclosures (Unerman and Zappettini 2014). Materiality analysis of sustainable reporting and corporate social responsibility reflects the needs of stakeholders while including items that have a direct or indirect impact on material issues of organizations' activities regarding sustainability (Sardianou et al. 2021). Thus, materiality considers the significance of social, economic, and environmental impacts of a company in conjunction with the consequences on stakeholders' decisions (Saenz 2019).

Stakeholders are consulted through various methods to establish the materiality issue and to prioritize them like surveys, interviews, web forums, company-investors meetings, customer satisfaction surveys, professional networks, social networking (IPIECA 2020). Stakeholders' opinions are important for the company both during the initiation of the report preparation process, during the report preparation phase, and after publication for obtaining feedback.

OMV Petrom developed the Sustainability Strategy 2019–2025 based on five pillars and 15 specific targets for 2025 (Fig. 3). In addition, OMV Petrom endorsed the World Bank's initiative "Zero routine flaring by 2030."

The sustainability strategy is aligned with the SDGs, but in order to potentiate the positive effects on the local communities and the Romanian economy, following an internal survey, the priority objectives were established: Quality Education (SDG 4), Decent Work and Economic Growth (SDG 8), Industry Innovation and Infrastructure (SDG 9), Responsible Consumption and Protection (SDG 12), Climate Action (SDG 13).

Considering the complex operations carried out by the companies in the energy sector, the activity of this company has implications on numerous categories of stakeholders that are presented in Fig. 4.

An important category of stakeholders for energy companies are suppliers, which is why these enterprises (OMV Petrom) have developed a Supplier Code of Conduct that seeks to promote the principles of sustainable development in these entities.

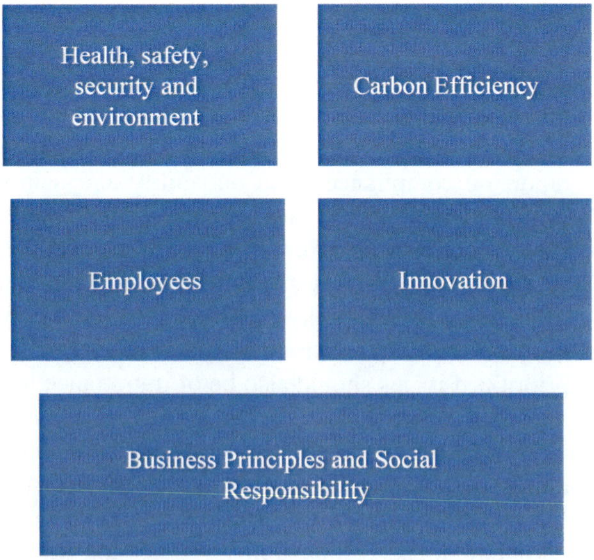

Fig. 3 Sustainability Strategy 2019–2025 of OMV Petrom. *Source* Authors based on information of OMV Petrom

Fig. 4 Stakeholder map. *Source* Authors based on information of OMV Petrom

The analysis of the sustainability reports available on the companies' websites allowed the identification of the main materiality topics, the impact produced, and the associated risks. The prioritization of materiality topics is done based on consultations with stakeholders, the final list being approved by the companies' management.

Non-financial reporting is done using several indicators according to international standards. Environmental performance can be monitored with the help of indicators such as Chemicals used in the manufacturing process, energy intensity, the total amount invested in renewable energy, total water withdrawal by source, direct GHG emissions, GHG intensity, reduction of GHG emissions, other significant air emissions, waste and disposal method, total number and volume of significant spills. In order to present relevant information regarding social performance, the listed companies use indicators like occupational injury and illness incidents, social investment, local hiring practices and performance, local procurement and supplier development, transparency of payments to host governments, workforce diversity and inclusion, or workforce training and development (Fig. 5).

The other companies in the index basket have less relevant information for assessing non-financial performance in the sense that the CSR section presents information on donation and sponsorship policy and details some charities with impact on local communities, sports, or cultural activity. Companies like Conpet and TRANSGAZ opted for the publication of the non-financial statement, which, however, presents in a very concise manner certain information on the impact on the environment and social performance.

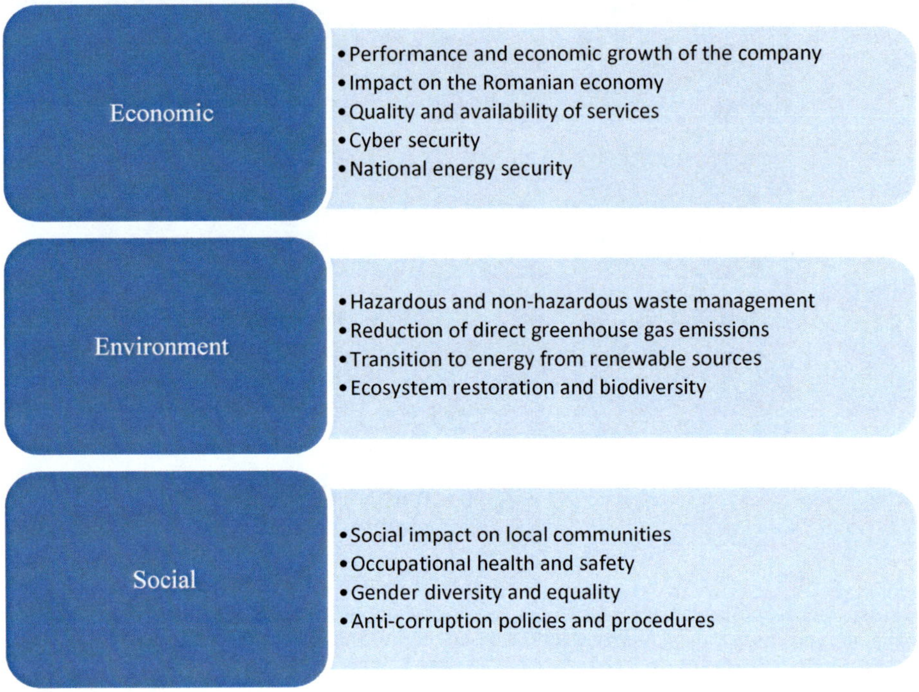

Fig. 5 The main materiality issues. *Source* Authors based on sustainability reports of selected companies

Given the impact they have on the environment, energy companies must not only comply with legal regulations in the field but also try to behave socially responsibly by publishing relevant information in this regard. Social and environmental performance reporting is a concern for companies that generate negative externalities. More and more studies reveal the positive impact that disclosure of relevant non-financial information has on the financial performance of companies (Yang et al. 2019; Akbar et al. 2021; Qureshi et al. 2021).

5 Conclusions

The non-financial behavior of energy companies has improved in recent years, given the information presented on the sites of these entities in specific sections, but also the data presented in the CSR or sustainability reports. More and more companies have started to present increasingly complex information in sustainability reports or non-financial statements published either as a result of the group strategy (they are part of transnational groups) or as a necessity to comply with the European directive on disclosure of social and environmental information.

The query of the GRI SDD database revealed a low interest of the Romanian energy companies compared to other European companies in the same field. The leaders in non-financial reporting are the most traded companies in the index structure, namely, OMV Petrom, Romgaz, and Electrica. Although most companies in the index structure are state-owned companies and their behavior is not similar, there are notable differences.

Even if the Bucharest Stock Exchange (BSE) has been a partner of the United Nations (UN) Sustainable Stock Exchanges (SSE) initiative since 2015, its involvement in promoting sustainable development is low compared to other stock exchanges (SSE 2021). Despite its commitment to launching a corporate governance index, this index has not been released. In the annual report of the administrators for 2020, the Bucharest Stock Exchange reexpresses its commitment to launching a specific index with an eligibility criterion from the environmental and social points of view.

At the Bucharest Stock Exchange, the company listing does not require the fulfillment of eligibility criteria regarding the environment and the social environment. Considering the trend regarding the provision of the most complex information to the stakeholders, in order to be listed, the companies present in the issue prospectus relevant information regarding the social and environmental risks that may affect the activity of the issuers.

The Bucharest Stock Exchange, as a company listed on its own market, has opted for the publication of a Report on the Environment and the Social Environment as an integral part of the annual report of the administrators. This report is made in accordance with the requirements imposed by the EBRD's Environmental and Social Policy. Given the predominant use of GRI reporting standards internationally, the Bucharest Stock Exchange could set an example for listed companies and should report according to GRI like two other major European stock exchanges (London Stock Exchange and Deutsche Borse).

Companies in the energy sector should provide more complete information to stakeholders on non-financial performance. In this sense, the actions undertaken by the Bucharest Stock Exchange, such as the educational partnership "Corporate governance that creates value," are addressed to the members of the boards of directors for improving their competencies and abilities and consolidating the corporate governance culture in Romania.

In addition, the gradual fulfillment of the criteria imposed by the SSE would be a first step for consolidating the involvement of the Bucharest Stock Exchange for improving the performance on ESG (environmental, social, and corporate governance) issues of listed companies. Providing detailed information on non-financial performance will be essential for portfolio investors given the trend in the Romanian capital market along with socially responsible investments.

The authors are aware of the limitations of the research conducted given the small number of companies analyzed and the structure of the official BET NG index, but also the features of the energy market, which is characterized by an oligopoly situation. For this reason, as a future research direction, the authors consider extending the analysis of non-financial performance for companies listed on the Bucharest Stock

Exchange. In this way, an impact analysis will be carried out regarding the application of the European directive 95/2014 by the listed companies. In addition, the extension of the sample of analyzed companies will also allow the identification of some sectorial characteristics considering the great diversity of the companies listed on the local capital market.

References

Abbasi, K.R., Adedoyin, F.F.: Do energy use and economic policy uncertainty affect CO_2 emissions in China? Empirical evidence from the dynamic ARDL simulation approach. Environ. Sci. Pollut. Res. **28**(18), 23323–23335 (2021)

Akbar, A., Jiang, X., Qureshi, M.A., Akbar, M.: Does corporate environmental investment impede financial performance of Chinese enterprises? The moderating role of financial constraints. Environ. Sci. Pollut. Res. 1–11 (2021)

Andrei, J.V., Panait, M., Voica, C.: Implication of the CSR and cultural model features in Romanian energy sector. Industrija **42**(4), 115–131 (2014)

Ates, S.: The Country-Level Determinants of Sustainability Reporting in Emerging Markets. In Financial Management and Risk Analysis Strategies for Business Sustainability, pp. 173–193. IGI Global (2021)

Balluchi, F., Lazzini, A., Torelli, R.: Credibility of environmental issues in non-financial mandatory disclosure: Measurement and determinants. J. Clean. Prod. **288**, 125744 (2021). https://doi.org/10.1016/j.jclepro.2020.125744

Beleneși, M., Bogdan, V., Popa, D.N.: Disclosure dynamics and non-financial reporting analysis. the case of Romanian listed companies. Sustainability **13**(9), 4732 (2021)

Bellantuono, N., Pontrandolfo, P., Scozzi, B.: Guiding materiality analysis for sustainability reporting: the case of agri-food sector. Int. J. Technol. Policy Manage. **18**(4), 336 (2018). https://doi.org/10.1504/ijtpm.2018.096181

Beske, F., Haustein, E., Lorson, P.C.: Materiality analysis in sustainability and integrated reports. Sustain. Account. Manage. Policy J. **11**(1), 162–186 (2020). https://doi.org/10.1108/sampj-12-2018-0343

Calabrese, A., Costa, R., Levialdi, N., Menichini, T.: A fuzzy analytic hierarchy process method to support materiality assessment in sustainability reporting. J. Clean. Prod. **121**, 248–264 (2016). https://doi.org/10.1016/j.jclepro.2015.12.005

Caputo, F., Leopizzi, R., Pizzi, S., Milone, V.: The non-financial reporting harmonization in Europe: evolutionary pathways related to the transposition of the directive 95/2014/EU within the Italian context. Sustainability **12**(1), 92 (2020)

Carpejani, P., Pinheiro de Lima, E., Gouvea da Costa, S., Machado, C., Tortato, U.: The contribution of the materiality process to a clean production. DEStech Transactions on Engineering and Technology Research. https://doi.org/10.12783/dtetr/icpr2017/17688 (2018)

Curtó-Pagès, F., Ortega-Rivera, E., Castellón-Durán, M., Jané-Llopis, E.: Coming in from the cold: a longitudinal analysis of SDG reporting practices by Spanish listed companies since the approval of the 2030 agenda. Sustainability **13**(3), 1178 (2021)

Di Vaio, A., Varriale, L.: SDGs and airport sustainable performance: Evidence from Italy on organisational, accounting and reporting practices through financial and non-financial disclosure. J. Clea. Prod. **249**, 119431 (2020). https://doi.org/10.1016/j.jclepro.2019

Escamilla-Solano, S., Fernandez-Portillo, A., Paule-Vianez, J., Plaza-Casado, P.: Effect of the disclosure of corporate social responsibility on business profitability. a dimensional analysis in the Spanish stock market. Sustainability **11**(23), p. 6732 (2019)

European Commission: Corporate sustainability reporting. Retrieved June 4, https://ec.europa.eu/info/business-economy-euro/company-reporting-and-auditing/company-reporting/corporate-sustainability-reporting_en (2021)

Feltham, G.A., Ohlson, J.A.: Valuation and clean surplus accounting for operating and financial activities. Contemp. Account. Res. **11**(2), 689–731 (1995)

Formisano, V., Fedele, M., Calabrese, M.: Materiality matrix: a comparison between relevant indicators for banks and stakeholder. In: Toulon-Verona International Conference Proceedings "20th Excellence in Services", ISBN 9788890432774 (2017)

García-Sánchez, I.M., García-Sánchez, A.: Corporate social responsibility during COVID-19 pandemic. J. Open Innov. Technol Market Complex. **6**(4), 126 (2020)

García-Sánchez, I.M., Raimo, N., Vitolla, F.: Are environmentally innovative companies inclined towards integrated environmental disclosure policies? Adm. Sci. **11**(1), 29 (2021)

Gigauri, I.: Corporate social responsibility and COVID-19 pandemic crisis. Int. J. Sustain. Entrep. Corp. Soc. Responsib. **6**(1), 30–47 (2021). https://doi.org/10.4018/ijsecsr.2021010103

Gigauri, I., Djakeli, K.: Expecting transformation of marketing during the post-pandemic new normal. Int. J. Sustain. Econ. Manag. **10**(2), 1–18 (2021). https://doi.org/10.4018/ijsem.2021040101

Hsu, C.-W., Lee, W.-H., Chao, W.-C.: Materiality analysis model in sustainability reporting: a case study at Lite-On technology corporation. J. Clean. Prod. **57**, 142–151 (2013). https://doi.org/10.1016/j.jclepro.2013.05.040

Hysa, E., Kruja, A., Rehman, N.U., Laurenti, R.: Circular economy innovation and environmental sustainability impact on economic growth: an integrated model for sustainable development. Sustainability **12**(12), 4831 (2020)

IPIECA: https://www.ipieca.org/media/5115/ipieca_sustainability-guide-2020.pdf. Accessed 4 June 2021 (2020)

Ismail, H., Mahmood, Z.: CSR profile of developing nations: a content analysis of CSR reports of listed companies in Pakistan. Pak. J. Soc. Sci. (PJSS) **39**(4) (2019)

Karaman, A.S., Orazalin, N., Uyar, A., Shahbaz, M.: CSR achievement, reporting, and assurance in the energy sector: Does economic development matter? Energy Policy **149**, 112007 (2021). https://doi.org/10.1016/j.enpol.2020.112007

Koseoglu, M.A., Uyar, A., Kilic, M., Kuzey, C., Karaman, A.S.: Exploring the connections among CSR performance, reporting, and external assurance: Evidence from the hospitality and tourism industry. Int. J. Hosp. Manage. **94**, 102819 (2021). https://doi.org/10.1016/j.ijhm.2020.102819

Latif, B., Mahmood, Z., Tze San, O., Mohd Said, R., Bakhsh, A.: Coercive, normative and mimetic pressures as drivers of environmental management accounting adoption. Sustainability **12**(11), 4506 (2020)

León, R., Ferrero-Ferrero, I., Muñoz-Torres, M.J.: Environmental performance assessment in the apparel industry. a materiality-based approach. Lecture Notes in Business Information Processing, vol. 254, pp. 51–60. Springer (2016). https://doi.org/10.1007/978-3-319-40506-3_6

Lubinger, M., Frei, J., Greiling, D.: Assessing the materiality of university G4-sustainability reports. J. Public Budg. Account. Financ. Manag. **31**(3), 364–391 (2019). https://doi.org/10.1108/jpbafm-10-2018-0117

Mahmood, Z., Uddin, S.: Institutional logics and practice variations in sustainability reporting: evidence from an emerging field. Account. Audit. Account. J. (2020)

Matei, M.: Responsabilitatea socială a corporaţiilor şi instituţiilor şi dezvoltarea durabilă a României. Expert Publishing House, Bucharest (2013)

Nicolo, G., Zanellato, G., Tiron-Tudor, A.: Integrated reporting and European state-owned enterprises: a disclosure analysis pre and post 2014/95/EU. Sustainability **12**(5), 1908 (2020)

Ohlson, J.A.: Earnings, book values, and dividends in equity valuation. Contemp. Account. Res. **11**(2), 661–687 (1995)

Petrescu, A.G., Bilcan, F.R., Petrescu, M., Holban Oncioiu, I., Türkeș, M.C., Căpuşneanu, S.: Assessing the benefits of the sustainability reporting practices in the top Romanian companies. Sustainability **12**(8), 3470 (2020)

Pizzi, S.: The Relationship between non-financial reporting, environmental strategies and financial performance. Empirical evidence from Milano stock exchange. Adm. Sci. **8**(4), 76 (2018)

Qureshi, M.A., Akbar, M., Akbar, A., Poulova, P.: Do ESG Endeavors assist firms in achieving superior financial performance? a case of 100 best corporate citizens. SAGE Open **11**(2), 21582440211021600 (2021)

Raimi, L., Isiaka, A.S.: Regional Review: Africa: CSR in Sub-Saharan Africa: Emerging Trends, Perspectives, and Debates. The Palgrave Handbook of Corporate Social Responsibility, pp. 1–26 (2020)

Rezaee, Z., Tuo, L.: Voluntary disclosure of non-financial information and its association with sustainability performance. Adv. Account. **39**, 47–59 (2017). https://doi.org/10.1016/j.adiac.2017.08.001

Saenz, C.: Creating shared value using materiality analysis: strategies from the mining industry. Corp. Soc. Responsib. Environ. Manag. (2019). https://doi.org/10.1002/csr.1751

Said, R.M., Theng, L.T., Senik, R., Yusri, Y., San, O.T.: The state of sustainability disclosure and effects on companies' financial performance. Pertanika J. Soc. Sci. Humanit. **23**(S), 99 (2015)

Sardianou, E., Stauropoulou, A., Evangelinos, K., Nikolaou, I.: A materiality analysis framework to assess sustainable development goals of banking sector through sustainability reports. Sustain. Product. Consum. **27**, 1775–1793 (2021). https://doi.org/10.1016/j.spc.2021.04.020

Shahzad, U., Radulescu, M., Rahim, S., Isik, C., Yousaf, Z., Ionescu, S.A.: Do Environment-related policy instruments and technologies facilitate renewable energy generation? Exploring the contextual evidence from developed economies. Energies **14**(3), 690 (2021)

Siminica, M., Sichigea, M., Craitar, A.: The impact of non-financial reporting on stock price: a case study of Romanian and Bulgarian listed companies. In Essential Issues in Corporate Social Responsibility, pp. 157–176, Springer, Cham (2020)

Slacik, J., Greiling, D.: Compliance with materiality in G4-sustainability reports by electric utilities. Int. J. Energy Sect. Manage. **14**(3), 583–608 (2019). https://doi.org/10.1108/ijesm-03-2019-0010

SSE, Sustainable Stock Exchange: https://sseinitiative.org/stock-exchange (2021)

Tarquinio, L., Posadas, S.C., Pedicone, D.: Scoring nonfinancial information reporting in italian listed companies: a comparison of before and after the legislative decree 254/2016. Sustainability **12**(10), 4158 (2020)

Ting, P.-H.: Do large firms just talk corporate social responsibility? – The evidence from CSR report disclosure. Finance Res. Lett. **38**, 101476 (2021). https://doi.org/10.1016/j.frl.2020

Tiron-Tudor, A., Nistor, C.S., Ştefănescu, C.A., Zanellato, G.: Encompassing non-financial reporting in a coercive framework for enhancing social responsibility: Romanian listed companies' case. Amfiteatru Econ. **21**(52), 590–606 (2019)

Tzouvanas, P., Kizys, R., Chatziantoniou, I., Sagitova, R.: Environmental disclosure and idiosyncratic risk in the European manufacturing sector. Energy Econ. **87**, 104715 (2020). https://doi.org/10.1016/j.eneco.2020.104715

Unerman, J., Zappettini, F.: Incorporating materiality considerations into analyses of absence from sustainability reporting. Soc. Environ. Account. J. **34**(3), 172–186 (2014). https://doi.org/10.1080/0969160x.2014.965262

Vartiak, L.: CSR reporting of companies on a global scale. Proced. Econ. Finance **39**, 176–183 (2016). https://doi.org/10.1016/s2212-5671(16)30276-3

Voica, M.C., Stancu, A.: corporate social responsibility reporting: background, evolution and sustainability promoter. Sustain. Manage. Manag. Eng. 109–155 (2021)

Voica, C., Panait, M., Rădulescu, I., Zefinescu, C.: The environmental component of CSR specific to energy companies listed on bucharest stock exchange. In: The International Conference 5th Economic Scientific Research–Theoretical, Empirical and Practical Approaches ESPERA, May 24–25, 2018, Bucharest, Romania, Proceedings ESPERA 2018, PeterLang, Berlin, pp. 511–521 (2019)

Vollero, A., Palazzo, M., Siano, A., Elving, W.J.: Avoiding the greenwashing trap: between CSR communication and stakeholder engagement. Int. J. Innov. Sustain. Dev. **10**(2), 120–140 (2016)

Vollero, A., Siano, A., Palazzo, M., Elving, W.: Corporate Communication and CSR; comparing Italian and Dutch energy companies on anti-greenwashing strategies. In CSR Communication conference 2011: The 1st international CSR Communication conference (2011)

Whitehead, J.: Prioritizing sustainability indicators: using materiality analysis to guide sustainability assessment and strategy. Bus. Strateg. Environ. **26**(3), 399–412 (2016). https://doi.org/10.1002/bse.1928

Yang, M., Bento, P., Akbar, A.: Does CSR influence firm performance indicators? Evidence from Chinese pharmaceutical enterprises. Sustainability **11**(20), 5656 (2019)

Resilience and Recovery: The Impact of COVID-19 Pandemic on the Global Cruise Tourism

Vlăsceanu Carmen Florentina and Țigu Gabriela

Abstract This article examines the scientific approach of the cruising industry's path toward recovery and resilience to the short- and long-term effects generated by the global pandemic crisis. The paper also discusses aspects pertaining to the actual state of the industry and the economic impact of the suspension of cruise operations for the past year. The methodology focuses on reviewing the industry's response to the unprecedented events, analyzing the business strategies, and closely observing how the major cruise operators position their brands and work toward future regeneration. Considering that cruises had been, for the past two decades, the fastest-growing sector of the global travel industry, it is important to consider the consequences the crisis had on the cruise companies' supply and value chains. The article provides a descriptive observation based on the developments within the cruising sector in terms of theory and practice underlining the counteractive measures recently adopted in order to improve the risk mitigation strategies and enhance their decision-making processes in unpredictable circumstances. Conclusions are drawn resulting from examining the impact of COVID-19 and the industry's response to the pressure of a series of influential factors and market determinants under uncertain conditions within the current transformational global business context.

Keywords Business resilience · Global business context · Uncertainty conditions

1 Introduction

The rapid spread of the virus in January 2020 determined the World Health Organization (WHO) to declare it an epidemic followed by the official recognition in March that the illness is a global pandemic (Chowdhury et al. 2021).

V. C. Florentina (✉) · Ț. Gabriela
Bucharest University of Economic Studies, Bucharest, Romania

Ț. Gabriela
e-mail: gabriela.tigu@ase.ro

A. M. Dima and M. Kelemen (eds.), *Digitalization and Big Data for Resilience and Economic Intelligence*, Springer Proceedings in Business and Economics, https://doi.org/10.1007/978-3-030-93286-2_15

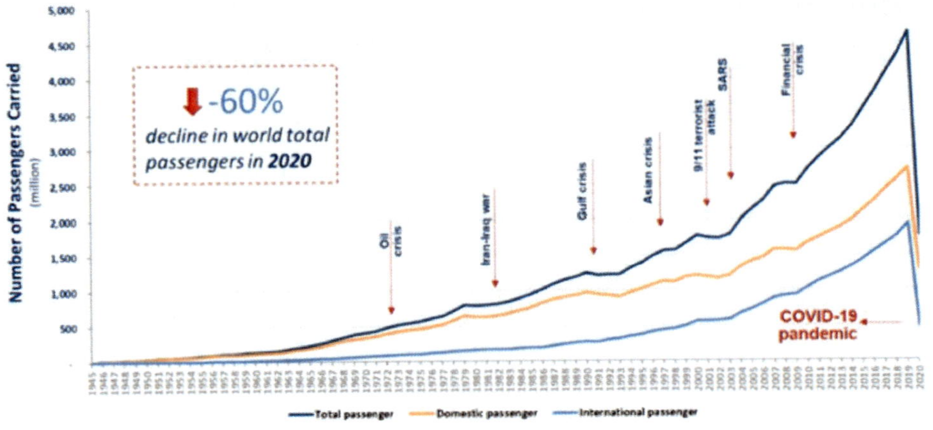

Fig. 1 World passenger traffic evolution 1945–2020. *Source* ICAO, 2021

Since the last year, governments, world organizations, researchers, and policy-makers have united, as the COVID-19 pandemic posed significant challenges to global safety in public health (Wang and Su 2020), in order to address the various dimensions of the pandemic, which has expanded far beyond the health realm and is affecting every aspect of the population well-being (Fig. 1).

According to an impact analysis report issued by the International Civil Aviation Organization (ICAO 2021) the international air traffic recorded numbers that were similar to those of 2003, causing the industry a 60% drop in 2020.

On a global scale, the cruise industry had been affected significantly by the COVID-19 pandemic and, at the beginning of last year, it suffered major restraints, from border closures in the most important cruise markets of Europe, North and South America, and Asia–Pacific region, to suspended sailings, which set the entire industry on a sudden halt.

This tremendous downfall had replaced the previously forecasted projections of the cruise industry's recent explosive development turning it into a major loss of estimated tens of billions of US dollars and plummeted two-digit shares of cruise companies. The predicament of the industry determined ripple effects into the global economy and the local economies of travel destination countries.

2 Literature Review

From the early days of the pandemic, the number of infected people had increased to 131.934 million at the time this article was written in April 2021, and over 2.87 million deaths had been recorded worldwide (Worldometer 2021).

Cruises to some extent present a relatively high degree of vulnerability due to the age demographics of some customer segments and the early stage of the virus breakout on some of the cruise ships was characterized by a rapid spread among its passengers. The situation took a dramatic downturn when some of the cruise ships were denied docking in certain ports in order to eliminate the contamination risk of the locals. Among the measures taken by the governments to fight the pandemic by far the most popular were transportation restriction and reduced freedom of movement (Bruinen de Bruin et al. 2020; Beck and Hensher 2020; Chinazzi et al. 2020; de Haas et al. 2020; Aldila et al. 2020) in addition to the quarantine measures, compulsory social distancing, and massive testing.

As the cruise operators received the "100 days No Sail Order" issued by the Centers for Disease Control and Prevention (CDC) in last year's spring, the impact on the tourism regions has been dramatic, particularly because local communities solely depend on the income infusion into their economies generated by the cruise industry. Within a few months, the cruise industry witnessed unprecedented and dramatic transformations triggered by the global pandemic, from the fastest growing sector of global tourism into a paralyzed state of upholding. The disruptive impact of the COVID-19 outbreak has devastating implications defying the previously forecasted growth and challenging the future recovery trend. However, successful may have been the restrictive measures taken to combat the effects of the pandemic (de Haas et al. 2020; Cohen 2020; Pirouz et al. 2020), they are extremely controversial as they drastically affected the economies around the world by the prolonged activity paralysis experienced in all the economic sectors. Following the cruise industry's pause, its dimensions and role within global tourism had become very clear.

Resilience by definition is referred to as the ability to recover from adversity and harsh conditions, and a good crisis management to overcome incertitude is essential for effective leadership. While the nature of adversity has its significance, by far the most important aspect is how the crisis is being dealt with and resilience plays a crucial role in helping the recovery process (Ackerman and Maslin-Ostrowski 2002; Greene 2002). Research demonstrated a direct relationship between stress as a factor and the ability to attain resilience in a prolonged state of adversity (Heifetz and Linsky 2004; Patterson et al. 2002). *Resilience theory* received much attention from many types of research (Garmezy and Masten 1986) studying the impact of adversity on life experiences. (Ginsburg 2011), pediatrician and human development expert, proposed the seven interrelated components of resilience namely competence, confidence, connection, character, contribution, coping, and control.

The greatest challenge suffered by mankind since the end of World War II is represented by the COVID-19 pandemic, which has rapidly spread around the globe, placing the entire world in a severe crisis, in which solidarity and leadership might be the key elements of finding solutions. Lockdown measures caused workplace displacements and business closures, which resulted in major supply and value chain disruptions. In tourism and hospitality-related sectors, the impact is devastating, with a drop of over 90% in business activity (Fernandes 2020) determined by the sudden stop of the global travel industry, as air and cruise traffic had been restricted in the early stages of the outbreak and later on, even banned.

So how did the cruise industry handle these unfortunate circumstances? How could the industry minimize the loss, mitigate the risks and ensure continuity of their future operations? The downturn of events presented the industry with the opportunity of months-long planning under the guidance of leading public health experts, such as the World Health Organization (WHO), US Centers for Disease Control and Prevention (CDC), the World Federation of Public Health Association (WFPHA) in order to elaborate enhanced public health protocols. In November 2020, CLIA was announcing a prolonged voluntary suspension of cruise operation of all member organizations until December 31st motivating their decision as taking the time to prepare and adapt the onshore and shipboard cruise operations to the new public health and safety regulations.

Since the very beginning, the pandemic had a devastating impact upon hundreds of thousands of passengers and crew members, the latter being stranded at sea for months in a row before being repatriated to their home countries. Their prolonged isolation had not only affected their well-being with intensive psychological implications, but also their livelihoods who are directly connected to the cruise operations. Besides sickness and death threatening lives, many people lost their jobs or earned reduced income (Ghosh 2020) causing greater economic depreciation and more future business closures. The impact on global tourism had been severe especially because over 50% of international tourists use air travel to reach their destinations (ICAO 2021). Countless people around the world suffer having lost their dear ones (Nicola et al. 2020) as governments are overwhelmed by the magnitude of this never-before-seen crisis. It has been a full year since April 2020, when the No Sail Order had been issued, and at the time of writing this article it is unclear when the cruise operations resume globally; in reality, only the future will unveil the actual costs, dimensions, and true impact of the pandemic.

3 Methodology

The research methods of this article focused on the qualitative analysis of the events evolution, which have gradually taken place from the inception of the SARS-CoV-2 outbreak until present times. Particularly, the attention was directed toward the cruise industry, representing the largest sector of global tourism, which had been severely affected by the dramatic unfolding of events. Previous scientific studies were investigated in addition to the continuous observation of the latest news bulletin, official declarations of cruise operators, and various declarations of the authorities in order to analyze the pandemic impact upon the cruise industry and evaluate the efficiency of the strategies employed in terms of resilience and recovery. Although the availability of scientific research in this field is limited, the existing literature pertaining to the global pandemic impact on the cruise industry was researched and referenced in the paper. It is unknown the extent of the true dimension of the negative economic and social impact of the prolonged restrictions and worldwide travel decrease (Leal Filho et al. 2020). While the scientific community has joined forces with governments and global health organizations, much research ought to be done on the actual scale of this pandemic and its multidimensional implications. Following our research, certain findings have been advanced in relation to some of the strategies employed by the cruising industry in their committed work towards the recovery path. A thorough review of the cruise lines news board and official communication over the past year since the COVID-19 outbreak had been declared a global pandemic allowed for accurate interpretation of the countermeasures adopted by the industry and estimate its future direction.

4 Analysis/Results Interpretation

The global pandemic exposed an existential crisis besides the health and safety threat of the population; it affected the world's sustainable development (Pirouz et al. 2020) and its well-being, causing by default a social and economic ripple effect.

The sudden and prolonged compulsory break highlighted the significance of the cruise industry and its importance within global economic activity. Table 1 presents the magnitude of the cruise industry at a global scale in a 2020 CLIA issued report pertaining to the total industry output in 2019, before the pandemic outbreak.

Nonetheless, the rapid response to the unprecedented global crisis and continued transformation made the cruise industry one of the most resilient segments of the global travel industry.

Resilience by definition is referred to as the ability to recover from adversity and harsh conditions and good crisis management to overcome incertitude is essential for effective leadership. *While* the nature of adversity has its significance, by far the most important aspect is how the crisis is being dealt with, and resilience plays a crucial role in helping the recovery process (Ackerman and Maslin-Ostrowski 2002; Greene 2002). Research demonstrated a direct relationship between stress as a factor and the ability to attain resilience in a prolonged state of adversity (Heifetz and Linsky 2004; Patterson et al. 2002). *Resilience theory* received much attention from extensive research (Garmezy and Masten 1986) studying the impact of adversity on life experiences.

Cruise lines have a long history of effectively managing various emergencies, and the industry has proven over the years an excellent ability to elaborate complex and efficient risk mitigation strategies. When the COVID-19 outbreak announcement was first made by the World Health Organization in March 2020, the cruise industry proactively acknowledged and tried to accommodate the risks imposed by the conditions that had placed our world in crisis and avoid unwanted negative consequences.

Table 1 2019 Global economic impact of cruise industry suspension

Criterion	Billions
Cruise passengers in 2019	29.7
Total output worldwide	$154.5
Number of jobs created	1,166.000
Wages & salaries created	$50.53

Source CLIA, 2020

As such, all the active members of the Cruise Lines International Association (CLIA, which accounts for 95% of the global oceanic cruise capacity) have taken the initiative to voluntarily suspend all their worldwide sailings.

Catastrophic times call for critical actions—The remarkable crisis management specific to the cruise industry is one of the factors that helped alleviate some of the immediate consequences generated by the COVID-19 breakout and shifted the focus toward finding solutions to eradicate the critical points. By comparison with other hospitality sectors, the cruise industry is known to be the best equipped and the most experienced in-crowd and crisis management, handling a broad array of situations, accidents, and unfortunate mishaps. Because cruise ships are massive floating hotels that carry a huge number of souls on board much like the population of a small town, it is, therefore, essential to have elaborated response measures, emergency procedures, and contingency plans. In an official statement issued by CLIA in 2020, it was highlighted that "the vast majority of more than 270 cruise ships within the CLIA member fleet were not affected by the virus." Ever since the very beginning of the COVID-19 outbreak, the cruise industry immediately responded with the appropriate emergency actions dictated by the severity imposed by the situation. In order to curb the spread of the virus at the end of January subsequent to the World Health Organization's declaration of a public health emergency, all the CLIA cruise operators declared upcoming modifications to the public health policy. From the early days of the outbreak enhanced health protocols were introduced and added to the existing medical treatment and sanitation procedures regularly performed on board. The instantaneous industry response was then followed by the suspension of cruise operations worldwide as an effective business tactic aiming for the health and safety of the passengers and crew, as well as reinforcing the consumer confidence level. To tackle the crisis and alleviate the undesired effects, passengers whose voyages were cancelled were given various options from receiving a full refund, or a future cruise credit of one hundred percent along with a ten percent bonus that might be used for 2021 cruises. By April 2020, it was becoming increasingly clear that the rapid spread of the virus was sweeping out everything in its path causing intensive cancellations of cruises and leading the industry to a temporary pause while leaving over 100,000 crew members stranded on ships (The Guardian 2020) as the travel barriers around the world were increasing and commercial air travel restrictions were being imposed by governments. In a tremendous joined effort, cruise operators managed to repatriate the crew, in some instances by ship, to their home countries (The Washington Post 2020). Ships are floating hotels and therefore self-sustaining for lengthy periods of time, which amplifies the importance of risk assessment as part of the hazard analysis and so priority has been given to the development of shipboard reliability plans. That includes HVAC air filtration (heating, ventilation, and air conditioning) designed to protect the passengers and crew from the potential and harmful spread of the virus capturing airborne particles and improve the air quality aboard the ships. From the prevention perspective, due to the highly contagious nature of the SARS-CoV-2 virus, it was necessary to increase and intensify the already existing ship cleaning procedures in accordance with the thorough USPH (US Public Health) hygiene inspections and introduce mandatory passenger screening at the check-in terminals with possible denial of boarding for incompliance. On the other hand, from the treatment perspective, the implementation of quarantine cells for ill passengers or crew is essential to facilitate the isolation and handling of illness cases. According to (CLIA 2020) preparedness for a safe start of the operations focused on three pillars:

1. the active implication of the scientific research experts to assist in efficiently handling the medical crisis;
2. the design and implementation plan of enhanced health and safety protocols issued by the experts in alignment with the regulatory public health organizations;
3. continuous monitoring of new scientific developments and constant improvement of shipboard health and safety.

There is no doubt that ever since the beginning of this health crisis the cruise industry had been working diligently for the safe return and phased resumption of the operations in various regions of the globe. As a consequence, in the second part of 2020, over 200 successful initial sailings and trials were organized in Europe and South Asia under the strict implementation of efficient health protocols (CLIA 2020). Even though the North American region remains officially inaccessible for cruises (The New York Times 2021), the overall sentiment among cruise customers is optimism and confidence (McKinsey and Company 2020) in the industry's resilience and ability to foster a safe environment aboard the ships.

Another aspect that cruise operators continued to improve is innovation and sustainability and the overall cruising industry has invested billions of US dollars to modify the ships with the latest technology that operates on cleaner fuels to reduce carbon emissions (CLIA 2020). The cruise industry pledged to achieve a 40% reduction rate in emissions by 2030, thus aligning their actions to the 17 United Nations Sustainable Development Goals.

Large amounts have been invested by the major cruise operators to equip the vessels with new environmental technologies among them advanced water treatment systems, liquefied natural gas LNG, and exhaust cleaning systems (EGCS). Besides the environmentally sound effects obtained by adding the new technical features aboard the vessels, it counteracts issues that help fight against COVID-19 transmission hazards.

The unexpected stop of cruise operations enabled some of the industry players to accelerate the sale of some of the less efficient ships aiming for an increase in operating expense efficiency level and a reduction in fuel consumption over the long-term (Carnival Cruise Lines, 2021). This drastic measure taken by the cruise operators comes in line with the commitment of renewing the company's fleet with environmentally efficient and technical upgraded cruise ships, and according to CLIA 2020, new ships are projected to debut in 2021.

Recently, as the industry joined forces with the scientific research community and after working closely with the national authorities in Europe and South Asia, under a firm commitment of following rigorous protocols some of the cruise ships have started to cruise.

5 Conclusions

It is considered that the sudden stop of all the business activities around the globe helped to successfully avoid the possible unfold of undesired events and increasing numbers of SARS-CoV-2 infections. Instead of continuing to cruise and deal with infection and death occurrences in a reactive manner, the cruising industry chose to suspend all their sailings, and later on it prolonged this measure by its own initiative.

The industry shifted its focus toward turning this unprecedented crisis into an opportunity to generate effective risk mitigation strategies and establish policies designed to assist cruise companies to proactively foresee and avoid high-risk situations. This rather severe and counteractive measure helped minimize the threat and spread of the disease to millions of passengers and crew, thus placing the cruise industry in a leadership position among the global tourism industry players. With the health and safety of the passengers and crew as the top priority, the ripple effects of the sudden suspension of global operations have shortly been noticed among the entire supply chain and cruise community, from cruise lines to port destinations, travel agents, airlines, suppliers, etc.

Over the last year, the cruise industry displayed resilience as the current circumstances demanded all their resources and abilities to be exerted to unprecedented levels. Research, novelty, and innovation became the focal point where cruise operators turned to attain new levels of exigency pertaining to onboard outbreak prevention measures in order to create a safe and secure operational framework. As part of the already existing emergency response strategy, cruise lines implemented elaborate protocols designed to monitor the passenger and crew health condition in order to prevent possible illness proliferation and provide its passengers round-the-clock medical care and support (Vlăsceanu and Tigu 2021). Cruise lines are known for their elaborate operational network employed in emergency situations that includes the active involvement of various crisis cells and medical facilities existent on board the vessels as well as a considerable number of shoreside professionals. Depending on the situation, it may be either the medical care department located at the company's headquarters, the local port agents or collaborating hospital units, US Coast Guard emergency services, etc. On board, the cruise vessels' priority number one has always been the safety and security of passengers and crew, and over the years cruise lines managed to have a successful approach in managing various infectious outbreaks such as norovirus, influenza, measles, H1N1, and efficiently prevent transmission of the disease on board. Nowadays with the Coronavirus outbreak, cruise lines are taking a proactive role of implementing precautionary testing and screening solutions of passengers and crew before their boarding, in addition to the procedures employed to ensure proper distancing in embarkation ports and communal areas around the ship. The cruise industry's resilience has been reflected in their committed approach to recovery and their decision to accept the risk of suspending all operations based on the potentially dramatic forecasted outcome if the cruising had continued throughout the initial outbreak phase. When global cruising resumes, the industry has to overcome all the challenges posed by the highly contagious disease with the help of already established prudent warning systems and coordinated effort of all the stakeholders along the supply and value chains. Equally important is for the tourism destinations to develop a recovery plan that allows resuming of operations in safe conditions as part of the sector growth stimulation framework. Following the creation of the vaccine and its extensive distribution over the past months, in Europe and Asia some cruise operators have slowly begun cruising under the official guidance of local authorities, the North-American cruise companies are waiting for the CDC's permission to deploy their fleet. On the road to recovery in a joint effort, industry leaders ought to ensure and closely monitor safety performance in order to eliminate possible consequences related to field failure and damage.

The goal of this article is to provide a glimpse of the cruise industry's resilience and a qualitative examination pertaining to the current state of the industry became compulsory to include within the research methodology. Some limitations became apparent during the course of the research, particularly related to the availability of scientific literature in this field, which shaped the qualitative nature of the article. The global environment of uncertainty created by the virus breakout caused reactive government responses to the crisis streaming down to all industries and economic sectors generating an overall state of upholding. Considerations might be extended pertaining to the contemporary period of time researched in our article, which is largely influenced by the continuous unfolding of events triggered by the pandemic outbreak.

Further research on this topic is recommended to be pursued following a thorough review of the contextual factors affecting the cruise industry and additional empirical analysis may be conducted taking into consideration the available data that highlights aspects related to the resilience and recovery of this industry in relation to the ongoing development of events.

References

Ackerman, R.H., Maslin-Ostrowski, P.: The Wounded Leader: How Real Leadership Emerges in Times of Crisis. Jossey-Bass, San Francisco, CA (2002)

Aldila, D., Khoshnaw, S., Safitri, E., Anwar, Y.R., Bakry, A., Samiadji, B.M., Anugerah, D.A., Gh, M., Ayulani, I.D., Salim, S.N.: A mathematical study on the spread of COVID-19 considering social distancing and rapid assessment: the case of Jakarta, Indonesia. Chaos Solitons Fractals **139**, 110042 (2020)

Beck, M.J., Hensher, D.A.: Insights into the impact of COVID-19 on household travel and activities in Australia–the early days under restrictions. Transp. Policy 76–93 (2020)

Bruinen de Bruin, Y., Lequarre, A.S., McCourt, J., Clevestig, P., Pigazzani, F., Zare Jeddi, M., Colosio, C., Goulart, M.: Initial impacts of global risk mitigation measures taken during the combatting of the COVID-19 pandemic. Saf Sci. **128**, 104773 (2020)

Carnival Cruise Lines, https://www.carnival.com.au/traveladvisory. Accessed 11 March 2021

CLIA, https://cruising.org/en-gb/news-and-research/research/2019/december/state-of-the-cruise-industry-outlook-2020. Accessed 6 April 2021

CLIA, https://cruising.org/en-gb/news-and-research/press-room/2020/september/clia-releases-2020-environmental-technologiesand-practices-report. Accessed 09 September 2021

Chinazzi, M., Davis, J.T., Ajelli, M., Gioannini, C., Litvinova, M., Merler, S., Pastore, Y., Piontti, A., Mu, K., Rossi, L., Sun, K., Viboud, C., Xiong, X., Yu, H., Halloran, M.E., Longini, IM. Jr, Vespignani, A.: The effect of travel restrictions on the spread of the 2019 novel coronavirus (COVID-19) outbreak. Science **368**(6489), 395–400 (2020)

Cohen, M.J.: Does the COVID-19 outbreak mark the onset of a sustainable consumption transition? Sustainability **16**(1), 1–3 (2020)

Chowdhury, M.A., Shuvho, M.B.A., Shahid, M.A., Haque, A.K.M.M., Kashem, M.A., Lam, S.S., Ong, H.C., Uddin, M.A. Mofijur, M.: Prospect of biobased antiviral face mask to limit the coronavirus outbreak. Environ. Res. **192**, 110294 (2021)

de Haas, M., Faber, R., Hamersma, M.: How COVID-19 and the Dutch 'intelligent lockdown' change activities, work and travel behaviour: evidence from longitudinal data in the Netherlands. Transp. Res. Interdiscip. Perspect. **6**, 100150 (2020)

Fernandes, N.: Economic effects of coronavirus outbreak (COVID-19) on the world economy, https://papers.ssrn.com/sol3/papers.cfm?abstract_id=3557504. Accessed 01 April 2021

Garmezy, N., Masten, A.S.: Stress, competence, and resilience: Common frontiers for therapist and psychopathologist, Behavior Therapy, vol. 17, 5th edn (1986)

Ginsburg R.K.: Building Resilience in Children and Teens: Giving Kids Roots and Wings. American Academy of Pediatrics (2011)

Ghosh, I.: The road to recovery: which economies are reopening? https://www.visualcapitalist.com/the-road-to-recovery-which-economies-are-reopening-covid-19/. Accessed 25 March 2021

Greene, R.R.: Resiliency: An Integrated Approach to Practice, Policy, and Research. National Association of Social Workers Press, Washington, DC (2002)

Heifetz, R.A., Linsky, M.: When leadership spells danger. Educ. Leadersh. **61**(7), 33–37 (2004)

ICAO, https://www.icao.int/Newsroom/Pages/2020-passenger-totals-drop-60-percent-as-COVID19-assault-on-international-mobility-continues.aspx. Accessed 06 April 2021

McKinsey & Company: The travel industry turned upside down – Insights, Analysis and Actions for Travel Executives (2020)

Nicola, M., Alsafi, Z., Sohrabi, C., Kerwan, A., Al-Jabir, A., Iosifidis, C., Agha, M., Agha, R.: The socio-economic implications of the coronavirus pandemic (COVID-19): a review. Int. J. Surg. (london, England) **78**, 185–193 (2020)

Leal Filho, W., Brandli, L.L., Lange Salvia, A., Rayman-Bacchus, L. and Platje, J.: COVID-19 and the UN sustainable development goals: Threat to solidarity or an opportunity?. Sustainability **12**(13), 5343 (2020). https://doi.org/10.3390/su12135343

Patterson, J.L., Patterson, J., Collins, L.: Bouncing Back: How your School can Succeed in the Face of Adversity, Larchmont. Eye on Education, NY (2002)

Pirouz, B., Haghshenas, S.S., Piro, P., Haghshenas, S.S.: Investigating a serious challenge in the sustainable development process: analysis of confirmed cases of COVID-19 (new type of coronavirus) through a binary classification using artificial intelligence and regression analysis. Sustainability **12**(6), 2427 (2020)

The New York Times: Why U.S. Cruises Are Still Stuck in Port: https://www.nytimes.com/2021/03/19/travel/coronavirus-cruises.html. Accessed 09 September 2021

The Guardian: https://www.theguardian.com/environment/2020/apr/30/no-end-in-sight-100000-crew-on-cruise-ships-stranded-at-sea-coronavirus. Accessed 09 September 2021

The Washington Post: https://www.washingtonpost.com/investigations/cruise-ships-crews-stuck-at-sea-paydays-dwindling-and-searching-for-a-way-home/2020/04/14/c7d9c498-78fb-11ea-a130-df573469f094_story.html. Accessed 09 September 2021

Vlăsceanu, C.F., Tigu, G.: Cruise industry: Enhanced health and safety protocols. In *7th BASIQ International Conference on New Trends in Sustainable Business and Consumption*. Foggia, Italy (2021)

Wang, Q., Su, M.: A preliminary assessment of the impact of COVID-19 on environment–a case study of China. Sci. Total Environ. **728**, 138915 (2020)

Worldometer, Reported cases and deaths by country, territory, or conveyance. https://www.worldometers.info/coronavirus/. Accessed 06 April 2021

Implications of the Migration Phenomenon in Romania

Liviu-Stelian Begu, Valentina Vasile, Andreea-Oana Enache, and Cristina Ioana Florescu

Abstract The migration of the population is a phenomenon related to the change of a person's place of living. The numerous existing forms of mobility have imposed a classification according to certain criteria, among which: the duration of the trip, its purpose, the distance traveled, or the degree of freedom of the person making the trip. Migrations involve a lasting or permanent change of residence and most of the time of the activity involves important changes in the lives of the engaged persons. These trips often require a change in the way of life of the people involved, are long-lasting or permanent, and almost always express an imbalance between the living conditions offered at the place of departure and those that exist or are expected to exist at the place of arrival. In order to highlight the current and future trends of migration, this paper will analyze its economic and social effects and the impact of COVID-19 on the migration phenomenon.

Keywords Migration phenomenon · Migratory flows · Pandemic migration

1 Introduction

The implications of globalization have socioeconomic, political, and cultural effects, eliminating countries' borders, thus contributing to the emergence of flows based on trade, financial capital, know-how, or human capital, which contribute to sustainable development globally and reduce disparities between developed and developing countries (IOM 2003).

L.-S. Begu (✉)
Bucharest University of Economic Studies, Bucharest, Romania
e-mail: liviu.begu@csie.ase.ro

V. Vasile · C. I. Florescu
The Institute of National Economy, Bucharest, Romania

A.-O. Enache
The National Institute of Economic Research "Costin C. Kirițescu", Bucharest, Romania

A. M. Dima and M. Kelemen (eds.), *Digitalization and Big Data for Resilience and Economic Intelligence*, Springer Proceedings in Business and Economics, https://doi.org/10.1007/978-3-030-93286-2_16

The current trends and evolutions of the migratory phenomenon need a good understanding of it, using analysis tools from several scientific sources to look at the phenomenon in all its complexity (Feraru 2011).

In the context of the health crisis, a new challenge for the migration phenomenon appeared in 2019, due to the rapid spread of the COVID-19 virus, which also generated a scientific interest in the economic and social implications caused by these problems.

The COVID-19 crisis has affected people's lives worldwide, both economically and especially socially, through the loss of human lives. The OECD believes that the most affected segment of a population is migrants. Studies show that they are most at risk of infection with the SARS-CoV-2 virus.

The COVID-19 pandemic produced multiple effects with a significant impact on migration as a phenomenon, migrants being the first exposed to several risks such as unemployment, illness, and even death [European Commission]. In 2020, the health crisis led to a massive decrease in global migration, the migration rate being half compared to the previous year. This is caused by community restrictions, which have led to a decrease in employment and an increase in the unemployment rate among migrants.

Economic, social, and political events influence migrant movements, and in the context of the COVID-19 crisis, migration is influenced by health restrictions. The existence of the SARS-CoV-2 virus causes problems in the economic field, destabilizes markets, and increases the labor shortage.

Migrants are a vulnerable segment of the population during crises, being the first to be affected by health restrictions or economic restructuring among employees. The power of movement of people is limited due to the pandemic and the increase in the number of outbreaks, and migrants are people at risk of infection and have difficulty receiving medical care.

In many countries, migrants, especially those without legal forms, do not have equal access to health care and may not receive COVID-19 care.

The aim of the paper is to identify the working hypotheses between the migration phenomenon and its implications on the Romanian economic market, in the context of the global health crisis.

2 Literature Review

Migration is a complex phenomenon and is highly studied globally, in its analysis being involved several scientific branches such as demographic, social, economic, territorial, and environmental (Borjas 2000; Nicolescu and Drăgan 2020).

The main concern of developing countries is the migration of those with higher education, the so-called "brain drain" and less the external mobility of workers, the former causing the loss associated with economic potential (Vasile 2012).

As seen from the outside, the countries with high migratory flows are trying to find levers to maintain and create new jobs of interest for the new generations of graduates of higher education and long-term education, which will give them the chance to develop, evolve, and prosper in their own country. These countries are less interested in the segment with a low level of training, their place being occupied in the labor market with immigrants from underdeveloped or developing countries (Boboc et al. 2014).

Labor market developments, technological progress, demographic balance, political conflicts, environmental changes, uneven development between countries, and health crises, will contribute to the existence of international migration (Kotaskova et al. 2020; Vasilescu et al. 2020).

The contemporary challenge for the global migration phenomenon is the emergence of a new virus, which has spread rapidly around the world, generating a pandemic with multiple effects, negative, worldwide, and indefinitely. Initially, the disease was identified in the Chinese city of Wuhan, being a virus in the coronavirus family, which spreads rapidly and can cause deaths (Chakraborty and Maity 2020).

Migrant movements generate demographic, social, cultural, and economic effects which, in the context of COVID-19 existence, shape migration areas (Massey et al. 1993). The existence of this virus exacerbates the economic crisis by increasing the health expenditures for reducing the number of outbreaks and the number of people affected.

As a result of the human movement, the virus first affected the neighboring countries of China, moving to countries in the United States and Europe, before reappearing in East Asia, where new cases of various strains of the disease have been identified (Guadagno 2020).

The spread of the virus and the problems generated by its existence cannot be attributed to migration (Kainz et al. 2020).

3 Methodology

The chosen methodology was mixed, consisting of two types: quantitative and qualitative. The qualitative one consisted in revising the scientific literature of numerous authors in order to have a better understanding of the topic at hand, namely, the influence of the COVID-19 pandemic on the migration phenomenon in Romania. The quantitative one was applied through objective testing by examining the relationship between the chosen variables: the number of emigrants, the working population, and the total population. Moreover, the data was analyzed through econometric procedures such as the VAR model, as it was the best suited (Jula and Jula 2019) for the chosen indicators. The VAR econometric model is described in the analysis subchapter.

4 Analysis

Like any other studied phenomenon, international migration can have both positive and negative effects for the countries involved. Romania is a former communist country, where migration is one of the most important socioeconomic phenomena (INS 2014).

After the 1990s, migration has been in a continuous expansion, in terms of migratory flows, but also of the targeted destinations. The universally valid reasons behind the decision to migrate have been socioeconomic.

From the perspective of the descriptive analysis of the migration phenomenon, between 1991 and 2019, Romania experienced important international migration flows with oscillating evolutions of both the number of immigrants and the number of emigrants, becoming a significant phenomenon for the Romanian society (Foerster-Metz et al. 2019).

In many countries, migrants, especially those who are not legally established, do not enjoy equal access to health care and may not receive COVID-19 care. In the case of Romania, for long-term migrants with low circularity, the health crisis has not led to the need for an emergency return to the country, while for short-term migrants staying in the destination country has not necessarily been an option.

In order to measure the impact of the number of working people and the population on migration, in the period 2011–2020, we carried out a VAR-type econometric analysis with the help of the EViews program. This method of analysis was chosen because through the common procedure (the least squares method) these indicators cannot be measured as the data present itself as being nonstationary without the possibility of being stationarized. All the data are taken from the Eurostat website. The values of the chosen indicators are given in Table 1.

The first type of analysis is the number of emigrants as a dependent variable, and the other two were considered independent variables.

Table 1 The number of emigrants, the working population and the total population in Romania in 2008–2019

Years	Emigrants	Employment	Population
2011	12,024	8673	20,199,059
2012	14,378	8725	20,095,996
2013	13,384	8710	20,020,074
2014	14,336	8762	19,947,311
2015	14,913	8718	19,870,647
2016	15,572	8569	19,760,585
2017	17,555	8689	19,643,949
2018	13,527	8641	19,533,481
2019	15,106	8639	19,414,458
2020	15,542	8613	19,351,318

Source Eurostat, 2021

$$\begin{aligned} \text{EMIGRANTS} = {} & 0.294916876208 * \text{EMIGRANTS}(-1) \\ & - 0.205937687455 * \text{EMIGRANTS}(-2) \\ & - 19.3647977549 * \text{EMPLOYMENT}(-1) \\ & + 12.7616337179 * \text{EMPLOYMENT}(-2) \\ & + 0.0336703999868 * \text{POPULATION}(-1) \\ & - 0.0361788905813 * \text{POPULATION}(-2) \\ & + 124044.266897 \end{aligned} \tag{1}$$

According to Eq. (1), a relatively weak inertial trend is observed on the two lags ($0.29 \neq 0$; $-0.02 \neq 0$), the dynamics being oscillating. The total number of employees has a direct and very strong influence on the number of emigrants on both lags, as demonstrated by their coefficients, which are well above 0 (19.36 and 12.76). In order to see which is the most significant indicator of all of those analyzed in the model, we will continue the econometric analysis by measuring the influence of the other variables in turn.

$$\begin{aligned} \text{EMPLOYMENT} = {} & -0.0424219500001 * \text{EMIGRANTS}(-1) \\ & - 0.00619333568139 * \text{EMIGRANTS}(-2) \\ & - 1.63770861138 * \text{EMPLOYMENT}(-1) \\ & - 2.11956480161 * \text{EMPLOYMENT}(-2) \\ & + 0.00567824983284 * \text{POPULATION}(-1) \\ & - 0.00542479838158 * \text{POPULATION}(-2) \\ & + 37532.5415791 \end{aligned} \tag{2}$$

If the total number of active populations in Romania is the dependent variable and the other independent (Eq. 2), it can be seen that the other two indicators do not have a significant influence on it. The total number of emigrants is in an indirect relationship on both lags (−0.04 and −0,006), and the population directly influences the number of employees (0,005) in lag 1 and indirectly in lag 2 (−0,005).

$$\begin{aligned} \text{POPULATION} = {} & -14.2159059979 * \text{EMIGRANTS}(-1) \\ & - 14.5664646274 * \text{EMIGRANTS}(-2) \\ & - 246.95446015 * \text{EMPLOYMENT}(-1) \\ & - 508.804097146 * \text{EMPLOYMENT}(-2) \\ & + 2.4214080008 * \text{POPULATION}(-1) \\ & - 1.46523108002 * \text{POPULATION}(-2) \\ & + 7902770.14502 \end{aligned} \tag{3}$$

In the case of the last equation (Eq. 3), it is observed that between the total value of the population (dependent variable) and the number of emigrants (independent variable), on both lags, there is an inverse relationship marked by the minus sign (−14.21 and −14.56). Between the total number of employees and the endogenous variable, the total active population, it can be seen that the fluctuation in these lags is extremely high, with the coefficients ranging from −246.95 to −508.80.

For all of the three equations, the confidence level is high: 94% for the first equation, 94% for the second, and 99% for the third, but the best case is found in the first equation due to coefficients attached to the total active population (Table 2).

According to the analysis presented, the number of emigrants of this country does not suffer modifications, as it shows a minor decrease in respect to the increase of the total number of employees, although this is not characteristic to the atypical economy like the one of Romania (INS 2014, 2019). Although over the years both the values of minimum and average wages have increased, this does not prevent young people from leaving the country in search of a better life. Moreover, Romania does not have a migration policy designed to determine the return of the population to the country and continues to be a country of emigration, the phenomenon of external migration continues to occur, along with declining birth rates, one of the main causes of population decline.

The phenomenon has also uniformly occurred in terms of the total active population and the total population in the sense of the existence of a decreasing number from one year to another. The reasons for the decrease by 0.99% in the total population of the country in 2020 compared to 2019 are the high number of deaths caused by COVID-19, a continuous decline in the birth rate, and the number of migrants who have continued to leave due to the precarious economic situation that Romania is currently facing. As it happened in other crises, too, migrants may be particularly vulnerable to the direct or indirect impact of COVID-19. Their ability to avoid infection, receive medical care, and cope with the economic, social, and psychological impact of the pandemic can be affected by a variety of factors: their living and working conditions, the linguistic diversity in the use of medical services, etc.

5 Conclusions

In the geographical landscape, one of the most dynamic components is the demographic one, which is reflected in the natural population movement (birth, mortality, marriage, divorce) and the migratory movement (emigration and immigration). Over time, migration has been influenced by a push-pull process; unfavorable conditions in one place push people to emigrate, and favorable conditions from other external locations attract them. Recent studies show that, especially in the last two decades, the phenomenon of the Romanians' external migration has been achieved more to carry out economic activities and less to change their home.

The correct measurement of the volume, meaning, structures, and intensity of the external migration movement, and its reasons and impact at the international, national, local community, family, and individual level is a difficult undertaking, all

Table 2 The Var model

Vector autoregression estimates			
Date: 07/06/21 Time: 00:07			
Sample (adjusted): 2013 2020			
Included observations: 8 after adjustments			
Standard errors in () & t-statistics in []			
	Emigrants	Emigrants	Population
Emigrants (−1)	0.294917	−0.042422	−14.21591
	(0.34920)	(0.01579)	(2.62109)
	[0.84455]	[−2.68690]	[−5.42366]
Emigrants (−2)	−0.205938	−0.006193	−14.56646
	(0.25464)	(0.01151)	(1.91136)
	[−0.80873]	[−0.53793]	[−7.62100]
Emigrants (−1)	−19.36480	−1.637709	−246.9545
	(13.5887)	(0.61439)	(101.997)
	[−1.42506]	[−2.66560]	[−2.42120]
Emigrants (−2)	12.76163	−2.119565	−508.8041
	(15.6307)	(0.70671)	(117.323)
	[0.81645]	[−2.99920]	[−4.33676]
Population (−1)	0.033670	0.005678	2.421408
	(0.05583)	(0.00252)	(0.41904)
	[0.60311]	[2.24957]	[5.77841]
Population (−2)	−0.036179	−0.005425	−1.465231
	(0.05619)	(0.00254)	(0.42176)
	[−0.64387]	[−2.13531]	[−3.47408]
C	124,044.3	37,532.54	7,902,770
	(251,187.)	(11,356.9)	(1,885,404)
	[0.49383]	[3.30481]	[4.19155]
R-squared	0.944268	0.949473	0.999910
Adj. R-squared	0.609877	0.646312	0.999367
Sum sq. resids	690,488.0	1411.510	38,901,944
S.E. equation	830.9561	37.57007	6237.142
F-statistic	2.823846	3.131913	1841.908
Log likelihood	−56.81436	−32.04340	−72.93996
Akaike AIC	15.95359	9.760851	19.98499
Schwarz SC	16.02310	9.830362	20.05450
Mean dependent	14,991.89	8667.625	19,692,728
S.D. dependent	1330.385	63.17309	247,836.8
Determinant resid covariance (dof adj.)		0.000000	

(continued)

Table 2 (continued)

Vector autoregression estimates			
Date: 07/06/21 Time: 00:07			
Sample (adjusted): 2013 2020			
Included observations: 8 after adjustments			
Standard errors in () & t-statistics in []			
	Emigrants	Emigrants	Population
Determinant resid covariance		0.000000	

Source Own computations based on the data gathered from Eurostat, 2021

the more so since in its various forms, international labor migration is becoming an important factor in the globalization of the labor market.

One of the arguments underlying the migration restrictions between the European Union and the countries that have entered the EU in the last waves concerns the so-called demographic pressure. Also, both the significant share of the working age population and the rather high unemployment rate have further influenced the region's migration potential. An important issue is the demographic vitality within the region and the possible consequences for international mobility, since over a relatively long period of time the demographic factor can have a significant contribution to the high mobility of the population. International migration flows are undoubtedly the most complex of the three data blocks. The indicators are built separately by category of persons, i.e., nationals of the country concerned (country under analysis) and foreign (other) nationals. At the same time, the migration flows of the people are distinguished by category, i.e., for work, studies, tourism, family reintegration, etc.

The movement of people, embodied by the permanent and temporary migration, represents a feedback regarding the evolution of the society, the national economies, and the local social environment. As in many other areas, direct and indirect effects can occur on multiple levels—demographic, economic, social, and cultural. Population aging and depopulation will generate change in many regions, including the rural and peripheral ones, and will have a strong impact on social and territorial cohesion, on the provision of public service, labor, and the real estate market. Other regions have growing populations and face different pressures. The significant intra-European migration following the EU enlargement and the immigration from mainly less developed third countries are specific challenges and opportunities, especially for the urban areas.

It is hard to estimate whether the population of the diaspora will want to return to the country once the pandemic passes, but it is certain that this will depend on the level of attractiveness of Romania and what the country will be able to offer to the emigrants.

Because of the present lack of data regarding the COVID-19 migration, this analysis will be developed in a future study at the moment when this data is available.

References

Boboc, C., Vasile, V., Ghiță, S., Covrig, M.: Romanian labour migration: employees perspective. In: 7th International Conference on Applied Statistics, Procedia Economics and Finance 10, pp. 244–248 (2014)

Borjas, G.J.: Economics of migration, International Encyclopedia of the Social & Behavioral Sciences (2000)

Chakraborty, I., Maity, P.: COVID-19 outbreak: Migration, effects on society, global environment and prevention, Science of the Total Environment (2020)

European Commission – Press release, Migration statistics update: the impact of COVID-19

Feraru, P.D.: "Migrație și dezvoltare: aspecte socioeconomice și tendințe", Editura Lumen [„Migration and development: socio-economic issues and trends", Lumen Publishing House] (2011)

Foerster-Metz, U.F.P., Golowko, N., Hell, C., Marquardt, K.: Creating talent pools through coopetition: a case study on vocational training programs in Romania. Manag. Marketing. Chall. Knowl. Soc. **14**(2), 203–219. https://doi.org/10.2478/mmcks-2019-0014 (2019)

Guadagno, L.: Migrants and the COVID-19 pandemic: An initial analysis, International Organization for Migration, No. 60, Migration Research Series (2020)

Institutul Național de Statistică (INS): „Migrația internațională a României" [National Institute of Statistics: "Romania's international"] (2014)

International Organisation for Migration (IOM): World Migration 2003 – Managing Migration: Challenges and Responses for People on the Move. Geneva (2003)

Jula, D., Jula, N.-M.: Econometrics, Ed. Mustang, București (2019)

Kainz, L., Banulescu-Bogdan, N., Newland, K.: The Divergent Trajectories of the Global Migration and Refugee Compacts, Implementation amid Crisis, Vol. December 2020 (2020)

Kotaskova, A, Belas, J, Bilan,Y., Ajaz Khan, K.: Significant aspects of managing personnel risk in the SME sector. Manag. Marketing. Chall. Knowl. Soc. **15**(2), 203–218. https://doi.org/10.2478/mmcks-2020-0013 (2020)

Massey, D.S., Arango, J., Hugo, G., Kouaouci, A., Pellegrino, A., Taylor, J.E.: Theories of international migration: a review and appraisal. Popul. Dev. Rev. (1993)

Nicolescu, A. & Drăgan, G. Integrating the non-EU immigrants into the EU labour market. An econometric analysis of some of the specific factors. Manage. Marketing. Chall. Knowl. Soc. **15**(3), 364–380. https://doi.org/10.2478/mmcks-2020-002 (2020)

Vasile, V.: Crisis impact on employment and mobility model of the Romanian university graduates. Proced. Econ. Finance **3**, 315–324 (2012)

Vasilescu, M.D., Marin, E., Begu, L.S., Enache, A.O.: Perceptions about immigrants and their integration in the European Union. Econ. Comput. Econ. Cybern. Stud. Res. **54**(4), 103–118 (2020)

The Importance of the Family Brand

Cioca Adriana, Wehbe Kassam, Popescu Delia, and Popescu Constanta

Abstract Under globalization aspects, the family brand recognition built over decades represents one of the most interesting marketing tools on which the family constantly worked. Based on the literature, the authors' research focuses on the innovative family type of businesses, where a gap regarding the main drivers behind a successful family brand was identified. In this regard, the paperwork addresses the research question related to the connection between the Research Department investment percentage and successful family business brand. The two directions of the authors' research are: firstly, identification and analysis of the psychological changes at the organizational levels, and secondly, examination of the most important financial criteria related to this purpose, on which structural equation was applied, by analyzing the relationship between their R&D investment and revenue with the aim to leverage the family brand importance and its efforts in regards to future generation recognition. The authors' results advance research to the extant family brand literature and will contribute to the discussion focused on the reverse symbiosis between family values and brand recognition.

Keywords Brand · Family business · Marketing · Innovation · Value · Campaign

1 Introduction

A family business is defined as the "backbone" of the world economy (Bird et al. 2002). Particular attention was paid to their performance through their own resources (Pounder 2015). The brand of a family business brings to light primarily the nature of the family that owns the business (Craig et al. 2008) and can be considered inimitable due to the uniqueness and history of the family. In a competitive environment, where end consumers have countless choices, an innovative brand of a family business can be a sustainable source of competition and can make a difference in the minds of stakeholders through the impression left by the services/products of the business

C. Adriana (✉) · W. Kassam · P. Delia · P. Constanta
Valahia University, Targoviste, Romania

A. M. Dima and M. Kelemen (eds.), *Digitalization and Big Data for Resilience and Economic Intelligence*, Springer Proceedings in Business and Economics, https://doi.org/10.1007/978-3-030-93286-2_17

(Anisimova 2007; Keller 2008; Binz Astrachan 2018). Exploring the idea of family brand in the business leads the authors' research on two parallel investigations: internal, related to what happens at the organizational level in the family business, and external, leveraging the family brand perception acknowledged by the stakeholders. (Binz Astrachan, 2014). Both directions of research are based on the involvement and influence of the family or family members who own/run the family business (Benavides-Velasco et al. 2013). The two researched directions are closely related to the continuous performance of the family business, which makes it different from all other non-family businesses.

1.1 Problem Statement

The marketing behavior of the innovative family businesses draws scholars' attention to the sensitive issues that the family has worked so far on, at the psychological levels that facilitated the communication between family and their business brands. Brand management is one of the most important catalysts that underlie the quality and performance of a family business, primarily by dominating the business niche and then positively, by influencing consumer behavior, namely, maximizing the trust in the brand used at the level of stakeholders (Binz Astrachan 2014). Irrespective of their existing or outsourced family business Research and Design departments, the authors identified a gap in the literature regarding the connections between investment dedicated for the Research and Design and recognition of the brand. The authors' assumptions are that the family plays an important role in the brand development, due to its uniqueness, values, traditions (Zellweger, 2012). The results of the study will contribute to the family business literature and will represent the base for the future development directions related to creative important sustainable ways of family brands.

1.2 Understanding of the Brand Concept

There are two important differentiations. The "*brand*" of a family business represents a name associated with a certain type of proven quality, which gained reputation over time, with immediate recognition by the stakeholders. "*Branding or brand management*" represents the way of doing it; *the way of developing the marketing strategies to keep the reputation and recognition of the Brand constant in front of the customers.* The perception of brand management has developed over time. Since ancient times, merchants have developed various graphic symbols, thus helping buyers to better distinguish similar products belonging to different merchants. For a long time, marketing campaigns have been limited by operations-oriented only towards the profit of companies, while highlighting price offers; Brand Management is based on two defining elements that cannot exist one without the other: *the transmitter* (the one who communicates and transmits information under the name of "brand") and *the receiver*, the one who receives and synthesizes the information (Brown et al. 2006; Bolton 2004; Wang et al. 2015). The importance of the family brand is strongly correlated with the managerial structure, financial capacity, as well as with the power of innovation. A successful brand management strategy in the family business has strategic value because it affects the future managerial decisions having a special impact on the financial performance of the company (Blombaeck and Ramírez-Pasillas 2012). *In general, family companies adopt different marketing strategies, by associating the elements that come from their own traditions, values, and responsibilities in order to create their own symbol to define them. The power of a brand is built on the capacity of stakeholders to be aware of the image of the brand that they create in their minds* (Brown et al. 2006; Zellweger et al. 2010). The authors investigated a couple of family brand management examples, such as: www.bacardi.com *"Heritage is at the heart of our company culture, our brands, and our products at Bacardi. Every item in our collections tells a unique story and brings to life the heritage of a brand, the spirits industry, and even cultural moments in time," (Jacqui Seargeant, Global Heritage Manager, Bacardi.) or "at our family company we have a unique way to create a new watch, we involve the family" (Patek Philippe /*www.patek.com*)*, give a quick recognition of the brand in the industry it belongs to Credit Swiss Report (2018), Blombäck (2009).

1.3 Marketing Campaign, a Strategic Tool of Branding

There are family businesses with brand innovation strategies that can be developed and customized, using marketing elements based on authenticity, rarity, and values (Eisenhardt and Martin 2000; Intihar and Pollack 2012) and considering the following:

- Establishing the brand with the target establishment of the business by the family;
- Family involvement in defining the business brand;
- Personalizing the brand through sensitive accents offered by your own family;
- Argumentation of the researched elements;
- Brand identity and authenticity;
- Awareness of the surrounding reality.

The brand of a business must remain constantly positive. The technique of continuous innovation of strategy or revitalization of the family brand is not easy and can be easily reversible. Today, marketing campaigns are built on the long-researched needs of stakeholders. Matching the elements of success will have the role of uniting the family with the quality of the business and implementing the information in the mind of the consumer (Beck 2016). The marketing campaign is built on the existing brand and has the role of introducing on the market the new products developed by the company, in order to make them easily recognized by consumers. It usually addresses a target audience and always has a message to convey. Another important aspect is the surrounding reality, to which the marketing campaign is addressed. Names were often used for certain products that had a different meaning than the message originally intended, in another country (Keller and Lehmann 2006; Basco 2014). Branding is defined by innovative graphics projects that render the symbolism (Logo) of the family business. The role of branding is to draw attention in a simplistic but clever way, with a memorizing impact on the final consumer. Many times, the consumer recognizes the symbol of the business brand and knows what to expect.

1.4 Family Brand Strategy Built on Family Heritage

By adopting different marketing strategies, family businesses have that competitive advantage that they have existed for decades, which makes the family heritage unique, with an identity that cannot be imitated, based on family history. Research has shown that introducing "family history" into the business brand can be associated for example, with the luxury industry or industries where handmade products are highly valued, thus creating, on the one hand, an image of quality, safety, and rarity in the consumer's mind, and on the other hand, the image of a key indicator associated with purchasing power and implicitly an indicator of business performance (Balmer and Gray 2003). Through brand strategy, the concept of institutionalized memory is realized in the minds of the stakeholders, with reference to the past, present, and future of what existed, survived, and will exist regarding the family heritage, traditions, and values (Menkes 2010). Thus, the message sent will associate in the minds of consumers the idea of stability and sustainability, quality and safeness to the products or services that the family business offers (Binz et al. 2017) *(e.g,. "William Grant & Sons" Independent family distillers since 1887,"turnover: £ 1,100 million, employees: 1,800, year of establishment: 1887, no. Generations in the family: 6, Beverage Industry,* www.williamgrant.com*)."*

1.5 The Family Branding Built on the Amalgam of Tradition, Value, and Innovation

There are family businesses that highlight the symbolism of their business by writing the year of their founding or summarizing the history of the family owning the business in a single message. This brand strategy aims to pass on to stakeholders the expertise gained over all these decades and to strengthen in the minds of stakeholders the confidence of what the family delivers through the business (e.g., *"John White & Son" one of the oldest families in Scotland who have invested and innovated continuously in the industrial business, in terms of equipment and weighing systems"*; always in the descriptions of the company will be found the words *"300 years of history," family business, founded in 1715,* www.johnwhiteandson.com). On the other hand, there is a clash between cultures and generations that drive the family and the business, which must be balanced. If, on the one hand, there is the tradition (past) that the family comes with, there is, on the other hand, a new generation (the future), which comes with new ideas related to the brand strategy, covering the business needs of the present and thus participating in the brand innovation process (Kahlert et al. 2017). The family business will always have the competitive and unique advantage in terms of the innovation process, through the constant large-scale involvement of numerous and different resources arising from: shareholder structure (concentration of decision-making power in one hand), a permanent collaboration of their own Research & Design departments with prestigious universities, financial independence, and others. In the same way, to revitalize the brand, employees must be considered, with an emphasis on the oldest and most loyal, who must adapt and incorporate new rules, trends, and values. Employees, part of the family business, are valuable assets who act daily with the purpose of the smooth running of the family business (Tasman-Jones, 2015a, b).

1.6 Family Brand Strategy Built on Values and Dedication

The first unique brand element of the family business is the family itself. Behind every business, there is the founding family or family members or the involvement of the second generation, the third one, and so on, who know very well the values and traditions that flowed for a long time from the family to the business they run daily (Orth and Green 2009). Compared to listed companies, where, as a rule, managerial leaders often change, especially shareholders, the family business always has a constant, namely the family, which is aware of its mission and the responsibilities they carry on their shoulders for the daily success of the business (Binz Astrachan 2014). The branding strategy places in the middle the family, which is seen as the energy source of all values and an image that confers the responsibility promoted by the business (e.g., *"C. & J. Clark International / British shoemakers since 1825," part of the retail industry, reached the 6th generation, today. The family is promoted as part of society, normal people who inspire trust, responsibility, and sustainability. "Warburton's family of bakers, turnover: £ 500 Mio, employees: 4,500 established in the year: 1876 generations in the family: 5, Industry: bakery, The family is promoted as part of society, normal people who inspire trust, responsibility and sustainability,* www.warburtons.co.uk,*)"* (BBC Business Tips from UK's Oldest Family Firms, 2020; Carrigan and Buckley 2008; Binz Astrachan and Astrachanet 2015a, b) (Fig. 1).

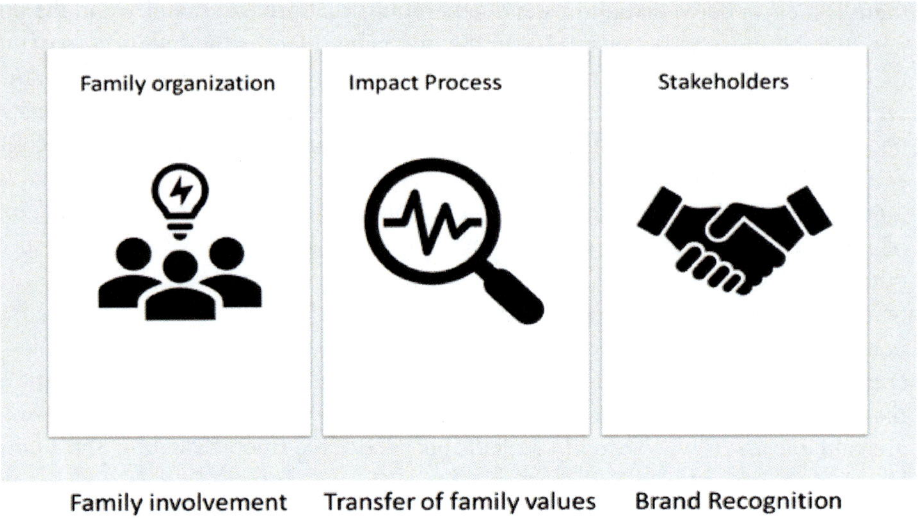

Fig. 1 Family firm impact on stakeholders. *Source* The Authors

2 The Consequences of Associating the Family Name with the Family Business Brand

Research so far has shown, according to Kashmiri and Mahajan (2014), that the family name behind the business used in the Brand of products denotes great satisfaction among consumers (corporate brand seen as "house of brands"; e.g., the fashionable house "Dior" or "Ferragamo"). The literature indicates a strong ethical behavior among consumers when the brand strategy is built with a focus on the family, according to Fig. 2, "The identity of Brand with the family business":

- *Family unity* seen through its business objectives, makes the family brand express the harmony and unity of the family seen over several generations. Moreover, the responsibilities of the family are honored regardless of the times; and decision-making when it comes to critical matters is seen as part of the family unit (e.g., *"the most important value for our family is unity" Jonny Wates, Wates Group Family Business /*www.wates.co.uk
- *Identifying family values* and exposing them to the public express the values that guide the family and the importance with which they treat the public (e.g., *Clarks, C. & J. Clark, founded in 1825,* www.clarks.co.uk*)*
- *Aligning the family with values*; the business highlights the tensions that are formed within the family business, more precisely between family members when it comes to business values. When these values and common visions of running the business are aligned, then the family makes even more commitments to the business they run. Moreover, the vision of long-term business goals makes the family even more involved in achieving their own goals. (e.g., *"The unlimited liability structure, with a cash and vote contribution, but no capital rights, makes you focus on things that*

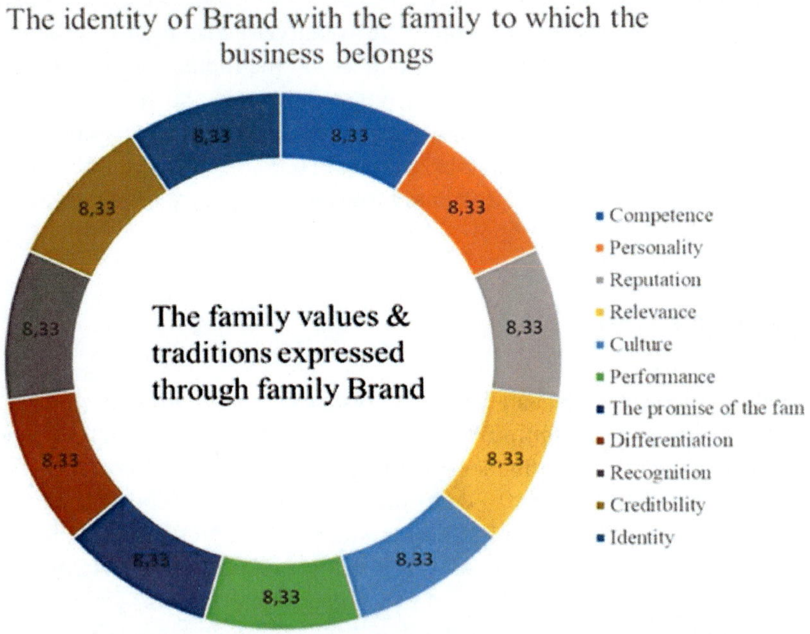

Fig. 2 The identity of the Brand with the family to which the business belongs. *Source* Authors, adapted from CB Astrachan et al. 2018, Brand identity in the family business

would go wrong, which served the bank very well. It aligns the family stakeholder group in an attempt to improve the condition of the bank for the next generation", "Bank, Family Business, 1672, Bella Hoare, C".www.hoaresbank.co.uk). The literature (Urde and Greyser 2014; Binz Astrachan 2018) suggests that there is a managerial mechanism that can be used to control the organizational brand, by mixing corporate identity (family business) with corporate reputation (family). The corporate brand communicates internally and externally. These two elements are interconnected by values, traditions, history, performance, quality, the level of influence of the family through the shareholder or management structure, and they emit a single common image, namely the one perceived by the stockholders. Figure 2 shows the corporate identity of the family Brand.

3 Research Questions

Based on the researched literature, the authors have formulated the following hypothesis:

- The Research & Design investment of the family business is strongly connected to its family brand.

In the next chapter, the authors would like to analyze and demonstrate how strongly a Research & Design department is influenced by the reputation of the own family Brand and how much the family is willing to invest in the R&D for continuous brand development. The assumptions of the authors are that family companies with strong innovation traditional behavior, which are recognized and appreciated in their business niche, are continuously oriented toward their family brand development.

4 Research Methods

The analysis of variance is a statistical analysis tool that divides an observed global variability found in a dataset into two parts: factors and random factors. Systematic factors have a statistical influence on the given data set, unlike random factors. Analysts use the ANOVA test to determine the influence of independent variables on the dependent variable in a regression study. The ANOVA test is the first step in analyzing the factors that affect a given data set. After the test is completed, the analyst performs an additional test on the methodical factors, which measurably contribute to the inconsistency of the data set. The analyst uses the results of the ANOVA test in the f-test to generate additional data consistent with the proposed regression model. The ANOVA test allows comparing two or more groups at the same time to determine if there is a relationship between them. The result of the analysis of variance formula, the F statistic (also known as the ratio), allows analyzing multiple data sets to determine the variability between and within samples. If there is no real difference between the test groups, called the null hypothesis, the result of the F-ratio statistic of ANOVA will be close to 1. The distribution of all possible values of the F statistic is the F distribution. It deals with a set of distribution functions and has two characteristic numbers, called the numerator degrees of freedom and the denominator degrees of freedom (Blombaeck and Botero, 2013; Fisher 1918; Encyclopedia Britannica 2020).

The authors used ANOVA because this test is useful for testing three or more variables. It is similar to multiple two-sample t-tests. However, this results in fewer Type I errors and a range of problems. ANOVA aggregates differences by comparing group means and includes the spread of variance in different sources.

The authors have conducted an analysis on the family business database, collected for the years 2015–2018 by reviewing 500 family businesses Index done by St. Gallen University in collaboration with E&Y, 2018 edition, and CS family companies report 2019, out of which d 120 family businesses based in Europe were selected. The selection criteria out of the 500 companies were:

- Family ownership with the shares between 25 and 50%;
- Family businesses after the first generation;
- Family members involved in the operational business roles;
- Innovative product companies with reputable brands and recognized products.

In this context, the authors have analyzed three financial dimensions of the 120 selected family companies:

- Yearly revenue;
- Percentage investment in R&D;
- % of revenues after 3 years investment in R&D;
- Analysis of the 120 family business companies.

For the statistic calculation, the authors have used the "Statistical Package for Social Sciences" (SPSS). The authors have calculated for the selected 120 companies the average values reported publicly by them on 4 years (2015–2018) for Research & Design (R&D) investment according to the revenues and turnover. The authors write the following mathematical formula:

$$\begin{aligned} \text{R\&D\%(avr2015} - 2018) &= \text{a} + \text{b} * 2015\text{REV} - \text{c} * 2016\text{REV} + \text{d} * 2016\text{REV} \\ &\quad - \text{e} * 2018\text{REV} + \varepsilon \end{aligned}$$

$$\begin{aligned} \text{R\&D\%(avr2015} - 2018) &= \text{the average of percentage the Research and Design} \\ &\quad \text{invested according to the revenue over the last 4year:} \end{aligned}$$

2015REV = revenue of the year 2015.
2016REV = revenue of the year 2016.
2017REV = revenue of the year 2017.
2018REV = revenue of the year 2018.

5 Findings

From the illustration above (Table 1, Regression Statistics), the model R-squared value is high (0.78). This indicates that our model explains 78% of the variance in our dependent variable (R&D AVR). The remaining 22% refers to the dynamics of the industry to which the family business belongs and how much they invested in R&D in the last 4 years. Thus, our model fits the data well. It is important to examine the reliability of independent variables in checking the relation between the R&D

Table 1 Regression statistics

Regression statistics	
Multiple R	0.883937
R square	0.781344
Adjusted R square	0.672016
Standard error	0.037021
Observations	120

Source The authors

Table 2 ANOVA

ANOVA	df	SS	MS	F	Significance F
Regression	40	0.03918	0.009795	7.146793	0.009429922
Residual	80	0.010964	0.001371		
Total	120	0.050145			

Source The authors

investment and the increase in revenue. This is done by observing the F-statistic. The p-value of the F-statistic is less than 1%. Thus, the goodness of fit is high, which means that our model is checked. This also indicates that our sample data provide enough evidence to conclude that our independent variables improve the model fit hypothesis:

i.e.,

$$\begin{cases} H_0 : \beta_i = 0 \\ H_1 : \beta_i \neq 0 \end{cases} \quad \mathrm{i} = 1,\ 2,\ 3,\ 4,\ 5$$

For the calculation of the variance analysis, the authors apply ANOVA statistical model in Table 2.

$F\,(5{,}120) = 7.14$, $p < 0.05$)

The results indicate that the observed difference is the result of a sampling error (chance) with a probability of 5% or less. Furthermore, although it does not indicate certainty, it indicates that the null hypothesis is less than 5% to be correct, so if the p-value is less than or equal to 0.05, we reject the null hypothesis and accept the alternative hypothesis. Then the authors analyze the importance of the p-value, in Table 3, as follows:

As it can be observed, p-value is <0.05, therefore the authors reject the null hypothesis and accept the alternative hypothesis. Using the statistical interpretation, the authors conclude that the model is significantly important and rewrite the results as follows:

$$\begin{aligned} \mathrm{R\&D\%(avr2015-2018)} &= 0.084 + 0.016 * \mathrm{2015REV} - 0.04 * \mathrm{2016REV} \\ &\quad + 0.046 * \mathrm{2016REV} - 0.022 * \mathrm{2018REV}. \end{aligned}$$

Good, quality, and recognizable products bring the brand further, to the next generations, which means survival and recognition of the family business, by its brand. Notwithstanding the Research & Development department, investment percentage is based on revenue. The authors demonstrated that R&D affects the revenue, which can also have consequences on the brand. The authors conclude that for the innovative family businesses this relationship is reversible, threatening even the existence of the family business in the market. By not investing in R&D, the family brand will be strongly affected, e.g., products too old on the market, no products/services in line with the market trends, no improvement of the quality, etc. The innovative

Table 3 Analysis of p-value

	Coefficients	Standard error	t Stat	P-value	Lower 95%	Upper 95%	Lower 95,0%	Upper 95,0%
Intercept	0.08422	0.016514	5.100004	0.00093	0.0461392	0.122301	0.046139	0.122301
2015	0.015723	0.003137	5.011612	0.001038	0.0084883	0.022958	0.008488	0.022958
2016	−0.03951	0.008563	−4.61401	0.001724	0.0592549	−0.01976	−0.05925	−0.01976
2017	0.047426	0.009261	5.121246	0.000906	0.0260709	0.068781	0.026071	0.068781
2018	−0.,02,202	0.004419	−4.98215	0.001077	0.0322079	−0.01183	−0.03221	−0.01183

Source The authors

heritage of the business comes with great responsibility for the family involved in the managerial roles to constantly develop their products, implicitly their family brand. When the expectations of the stakeholders are already positively formed for a particular family brand, the family behind the business has nothing left but to preserve the importance brand level by continuous development. In other words, there is a positive relationship between the revenue and the research and development investments. *This research encourages organizations to invest in research and development since this investment will increase their revenues.*

The authors used this model by selecting and presenting the identified financial criteria to compare the investment in Research & Development to revenue. The authors consider their model contains efficient data to demonstrate *the powerful connection between Research and Design and successful business brand.* In this regard, the authors see a limitation in their study as concerned the above mentioned identified financial criteria and express their further development directions as follows:

- Increase number of industries;
- Increase number of family business companies;
- Select the family companies with ownership between 75 and 100%;
- Select companies after the second generation.

6 Conclusion

In the globalization context, a family brand cannot survive without family involvement in the continuous development of the brand work. The commitment of the family offers a competitive advantage over all other non-family businesses on the market. First of all, through the family that owns the business, which expresses history, tradition, durability, quality, importance, value, trust, and second of all, by the transfer of these cultural values into their products/services with great recognition and appreciation by the stakeholders. On the other hand, the dynamic family businesses with an innovative specific business are obliged by their environment, to keep up with the market trends and to invest much more than all the other types of business, in Research and Design. The purpose is to keep the level the quality on the market and to continuously contribute to its improvement and thus, to their family brand reputation. The decision of the percentage allocation for the Research and Development is in the hands of the family members' decision-makers, who have the responsibility, the power, and the expertise to allocate the funds for the necessary/selected business segments to be innovated or improved. Such a reckless decision is reversible and can have a considerable impact on the company's performance, can lead to a loss in revenues up to affecting the family brand, even closing down of the family business. The heritage of the family brand represents the biggest challenge of the family and lies in the continuous identification with their brand by permanent submission of their efforts at the psychological, social, and financial level contributing in this way to the sustainable family business brand. Through this symbiosis, the brand brings immediate recognition and credibility, and the family's reputation remains intangible.

References

Anisimova, T.A.: The effects of corporate brand attributes on attitudinal and behavioral consumer loyalty. J. Consum. Mark. **24**(7), 395–405 (2007)

Balmer, J.M.T., Gray, E.R.: Corporate brands: what are they? What of them? Eur. J. Mark. **37**(7/8), 972–997 (2003)

Basco, R.: Exploring the influence of the family upon firm performance: does strategic behavior matter? Int. Small Bus. J. **32**(8), 967–995 (2014)

BBC Business Tips from UK's Oldest Family Firms.: www.bbc.co.uk/news/magazine-25711108. Accessed 03 May 2020, 19.00 pm

Beck, S.: Brand management research in family firms - a structured review and suggestions for further research. J. Family Bus. Manag. **6**(3). https://doi.org/10.1108/JFBM-02-2016-0002. Accessed on 11 May 2020, 20.40pm (2016)

Benavides-Velasco, C.A., Quintana-García, C., Guzmán-Parra, V.F.: Trends in family business research, Small Bus. Econ. **40**(1), 41–57 (2013)

Binz Astrachan, C.: Branding the Family Firm: An Empirical Exploration of the Antecedents and Consequences of Family Firm Brand Promotion. Unpublished. doctoral dissertation. Private Universität Witten/ Herdecke, Witten, Germany (2014)

Binz Astrachan, C., Hair, J., Wanzenried, G.: Assessing the attractiveness of family firm employers: An empirical exploration of managers' attitudes towards working in family-owned companies. In: 14th annual IFERA world family business research conference (2014)

Binz Astrachan, C., Astrachan, J.: Family Business Branding: Leveraging Stakeholder Trust. IFB Research Foundation, London (2015a)

Binz Astrachan, C., Astrachan, J.H.: Family Business Branding Leveraging stakeholder trust (2015b)

Binz Astrachan, C.: Branding the family firm: a review, integrative framework proposal, and research agenda. J. Fam. Bus. Strat. (2018). https://doi.org/10.1016/j.jfbs.2018.01.002

Binz, C.A., Ferguson, K.E., Pieper, T.M., Astrachan, J.H.: Family business goals, corporate citizenship behavior and firm performance: disentangling the connections. Int. J. Manage. Enterp. Dev. **16**(1–2), 34–56 (2017)

Bird, B., Welsch, H., Astrachan, J.H., Pistrui, D.: Family business research: the evolution of an academic field. Fam. Bus. Rev. **15**(4), 337–350 (2002)

Blombäck, A.: Family business: A secondary brand in corporate brand management. Working Paper (2009)

Blombäck, A., Botero, I.C.: Reputational capital in family firms: Understanding uniqueness from the stakeholder's point of view. In: K.X. Smyrnios, P.Z. Poutziouris, S. Goel (Eds.). Handbook of research on family business, 2nd ed, pp. 677–693. Edward Elgar Publishing, UK (2013)

Blombäck, A., Ramírez-Pasillas, M.: Exploring the logics of corporate brand identity formation. Corp. Commun. Int. J. **17**(1), 7–28 (2012)

Bolton, R.N.: Linking marketing to financial performance and firm value. J. Mark. **68**(4), 73–75 (2004)

Brown, T.J., Dacin, P.A., Pratt, M.G., Whetten, D.A.: Identity, intended image, construed image, and reputation: an interdisciplinary framework and suggested terminology. J. Acad. Mark. Sci. **34**(2), 99–106 (2006)

Carrigan, M., Buckley, J.: 'What's so special about family business?' An exploratory study of UK and Irish consumer experiences of family businesses". Int. J. Consum. Stud. (2008). ISSN 1470-6423. https://doi.org/10.1111/j.1470-6431.2008.00696.x

Craig, J.B., Dibrell, C., Davis, P.S.: Leveraging family-based brand identity to enhance firm competitiveness and performance in family businesses. J. Small Bus. Manage. **46**(3), 351–371 (2008)

Eisenhardt, K.M., Martin, J.A.: Dynamic capabilities: what are they? Strateg. Manag. J. **21**(10–11), 1105–1121 (2000)

Encyclopaedia Britannica. Sir Ronald Aylmer Fisher. Accessed 10 Auguest 2020 (2020)

Fisher, R.: The correlation between relatives on the supposition of mendelian inheritance. Trans. Royal Soc. Edinb. **52**(2), 399–433 (1918)

Intihar, A., Pollack, J.M.: Exploring small family-owned firms' competitive ability: Differentiation through trust, value-orientation, and market specialization. J. Family Bus. Manag. **2**(1), 76–86 (2012)

Kahlert, C., Botero, I.C., Prügl, R.: Revealing the family: Effects of being perceived as a family firm in the recruiting market in Germany. J. Family Bus. Manag. **7**(1), 21–43 (2017)

Kashmiri, S., Mahajan, V.: A rose by any other name: are family firms named after their founding families rewarded more for their new product introductions? J. Bus. Ethics **124**(1), 81–99 (2014)

Keller, K.L., Lehmann, D.R.: Brands and branding: Research findings and future priorities. Marketing Sci. **25**(6), 740–759 (2006)

Keller, K L.: Strategic Brand Management: Building, Measuring and Managing Brand Equity, 3rd ed. Pearson, Upper Saddle River (2008)

Menkes, S.: Heritage Luxury: PAST becomes the Future. The New York Times, November 8; www.nytimes.com. Accessed 14 May 2020, 12.32 (2010)

Orth, U.R., Green, M.T.: Consumer loyalty to family versus non-family business: the roles of store image, trust and satisfaction. J. Retail. Consum. Serv. **16**(4), 248–259 (2009)

Pounder, P.: Family business insights: an overview of the literature. Journal of Family Business Management **5**(1), 116–127 (2015)

Tasman-Jones, J.: Brand camp: How to market a family business. Campden FB, http://www.campdenfb.com/article/brand-camp-how-marketfamily-business (2015a)

Tasman-Jones, J.: Brand camp: How to market a family business. Campden FB. http://www.campdenfb.com/article/brand-camp-how-marketfamily-business (2015b)

The Credit Swiss Report.: September 2018, file:///C:/Users/CA979/Downloads/the-cs-family-1000-in-2018%20(2).pdf. Accessed 20 August 2020

The Report 2019 EY and University of St Gallen Global Family Business Index.: https://familybusinessindex.com/ [accessed on 12.08.2020, 18.40].

Urde, M., Greyser, S.A.: Thenobelprize: A 'heritage based' brand-oriented network. Harvard business school working papers series, 15, pp. 15–010 (2014)

Wang, D.H.-M., Chen, P.-H., Yu, T.H.-K., Hsiao, C.-Y.: The effects of corporate social responsibility on brand equity and firm performance". J. Bus. Res. **68**(11), 2232–2236 (2015)

www.telegraph.co.uk/news/uknews/11697716/Tesco-under-attack-for-offering-bacon-flavoured-Pringles-as-part-of-Ramadan-promotion.html. Accessed 14 May 14.00

Zellweger, T.M., Eddleston, K.A., Kellermanns, F.W.: Exploring the concept of familiness: introducing family firm identity. J. Fam. Bus. Strat. **1**(1), 54–63 (2010)

Zellweger, T.M., Kellermanns, F.W., Eddleston, K.A., Memili, E.: Building a family firm image: how family firms capitalize on their family ties. J. Fam. Bus. Strat. **3**(4), 239–250 (2012)